NOT A NUMBER

Patrick McGoohan - a life

First published in the UK in 2011 by SUPERNOVA BOOKS
80 Hill Rise, Richmond, TW10 6UB
www.supernovabooks.co.uk

Reprinted 2015, 2016, 2020, 2022

With thanks to Jack Timney, Martin Gilbert, Simon Smith, Lesley Mackay, Jackie Glasgow, Neil Gregory, Richard Turk, Laurane Marchive, Thomas Skinner, Jaimie Henderson, Sumedha Mane, Hayley Hatton and Richard Chapman.

Printed by 4 Edge, Essex, UK on sustainably resourced paper.
ISBN: 978-0-9566329-2-0 (print)
ISBN: 978-0-9566329-3-7 (ebook)

NOT A NUMBER
Patrick McGoohan - a life

Rupert Booth

SUPERNOVA
BOOKS

To Ness, who made it happen, and to Sir who always listens;
both are exceptional people.

Several people have very kindly given me their time during the writing of this book so, in alphabetical order, I would like to thank:

Alvin Rakoff, Cheryl Robson, Eric Mival, J.M. Sykes, Jackie Bennett, John Wyver, Katrina MacGregor, Keith Farnsworth, Larry Green, Mateo Latosa, Nigel Cave, Paul Duane, Robert Fairclough, Roger Goodman and the many researchers, writers and journalists who have gathered information on McGoohan and especially *The Prisoner* over the years including Steven Ricks, Andrew Pixely, Ian Rakoff and Moor Larkin amongst others.

Special thanks for the time and effort they have put in to this book to Rebecca Gillieron, Vanessa Champion and Rick Davy, all of whom rock a great deal.

CONTENTS

INTRODUCTION
Meeting the Man

It was 2000. I was in a large hall crowded to capacity. The event was the annual 'Cult TV' convention, where like-minded fans get together to drink enormous quantities of beer and meet celebrity guests from the TV shows that have enthralled them. I'd come to this particular event for one reason, their guest of honour was to be Patrick McGoohan: actor, writer and director best-known for his work on *The Prisoner* and *Danger Man*. McGoohan was a notoriously reclusive figure and so this was probably a once in a lifetime opportunity to meet a man who had fascinated me since I had first seen his most famous work ten years previously.

The organiser came on stage to welcome everyone. He looked shifty. I started to smile, I knew exactly what was coming. In disappointed tones he announced that the big draw of their show would not be attending after all. McGoohan had developed a serious case of 'other work commitments' and had sent a polite letter which was dutifully read out to give us a tiny shred of personal contact. The sense of disappointment in the room was profound but while I shared it, my smile was spreading. This was exactly what you would expect of him. McGoohan was someone for whom the word 'mercurial' had surely been invented. A reluctant star of television in the 1960s, following the spy thriller series *Danger Man*, McGoohan famously turned down the roles of both James Bond and Simon Templar in *The Saint*, enabling both Sean Connery and Roger Moore to rise to stardom. This was a man who had apparently thrown it all away when he made *The Prisoner*, his own show, taking a stand against conformity, screaming for the rights of the individual to be an individual. This was a man who reportedly had to leave the country and hide in Switzerland until the furore died down; who then relocated to the States, shunning publicity and taking only the roles which he wholeheartedly believed in.

I never did get to meet him. But in 2004, the first novel in a series based on *The Prisoner* was released by Powys Media, co-authored by myself and Jonathan Blum. During the eighteen month period we spent writing the book, we spent a great deal of time analysing 'Number 6', the central character, played by McGoohan, in order to write his part properly, and came to the conclusion that on the page, Number 6 isn't much of a character at all. He snarls, he gets angry, he's witty and urbane then suddenly animalistic, but he remains strangely devoid of personality on the page. Without McGoohan's fantastically intense performance he becomes something of a one-note character. It took a great deal of work to bring McGoohan's physical presence back to the character and, as we wrote, Jon and I both realised just how much of himself McGoohan had invested in the part and in the series itself.

Jon went so far as to send McGoohan a letter and a copy of the manuscript. Quoted in an interview that we did for the excellent *Prisoner* fansite The Unmutual[1] he said:

> 'We sent him the manuscript with a somewhat crawly letter, saying we wanted to make him proud – I suspect maybe we should have said, "Here we are, this is our individual take on *The Prisoner*, what do you think?" Then at least he would have had to respect our guts!'[2]

Perhaps if we had opened the letter with the words, 'Right, here's what we've done, you either like it or not,' we might have elicited a response from the conscientious hellraiser.

In January 2009, I heard that McGoohan had died. Considering the fact that he has a global fanbase which goes from strength to strength, with the many *Prisoner* fan conventions held from Portmeirion – where the series was filmed – to Argentina attracting hundreds of obsessed followers (often in full character and costume), there was surprisingly little coverage in the mainstream media. On *Newsnight*, Jeremy Paxman offered the only televised tribute. In the 60s, McGoohan had been one of the biggest actors in the country for his role in the spy thriller *Danger Man* followed by his endlessly-debated, hugely-divisive, seventeen-part-series *The Prisoner* – the ending of which had caused genuine outrage and resentment. Moreover, the recent US remake of *The Prisoner* starring Ian McKellan and Jim Caviezel had won him a whole new generation of fans in 2010. I was outraged that his passing had occurred without a fitting tribute and immediately started laying the groundwork for a TV documentary. I wanted to explore the reasons behind his enduring appeal to myself and to so many others.

During my research, I found myself becoming more and more fascinated by this 'professional enigma'. Many actors are surprisingly shy characters who seek the limelight only because they need a platform for their art; they are forced into the public sphere because they have a message to communicate. McGoohan certainly fell into the category of reluctants; there are frequent references to his contempt for the 'fame game' and the inevitable media circus that surrounds such a high profile performer.[3] But there was more to his situation than a simple lack of confidence. He didn't come over as being particularly shy, in fact, he could be extremely opinionated in the interviews he did agree to give. Something else was going on here. Most obviously, McGoohan harboured a burning desire to protect his family from scrutiny, an attitude which showed great love and unselfishness. McGoohan saw no reason why his chosen career should impact upon his normal family life.

In *Not A Number*, my intention is not to write a hagiography, nor to present a detailed rundown of McGoohan's work, but to try to find out what was really going on behind the steel blue eyes. His acting was intuitive, he had received no formal drama training, his writing equally so: pointed, forceful and original. His direction was confident and assured, exhibiting an innate grasp of storytelling. It's almost as if he was made for the medium; born a creature of television and film. Everything about him points to a man driven from within to create and to express, to interpret and communicate. He put himself in the position of the everyman though he was never simply one of the masses. Indeed, Number 6, which remains his most famous character, often came across as being practically superhuman. Contrary to his stated desire to represent every one of us in *The Prisoner*, McGoohan was one of the most ferociously individual people of his generation.

It's remarkable that for such an individual vision, the themes of *The Prisoner* are so universal.

Many commentators preface their introductions to a piece on McGoohan with the word 'enigma' but to describe him as such seems to me at best lazy and at worst untrue. He was undeniably cautious of interviews and made sure that, on the whole, questions were steered away from his family and focused on the work, echoing Number 6's mantra: 'My life is my own'. Every high profile actor has to play the publicity game and McGoohan understood the importance of publicising his appearances even if he was sometimes uncomfortable in doing so. Indeed, even after *The Prisoner*, when his career was less high profile, he still gave few, though surprisingly in-depth, interviews. He could certainly be mercurial and imperiously intellectual and was easily bored with routine questions, but when confronted with a line of inquiry that engaged him, he was more then prepared to give thoughtful, considered and apparently honest answers.

Yet – a paradox to the very last – McGoohan could also be unashamedly un-intellectual. When asked whether Kafka or Kierkegaard had influenced *The Prisoner* he dismissively announced that he had never read either and had no interest in doing so[4]

He was noted as being for the most part very down-to-earth, with a strong work ethic, someone who was not afraid of his roots, but was no working class hero either. His personal assistant during the 1960s once referred to him being a 'man's man',[6] someone who enjoyed a quiet drink with his friends, shunned the high profile events he was constantly invited to and remained dismissive and distrustful of the limelight that most actors enjoy exploiting. McGoohan preferred his work to speak for itself.

What many journalists seem to have missed when discussing McGoohan is that he in effect gave a very revealing and decidedly epic seventeen-hour-long interview in his best known work *The Prisoner*. From using his own handwriting for the character, to the same date of birth, the same belief system and the same dogged persistence and ferocious individuality, McGoohan cast himself onto the screen as Number 6 and laid himself bare (though the on screen confessional is masked by the tropes and performance codes of the man in the white hat).

Since the making and interpretation of *The Prisoner* has been the focus of McGoohan's life and career, I intend to explore this TV series more deeply than some of the other aspects of his life; not just because information is sparse but because it came to define the actor. He once wryly remarked in the 1990s that 'Mel Gibson will always be *Mad Max* and I will always be a number'.[5]

Of course, McGoohan knew perfectly well that his own series was a gamble with his career. Superficially at least, this was a gamble that he lost. After the series had concluded, the audience was, on the whole, furious that he had not offered a straightforward conclusion to the narrative and his stock fell considerably. Yet McGoohan was unrepentant; he had said what he felt had to be said over the course of the seventeen episodes. He continued, after the series, to accept only those film and television roles that he specifically chose, with even the occasional stage appearance. However, the public's perception of him had changed. He was no longer the suave, sexy young man who had wowed audiences as John Drake in *Danger Man*. He was, in the words of critic Victor Lewis Smith:

> 'Patrick "I'm stark raving mad" McGoohan: the man who made that silly series with the big white balloon that chased people around and swallowed them whole, the series that made no sense and had housewives all over the country moping, "Oh but he was *so* good in *Danger Man*. What went wrong?"[6]

But then, McGoohan had never been the suave sex symbol. At least not in his mind. He had nothing but contempt for such prescriptive labels and certainly had no interest in promoting himself in that way. He had two great obsessions: his work, in whatever form it took, and his family. He was devoted to his wife Joan and to his three daughters, refusing to appear in romantic scenes in case it upset them. There was never even a hint of any other liaisons or scandal in his private life, which was highly unusual for such a high profile performer, though he would no doubt have had the option to indulge on many occasions.

Actresses and co-workers often found him charming but reserved with them, chaste and respectful.

Yet as with many driven artists, there was another side to him. He had a sharp tongue and frequently used it, lashing out at times for no reason. He began to drink very heavily, apparently during the making of *The Prisoner*, no doubt to help him cope with the stresses he had placed himself under. When drunk, he became a snarling, terrifying demon, unpredictable and aggressive, called a 'bully' by many of those who worked on *The Prisoner* with him. Like most people, McGoohan had certain vices he had trouble controlling, and his drinking reached legendary proportions in the 1970s and 80s. At this point, under stern advice from his doctor, he managed to give it up completely.

McGoohan meant many things to many people. He was an intensely popular actor with the public (until *The Prisoner*), compelling, powerful and never off the screen for long. He was admired by friends and co-workers for his innate skill and professionalism. Directors found him to be a willing collaborator, always keen to bring his own ideas to a performance. To fans of *The Prisoner* he became a legend, a towering figure who maintained a discreet distance from them, refusing to explain his show and often showing contempt towards those who were determined to analyse it to death to discover its 'true meaning'. Yet he gratefully accepted the honorary presidency of the fan club Six Of One and seemed pleased that there was such dedication to his masterpiece. *The Prisoner* is a very inclusive series and we are invited to share Number 6's righteous outrage at the treatment handed out to him by the Village. McGoohan calls out to us to stand up and (as it were) be counted, to say: 'Hey, you can't do that to me!'. In some interviews, he seems to have been positively delighted to have been so vilified by the members of the public who were upset enough to jam the switchboards at ATV after the conclusion of the show. He was happy to be a figure who provoked rage because, as he saw it, rage was a much better response than complacency.

At the end of the day, only two things can be said about Patrick McGoohan with great certainty. He was a devoted family man and a dedicated artist. The two rarely go hand-in-hand but then he was not one for following the rules.

I decided to write this book out of a very deep admiration for McGoohan. I was first introduced to his work when a friend loaned me tapes of *The Prisoner* in the late 1980s and was captivated by his vision as so many others have been. I joined the fan club Six Of One almost immediately and devoured every book and magazine article I could find about the series, then later about the man himself. He inspired me as both an actor and writer and helped to shape my own beliefs about society and freedom, with his views confirming and strengthening my own. I suspect that had he been alive, he would have detested the very idea of this book. However, during my research, I feel that I have come to know him for the brilliant yet flawed individual he was and my respect for him has not dimmed.

The world could do with more people like Patrick McGoohan.

CHAPTER 1
An Actor is Formed

On March 19th 1928, the world changed ever so slightly. Patrick Joseph McGoohan was born to Irish parents in Astoria, New York. In the early 20s, Astoria was the home of America's burgeoning film industry before, during the course of the decade, it migrated slowly to Hollywood. Considering the career path he would take, it seems only right that McGoohan should have been born amidst the experimental bustle of the new and exciting industry, though he would hardly have had time to take any of it in.

McGoohan's parents relocated to their farm in Mullaghmore, County Sligo, Ireland when he was only a few months old. Thomas and Rose McGoohan had emigrated to the States in 1925 to look for employment. His father dug ditches and eventually worked for the Edison company while his mother found employment in Macy's, but both had become increasingly homesick and with the birth of their first child wanted to return to their roots. In an interview with Arnold Hano for a US version of *TV Guide* in 1977, McGoohan outlined the events of his earliest months:

> 'My father had ten shillings in one pocket and a change of collar in the other. My father did not take to the pace of New York. He farmed in Ireland, in County Leitrim, the poorest county in Ireland. Its only export is people. He made the farm go for eight years and they emigrated again, this time to England.'[1]

Life on the farm appealed to the boy who felt at home with nature, taking a deeper pleasure in the simplicity and complexity of his surroundings than might be expected from a child so young. With forty acres of land to roam in, he was given complete freedom to explore in relative safety and had fond memories of the white farmhouse with its suitably rustic thatched roof. McGoohan described some of his earliest memories to Jeannie Sakol in an interview for *Cosmopolitan* magazine in 1969:

> 'Rich in the simplicity and discipline of country life. Fat rambling roses that covered the garden wall in summer, their scent flowing indoors to mingle with the other smells of peat fires, oatmeal cookies and new mown hay.'[2]

Even in this nostalgic description of a pastoral paradise, there is an edge of steel as he also recalls the 'discipline of country life'. This propensity for discipline proves to be a key component of his character in later life. Both cast and crew who worked with him on the projects that he commandeered in the 60s speak of a man who was dedicated to his art, flawlessly prepared and who saw no excuse for laxity or laziness. This early sense of discipline was no doubt reinforced by his very Catholic upbringing. His parents were both extremely devout and would have passed on their beliefs to McGoohan and his four sisters, all of whom were younger than him. Very little is known about these sisters, bar their names, but there is an intriguing story included in the obituary that *The Times* published when McGoohan died in 2009. They had once ganged together to get their shy elder brother a girlfriend, with whom he 'walked out' for a few months (largely one feels, out of a sense of duty).

McGoohan would send his own daughters to a Catholic school in the 60s, presumably wanting them to be taught the same belief system as his own, before allowing them the freedom to make up their own minds.

McGoohan offered another glimpse into his early years in an interview given to Rupert Butler in the mid 60s for a US TV company's publicity brochure, recalling the sights and smells of his earliest home:

> '…the stone-floored kitchen, sides of bacon hanging from rafters, the peat fires. ["Above all," he says, "the peat fires."] Going through his

head still are the sweet brogues of the storytellers who came to weave their wonders in the Irish evenings.'[3]

The practice of oral storytelling for entertainment has all but vanished save for formalised occasions, replaced first by radio, then television and more recently the internet. But in the early 1930s it was a popular pastime and an important way of handing down folk tales. McGoohan took an early delight in being 'spirited away' on journeys to unknown places filled with new and interesting people, creatures and trials. He seems to have developed a leaning towards writing and storytelling from a very young age and by the time he was writing his own material for series such as *Danger Man* and *The Prisoner* he had a finely-tuned prose style, edited and pared-down with the delicious turn of phrase that one would ascribe to an experienced professional.

Parental Influence

In the autumn of 1965, *Woman* magazine published a four-part article written by a journalist called Joan Reader and apparently dictated by McGoohan himself. This is the nearest that one comes to a written autobiography. It's a delightful piece to read and no doubt rubs salt into the wounds of fans who wish he had put pen to paper to tell the story of his life. But his life was his own and by all accounts the thought of such a work would quite simply be distasteful to him. Considering the fact that this article was written at a point when *Danger Man* had already brought him the international fame and resulting intrusions that he so despised, it is altogether surprising that he was willing to go into so much biographical detail.

Though substantially self-authored, it cannot be known to be accurate. McGoohan may have altered the details in his favour slightly or to facilitate better and more engaging storytelling and Joan Reader no doubt edited the text to some degree to suit the magazine's style and remit. However, as the piece is a direct account of his teenage years and onwards, even if it cannot be 100 per cent authenticated, it is of tremendous value to the researcher. In the article, Patrick dictated the story of how his parents had met.

'He had been playing the fiddle with the band when he noticed this girl who was always laughing and always the centre of attention. She was dancing with one of the local blades who had a fair reputation in County Leitrim.

When they struck up the jig "Haste to the Wedding", that was it. My father wasn't going to play it, he was going to act upon it.

He put down his fiddle, walked over to the pair in the middle of the floor and with a brief, "Just a minute, boyo!" to his rival, whisked this girl off – towards their own wedding.'[4]

It was a story which would later inspire McGoohan's one-and-only proposal of marriage to the woman who was to be with him till the end of his life. Indeed, a predilection towards impulsive behaviour would seem to be a trait that Patrick very much inherited from his father. This was a trait that would get him into trouble on occasion but which also helped to shape the man he became, in no small part contributing to his achievements and successes. Though there is little information available about McGoohan's parents and the influence they must have had on his life, the few insights that he is willing to offer show that he had a happy childhood and had a great respect and love for both his mother and father.

One slightly disturbing insight into his upbringing comes from an unguarded and revealing comment McGoohan made in an interview with Peter Tipthorpe, editor of *Photoplay*, during his time as a contract player for Rank Studios. At that time, the studio was desperately trying to cultivate a 'tough guy' image for McGoohan, since he would have little to do with their publicity schemes. While using the interview to rail against this portrayal, McGoohan said:

'I'm not a tough guy and I'm not a beast. I'm soft-hearted, gentle and understanding. I don't even beat my wife!'[5]

What is surprising about this admission is that McGoohan should think it noteworthy and sufficiently unusual to mention that he did not beat his wife. Unfortunately, in the community he grew up in such domestic abuse of women was almost ritualised and certainly accepted during McGoohan's formative years. At that time, working class communities in Country Leitrim were resolutely patriarchal. I'm not saying the practice was endemic in every home nor suggesting that Thomas McGoohan beat his wife, but these attitudes must have had an impact on McGoohan's early life.

In any case, McGoohan may have been speaking in jest. At the very least the statement indicates that, by the time of his marriage, he clearly thought it unacceptable to hit a woman, regardless of his childhood environment. As a young man he preferred to make up his own mind rather than be swayed by society's rules. (To even mention the topic betrays a certain naivety, bearing in mind that he was a respected actor and rising star whose career could have been damaged by any suspicion of domestic violence).

Relocation: Sheffield

McGoohan suffered badly from bronchial asthma in his childhood and while the fresh, clean air of the countryside greatly improved his condition, the family's next major move would undoubtedly have worsened it. The global economic depression of the mid 1930s brought the McGoohan family to the unhappy conclusion that they could no longer make a living out of the farm. With great reluctance they decided to abandon it for England, becoming County Leitrim's newest exports. After a childhood spent in a rural idyll, McGoohan must have been in for a shock when the family relocated to Sheffield, a dank industrial city that lived up to the 'dark Satanic mills' cliché of the Northern working town. This was some years before the passing of the Clean Air Act of 1956 and the industrial chimneys belched out choking smoke and fumes with daily regularity. However, the actor later reminisced that his time in Sheffield was one of the happiest periods of his life and the town became very special to him. It was a place to which he would return several times after he had moved on from its confines and experienced the bright lights of London.

Patrick was initially schooled at St Vincent's, a Catholic boys' school affiliated to a local youth club which regularly held elaborate amateur dramatics, then moved to De La Salle school in Pitsmoor. A strongly sports-based establishment, it may have been here that McGoohan first developed something of a talent for boxing.

With the coming of War, like a great many children from industrialised towns, McGoohan and his sisters were evacuated to the less vulnerable countryside – in their case, to Leicestershire. One can imagine McGoohan's delight at being in a rural environment once more and the fresh country air helped to combat his recurrent asthma. His home for this period was Ratcliffe College – originally established in 1847 as an independent Catholic boarding school – where his education would continue along those strongly Catholic lines which made a lifetime impression on him.

During his time at Ratcliffe, McGoohan was noted as being withdrawn and solitary, happiest when strolling the huge grounds of the school, lost in his thoughts. He excelled at mathematics and continued to box, though his achievements in this field appear to have been wildly exaggerated in later publicity material, some of which goes so far as to have him down as a 'boxing champion'. These two particular talents are referenced in the semi-autobiographical episode of *The Prisoner* 'Once Upon a Time', during which Number 6 is mentally regressed to childhood, recalling that at school he was 'very good with numbers' and proving to be proficient at boxing.

Once Upon a Time

It's interesting to consider what this episode might reveal about McGoohan's Ratcliffe years and indeed his early life in general, as having left school the character of Number 6 follows McGoohan's real life career path to a certain extent.

He is first seen with Number 2 (played by Leo McKern), taking the part of his father walking with his child in the park (analogous perhaps to the grounds of De La Salle college where McGoohan's father had obtained work as a bailiff). This paints a superficially settled picture of home life, before moving to the character's schooldays. Here Number 2 takes on the persona of a headmaster trying to elicit information about some minor misdemeanour from a recalcitrant pupil. Number 6 is honourable enough not to reveal the name of the culprit and accepts the punishment himself as a consequence. The character is shown to be accepting of his situations as the story progresses but always rebellious, at first quietly then openly. The episode inevitably takes in McGoohan's much over-vaunted boxing practice and adds a sidestep into fencing (it is not known if he was ever taught fencing at school but it seems entirely possible), before Number 6 relives the day he applied for a job at the bank. Number 2, as the bank manager, is contemptuous of the fact that Number 6 wants the position simply because it is 'a job'.

The narrative obviously differs hugely from McGoohan's own life, with only touchstones remaining, but two further scenes are interesting. One features McGoohan as a bomber pilot, charged with dropping the explosive device. McGoohan had always expected to be called up for the war effort but was too young when the time arose. Perhaps, because of his extreme sense of responsibility, he felt that he had been cheated out of doing said duty for King and country. Perhaps he felt he had missed out by not having the chance to prove that dedication and learn from the disciplines of the armed forces.

If McGoohan had entered the army, his career might have taken a quite different direction. No doubt he would have risen rapidly through the ranks due to his innate qualities of leadership and self-possession. However, I imagine he would rapidly have become dissatisfied with the authoritarianism of the organisation. McGoohan might have followed other recently-demobbed soldiers into entertainment careers, honing his acting skills in such organisations as ENSA. (This route would have presented definite advantages, with a network of 'war buddies' filtering into the entertainment industry in the late 40s and 50s.)

The other scene of note takes places during a fencing match between Number 6 and Number 2, now playing the instructor and always, in these scenarios, the elder authority figure. Having lost the protective rubber tip from his foil, Number 6 is goaded into taking a genuine stab at Number 2 but misses the mark and merely draws blood from the man's hand. Number 2 retorts that Number 6 is unable to prove that he is a man, that he is 'too scared'. This reads as a direct reference by McGoohan to himself, the shy boy unable to break out of his shell and prove what he could do until eventually enabled by the cloak of anonymity given to him by the stage.

Ratcliffe: Finishing School

To return to McGoohan's time at Ratcliffe, as with most of his boyhood years, there is a frustrating lack of information. In a recent interview for this book, his former classmate, old Ratcliffian JM Sykes shared his recollections:

> 'Although I was in the same year as McGoohan, I was in the A stream, whereas he was in the B stream, you may deduce from that that we had little in common, though I seem to remember him being an engaging conversationalist at mealtimes (we sat at fixed places in the refectory, he and I not far apart). He never, as far as I know, showed any interest in the stage at school; I can be fairly confident of that because I did, though I only played small parts (Stephano, to Norman Stevas's Ariel, would you believe?).'[6]

Mr Sykes was most apologetic to me that his memories of seventy years ago were sparse but, as I pointed out to him, even a tiny gem can be illuminating. Though shy and withdrawn during his time at Ratcliffe, McGoohan shows early evidence of his ability to hold an audience and of his desire to learn, to exchange information through engaging conversation. In later life, McGoohan was relentlessly questioning, arming himself with information and hiding his own secrets behind further questions. The desire to know, to answer the question 'Why?', was an unchanging aspect of his nature; he was forever challenging established facts and devising his own interpretations.

During his time at Ratcliffe, McGoohan was obviously an extremely thoughtful young man, but I suspect his chronic shyness prevented him from taking to the stage. He did, however (according to another fellow pupil), take considerable pleasure in using his carpentry skills to create sets and props. He would throw himself into backstage production duties with zeal and developed a real fascination for the creative artifice of stagecraft. This and similar formative experiences at the Sheffield Rep and other theatre companies like it would leave him with as much of an interest in the mechanics of production as with performance itself.

As with most educational establishments of the time, the college was heavily biased towards religion. McGoohan maintained his strongly Catholic beliefs during his time in education and indeed would carry them forward for the rest of his life. However, there was something within him that prevented him from taking the next step into the priesthood, the vocation to which his mother was most inclined for her son. Early on in the autobiographical *Woman* article, mentioned earlier, he states:

'Until my last year at school I had intended to become a Catholic priest. At the time when most boys were thinking about careers, I had thought only towards the self-discipline of a life dedicated to the Church. Material necessities like rent, meals, clothes, and pay packets, never entered my head.

Then, in my last term at school, I had realized that my sense of vocation for the priesthood was inadequate.

This left me with a singularly lopsided attitude towards an unexpected future which could suddenly include girlfriends, marriage and had to include a job.

I had a whole lot of catching-up to do.'[7]

There is a possibly apocryphal story in the 1969 *Cosmopolitan* interview with Jeannie Sakol where she states that 'with his four younger adoring sisters as congregation, he would deliver "sermons" and enjoy the prospect of a turned-around collar'. It seems that, at the final count, he felt his calling wasn't strong enough. Although his belief in God was held with great conviction, he might have suspected that the restrictions placed on a man of the cloth, particularly a Catholic priest, would leave him feeling hidebound and frustrated. He had a deep-seated dislike of authority figures and by now must have surely begun to question the Catholic church's highly restrictive stance on many issues.

Interviewed in the early 80s, McGoohan made the direct comment, 'I certainly believe in a God but I don't go around waving a flag about it.'[8] Doctrines and dogma were not for him yet he would carry at least one particular aspect of Catholicism with him: a very restrictive attitude towards sex. In later interviews, he stressed that this was a very personal belief rather than one that had been instilled within him, born from a feeling of responsibility resulting from his position as a mainstream actor. In fact, in later life McGoohan was even prone to criticise his beloved Catholicism, once commenting that within the church it was 'impossible to do anything that was not some form of sin.'[9] It was clearly acceptable for McGoohan to believe in the unprovable, the very definition of faith, but restrictions and rules devised by human beings had to be questioned, analysed and either repudiated or upheld. In a *Photoplay* interview with Mike Tompkins on the set of the short film *Ice Station Zebra*, McGoohan stated:

'A man must create pressure in his working life, something to which he can respond and must overcome. I question everything. I don't accept anything on face value. I argue because by arguing something good often results.

I've sometimes been accused of being difficult end edgy and complicated but only because I want the end product to be as perfect as possible. I haven't always endeared myself to some people perhaps.'[10]

Whatever it was that made him doubt his sense of vocation, the certainty of a career in the priesthood was suddenly removed. McGoohan was directionless. He was free. McGoohan's Catholicism was to stay with him throughout his life as was his desire for self-discipline and discipline in others. Throughout his career, though co-workers often complained about his temperament, there was rarely a bad word uttered about his professionalism. He was always willing to do as many of his own stunts as possible, taking risks to give added realism to whichever piece he was performing. His desire for excellence may well have been shaped by the positive Catholic ideals of self-improvement and perhaps his early desire to be a preacher stemmed from an innate need to stand up and perform to an audience.

By the time McGoohan left Ratcliffe in 1944, there was already a clear picture of the individualistic young man emerging. Here was a mind driven by curiosity to question everything around it, contained within an introverted figure that had not yet found a way of unlocking itself. This isolation would shape a very solitary aspect to McGoohan's personality, leading to him frequently being described as 'self-contained'. While this is in many ways a great strength, it may also hint towards his reluctance to delegate in later life, where he would take on more and more burdens for himself within his working life rather than trusting his colleagues. He had already rejected his expected future, though judging from later comments about how supportive his parents were of his early stage career, this does not appear to have caused any major upset with them. He was now ready and eager to embark on a life of work.

Factory Worker, Bank Clerk

'The Macintosh was one of those universal, mass-produced, putty-coloured garments that make the average Englishman about as distinguishable as a grain of sand in the Sahara. That was precisely why I liked it. As soon as I put it on – and I did so regularly, every weekend, rain or shine – I felt securely inconspicuous, practically invisible, and ready for an evening out.'[11]

In the profile of Patrick McGoohan that appeared in *Woman* magazine in 1965, the piece begins with McGoohan at the age of sixteen facing a quandary. He describes how every weekend he would head to the Sheffield Youth Club where he participated in physical training classes and table tennis. His interest went further than that, however, for after those activities was held a dance. Donning his protective raincoat and becoming the invisible man, he approaches the doors and for four weeks running comes across the cloakroom, with its helpful sign directing you to 'Remove your coat.'

'My problem was simple – but insurmountable. If you could have worn a rain mac into the dance hall I'd have gone in. But you couldn't, so I stayed outside. In a mac, you were one of a crowd, looking exactly like everybody else.

Without a mac – or so it seemed to me – you became an identifiable individual: Pat McGoohan, sixteen-and-a-half, six-feet-two. Just out of boarding school, big, clumsy, with no idea of how you went up to a strange girl and asked her to dance and even less idea of what you did with your feet if she said " yes".

The whole thing was impossible, and I wanted to do it.'[12]

To be chronically shy at the age of sixteen is hardly unusual but it's an interesting detail to factor into his later life, as many of his colleagues have observed that his shyness would remain with him. He was undoubtedly a very sensitive individual, running on heightened emotional responses. In part, this was to give him his particular gift as an actor. It is perhaps due to this sensitivity of actors that many of them are portrayed as prima donnas, drunks, expansive, voluble and magnetic people. It is also not unknown for actors to be insecure and shy of attention, paradoxically, considering the demands of their profession. There is that fascinating schizoid quality to a great many actors and few reach the levels of fame that McGoohan was to achieve in the 60s.

Also interesting in McGoohan's case is this desire to achieve the impossible, right there from the age of sixteen. This is a trait which would come to define the man in the eyes of many of his co-workers: a determination to achieve, coupled with a single-mindedness of purpose and drive that allowed him to do so. Indeed, one of the central themes of *The Prisoner* is that the individual must demonstrate the determination and the stamina to follow through on their convictions. It's a trait that recurs in several of McGoohan's most defining roles, at a time when he had achieved the financial stability to pick and choose the parts he wanted to play.

The solution to McGoohan's dance hall problem was to come from an unexpected source. Having wryly described how he would study the notice board beside the cloakroom and exit without ever managing to get to the double doors leading to the dance hall, McGoohan continued in the *Woman* article to describe how he was touched by a slightly divine intervention:

'The fourth Saturday saw me back again, more grimly determined than ever, when Father McDonagh, our priest, waylaid me. "Ah. Patrick. I thought you'd be coming to the dance."

"Yes, Father," I agreed, politely; after all, I was coming to the dance, wasn't I?

"Well. I wonder if Mr. Lodge here could have a word with you first – he wants some help with a play he's putting on." Still thankfully clad in the incognito of the macintosh. I shook hands with Mr. Lodge, and turned my back on the dance hall.'

Relieved of his first appearance at the dance hall, McGoohan was to find he felt surprisingly at home on the stage:

'The youth club play was called *The Thread Of Scarlet*. They were short of a bit-part player. "Nothing much," Mr. Lodge explained, almost apologetically, "just someone fairly big and strong who could look like a man, not a boy. Really all you have to do is to cart a couple of buckets of coal across the stage."

That was an overstatement. All I had to do was to carry one small bucket of coal from one side of the wings to the other, once. But it was enough to get me out of my mac, into rehearsals, and behind the footlights. By the time the entire family, my parents and my four younger sisters, all came to see this First – five-second – Performance, I'd discovered that being on a stage, sheltered by the bright glare of footlights, was a much better cloak of anonymity than a mere macintosh."[13]

The craft of acting is to subsume oneself beneath the character, follow and interpret the instructions in the text and from the director and become an integral part of the storytelling process. It is a world where the normal social rules cease to be applicable. If you have successfully portrayed hatred or jealousy then you are congratulated and welcomed. The forbidden becomes acceptable, the actor can commit mass murder or rape and be rewarded, they can express undying love to a colleague every night and think nothing of it during the day. Some receive a catharsis, others find a shield. It seems that for most of his career, McGoohan falls into the latter category with one very notable exception. His shyness was to stay with him throughout his life. In an interview printed in 1965 at the height of his *Danger Man* fame, he said:

'Certainly, I am self-conscious, trip over my own feet and so on. In company I tend to hide. Though I can get laughs on stage easily enough, I can never tell jokes in conversation.'[14]

Like many shy people, McGoohan was also very perceptive of the reactions of others, picking up instinctively on their unconscious body language, a valuable tool in the arsenal of any actor, but especially one who wishes to pursue naturalism. In the same article, the interviewer relates that:

'He was offering me a drink and quickly ran through the list of bottles he had, adding, "But I haven't offered you anything you like." He had sensed my reaction. He is sensitive to others.'

McGoohan was an incredibly sensitive person, arguably too sensitive. His behaviour could be unpredictable and in later life he would rely heavily on alcohol to control his moods. It has been suggested that McGoohan suffered from bipolar disorder to some extent. Often referred to as manic depression, the condition is characterised by excessive mood swings, sudden bursts of energy and creativity where a thousand projects are started and never completed, followed by depressive periods during which the subject is frequently angry, anxious, confused or melancholic. Both periods are usually separated by periods of normality and mood swings in either direction can be triggered by events in the life of the sufferer. The depressions are also characterised by a feeling of self-loathing, often irrational. This would be remarked upon as being part of McGoohan's make-up in several interesting asides in both personal interviews and in interviews with colleagues. Moreover, the fact that McGoohan started innumerable projects that appear to just fizzle out becomes apparent as one reads through the story of his life.

However, the condition is also linked with high achievers and original thinkers, both phrases that define McGoohan well. If McGoohan did suffer from bipolar disorder it is remarkable and to his credit that he managed to keep on functioning in his professional life, despite the later heavy use of alcohol as a crutch.

Whether or not this disorder contributed to his mood swings, by his own admission McGoohan found a great freedom from himself through acting, finally unlocking his Ratcliffian shell and finding a way to communicate and express himself anew to the world, through performance. Having made his stage debut, into a profession which he describes as a 'wide, confident world', McGoohan took his newfound fortitude back to the cloakroom of terror which had thus far thwarted him, shed his mackintosh as required and hurtled through the doors into a new and yet more terrifying experience, that of the dance itself.

'We were known to my sisters as "The Wallflowers' Delights" since the general method of picking partners was to make a bee-line for any girl who looked too scared and timid either to refuse, or to complain if we trod on them.

I wasn't even that selective. My eyes didn't travel as far as their expressions. I never looked at anything but their feet.'[15]

The article continues with McGoohan explaining that thanks to his recurring shyness, he never actually knew what the girl he learned to dance with looked like, although he could recognise her feet to this day. The article is laced with gentle self-mockery and honest observations about himself. He looks back on his younger self with the knowing wryness that one would expect from a man with twice the life experience reminiscing, but again it is surprising that he is so at ease with revealing these intimate details about his formative years.

What can be established is that his account ties in with established facts. By the time he was attending the weekly dance classes, McGoohan had taken his first employment as a labourer at a steel rope factory. He describes it in the article thus:

'Grey, bleak, miserably oppressive atmosphere … redolent of the "dark, satanic mills" of the 19th century. Over all the sickly metallic smell of iron filings.

Enter through tall, dark gates into blacksmith's shop … huge furnace, men wearing leather aprons and clogs. Camera moves across pitted yard to spindle factory where great bales of wire are rolled down. Youngsters being taught the knack of handling these bales without tearing their hands to ribbons...'

McGoohan was to spend a full year at the factory, graduating from the physical labour of the spindle factory through various departments before his flair for figures landed him a position in the accounting department. He later said that although he had nothing against the rope factory, the work was not for him and the prospect of staying in the same job for the rest of his life was completely anathema to the ambitious young man. He was not yet sure what he wanted to do with his life, however, and the need for financial security, coupled with his strong work ethic, drove him to seek employment at a local bank. He was expecting to be called up for national service at any minute, something that would have defined his life for the next two years, at least, but for some reason this did not happen. If he had ever attended an interview, no doubt his chronic asthma would have removed him from the selection process. McGoohan found a job where he could potentially use his talent for mathematics at the local bank, starting at the lowest level, a bank clerk:

'In the big general room behind the public counters I was allotted a place at the long table to address and lick envelopes, and to balance the accounts – of the stamp box.

It was a life of careful initialling, signing, and accurate arithmetic which began at 8.30 am and ended, if you were lucky, at 4 pm.

If you were unlucky you could be there till past midnight. This could happen if even one penny was adrift at the end of a day.'[16]

McGoohan goes on to describe how once he was responsible for such a mishap, but that due to the shortage of able-bodied men, many still posted overseas, it was easy enough to rise through the ranks at the bank. He eventually took on added responsibilities at another branch, allowing him to get out of the office from time-to-time and cycle the four miles to the second branch where he had become 'sub sub sub manager'. However, the stultifying atmosphere of the job was beginning to get to him and he had already discovered an outlet for his creativity which held his attention and interest a great deal more powerfully than his day job.

McGoohan had kept ties with St Vincent's school after he had left and now returned to its popular youth club, which was noted for its regular and high quality amateur dramatics. It was run by James Lodge – who had previously given McGoohan his first taste of the theatre as a coal carrier:

> 'James Lodge, the man who had persuaded me to carry the bucket of coal across the stage, produced the plays for St Vincent's Youth Club. He owned a cutlery works and the time he gave to the club was entirely voluntary. But, though he was an amateur, his standards were more professional than those of many producers I've worked for since.
>
> He taught me the disciplines and courtesies of the theatre which I need and value to this day. And he could make a stone act. He made me. Soon I was in all his plays.'[17]

Lodge was clearly of immense value to the young actor in waiting, guiding him and helping to shape his performance style. McGoohan's use of the term 'make' seems to suggest that Lodge took a hands-on approach, directly teaching his charges technique and stagecraft. Lodge appears to have been one of the two major influences on McGoohan's early acting and McGoohan would remain grateful to his mentor throughout his life, often crediting him with 'creating' the young actor and setting him on the road to success.

In a pattern that was to be repeated throughout McGoohan's career, exposure led to exposure, as he continued:

> 'Another amateur group, St Thomas', remembered me when their leading man became ill twenty-four hours before their show, *The Duke In Darkness*, was due to open.
>
> My four sisters took it in turns to sit up all night, hearing and cueing me. Next night I went on for St Thomas's, word perfect.
>
> After this, other groups had invited me to join them. I was a member of five different dramatic societies all through my banking days, rehearsing

or acting on an amateur stage nearly every night. But it had never occurred to me that such an enjoyable occupation could also be a job.'[18]

Barbara Bowles, one of McGoohan's co-workers at the bank recalled:

'I know when Pat McGoohan worked with us at the bank – when he went to the Playhouse he had to go as an ASM. The fact that he was a good actor had nothing to do with it. He started at the bottom and learnt the trade until he got the leading parts and then got London.'[19]

Life on the Farm

McGoohan was never afraid of hard work, nor of trying to find any short cuts to the top in his chosen profession. It was a time and indeed a place where boys would start in work as apprentices and learn the basics of their craft, whatever it may be, before finally winning a full-time job and starting their slow progression through promotion.

However, McGoohan was now chafing at the bit, finding that the rote of office work and the constant conversations from older men of forgotten dreams were beginning to wear him down:

'Those bank tea breaks were depressing me. Too often I heard the words: "If I had my time over again…" followed by the fading day-dreams of sailing a ship, building a bridge, emigrating, taking a chance. Such fragments of conversation always ended "…too late now of course… but only another ten, twelve, fifteen years till I can retire…"

They had chosen security and were not grumbling. I wanted to take my chance, before it was too late.

The day one of the chief cashiers made the heartening observation, "Well, McGoohan, you've already done two years towards your pension," was the day I bought the *Sheffield Telegraph and Star* and looked down the "Sits. Vacant" columns:

"Wanted: energetic young man with some experience to manage and re-organize Chesterfield."'[20]

McGoohan offered another interesting reason for wanting to leave in his interview for *TV and Radio Mirror*:

'I couldn't stand seeing all that money about ... and knowing that none of it was mine or ever likely to be. I decided if I couldn't get rich, I'd better get out of sight of all those bills, the temptation might be too much. So I packed it all up and went to work as a chicken farmer.'[21]

McGoohan rang the number in the advert, cycled the twelve miles to the farm and was accepted for the post. He seems to have revelled in his country life, taking great pleasure in the hard physical work which no doubt helped to keep his inventive and active mind occupied.

'I lived in digs with Mr and Mrs Brown who had a bungalow right opposite the farm. Mr Brown worked on track maintenance for the railway. Mrs Brown was a marvellous cook. Both in their fifties, they were childless, and were missing the wartime evacuee who had been like a son to them. They welcomed me and I loved them. I still do.

After the inactivity of the bank I went almost berserk with the sheer luxury of physical hard work. Each day, I began at 6 am and went on till 7.30 pm before going home to the bungalow to devour one of Mrs Brown's enormous and wonderful suppers. Sometimes I played chess with Mr Brown, or clipped his privet hedge for him. Then I slept and slept...'[22]

McGoohan appears to have found remarkable peace during his time with the Browns and was clearly accepted into a surrogate family unit by them. His reminiscences of early life are always laced with an appreciation for nature and no doubt McGoohan had many formative experiences on the farm, one of which he described in the same interview:

'The first time I saw a tiny chicken pecking its way out of an egg ... I realised just what a wonderful thing nature is. I thought, "This is the way life starts. This is the beginning of it all." It sounds corny but that little yellow powder puff gave me a reverence for the miracle of birth.'[23]

It is typical of McGoohan's curious mind to uncover the deeper meaning in such an event. He seemed to have such an emotional and spiritual experience that this informed his beliefs about the 'miracle' of birth for the rest of his life. Farm life suited McGoohan immensely. He was enthusiastic and excelled at the work, eventually being offered a partnership in the farm. The Browns treated him more like a friend than an employee. He was also within cycling distance of his family, ensuring that the family bond was not put under too much strain by his new location. In effect, McGoohan had the best of both worlds for a lad of his age, a place of his own away from home where he lived and worked, with family life close but not so close that it cramped his style.

Life on the farm must have impinged on his amateur acting though, if McGoohan's working day started at 6 am and finished at 7.30 pm. There would have been precious little time to fit in extracurricular activities. His acting may have ceased during this time altogether but, if so, McGoohan didn't seem to mind:

> 'I was happier then than I had ever been. My idea of the good life was a bucket full of chicken meal and a couple of dozen broody hens clucking contentedly around my feet. The fact was I'd almost become like one of them. I was cock of the walk ruling my own little roost.'[24]

The Sheffield Rep

Sadly, the work on the farm was to lead to a recurrence of McGoohan's asthma, possibly brought on by his proximity to the chickens. He described once how he suddenly found himself falling asleep amongst them and realised that he was no longer able to work for the Browns. His chronic condition eventually forced him to be bedridden for six months while recuperating from the attack and this seems to have become a crucial point in his life, giving him the spare time to think about what he really wanted to achieve. He decided that his overwhelming passion was for amateur dramatics.

McGoohan wanted to lose himself in the spotlight and make the leap from amateur to professional actor. The easiest way to accomplish that was to get a place at an established repertory group in one of the local theatres and he decided to target the legendary Sheffield Rep, based at the Playhouse.

'I had cycled past it, morning after morning, on my way to work. Now, unemployed, I strutted by at midday and noticed the doors were open.

I went in, past the box office, down a long corridor towards the stage where the producer, Geoffrey Ost, was taking a rehearsal. I waited for him in the wings. When he came off, a quiet, fairish man in a dark grey suit, and wearing glasses, he looked and sounded more like the architect he had originally trained to be than a first-class theatrical producer which, in fact, he was.

"Have you got a job?" I asked him, and was staggered by my own question.

Geoffrey, mistaking me for a professional actor, said: "Well now, what have you done?"

As I started listing the wire rope factory, the bank and the chicken farm it was his turn to be surprised. "I'm sorry," he interrupted hastily, "we don't take students."

"I'm used to starting any job with making tea, Mr. Ost," I told him. "I could sweep the stage, do odd jobs, anything as long as I can learn."

I became his first student, at £2 a week, then went home to see how my parents would take it.'[25]

To return briefly to 'Once Upon a Time', *The Prisoner* episode in which McGoohan's character seeks employment, this part of Number 6's life is analogous to this moment in McGoohan's. Number 6 applies for a position where 'secret work' is done, a job that he feels befits his talents. Parallels may be drawn between the simple way in which McGoohan attained his initial employment with Geoffrey Ost and the exchange between Numbers 6 and 2 which runs:

'I want a job.'
'You have it.'
'Thank you.'

Whilst the world of the theatre is hardly that of the international spy (or even the desk-bound civil servant who makes up the majority of the secret service) it is certainly to this day a substantially closed world to the layperson. Most people have little idea of how an actor arrives at their performance and McGoohan was certainly intrigued by this situation. Perhaps he preferred that world to be kept secret. He was certainly happy to talk about his work but rarely to dissect it or subject it to any kind of detailed analysis, possibly sharing the feeling of many actors that to give away too much is to destroy the illusion.

McGoohan had made an easy entry into the Sheffield Rep, impressing Ost largely on the strength of his determination and now he could really start working towards his ultimate goal. However, he later admitted to being somewhat nervous when revealing his new career plans to his parents. Their son, who had so far taken reasonable, realistic and ultimately conformist jobs, was now about to throw security away to take a gamble on a career that for most remains financially perilous. Fortunately, they were completely supportive, even though this meant they would have to subsidise him for the short term until he could make more money in a higher position in the theatre.

Given that acting and indeed an artistic bent seemed to run in the McGoohan family, it is perhaps less surprising that his parents should be so demonstratively in favour of his plan. One of the earliest known theatre programmes featuring McGoohan, from Easter 1945, shows Rose McGoohan appearing alongside her son in the St Vincent's production of *Pride and Prejudice,* in which she played Maggie, while Patrick took the leading role of Mr Darcy. McGoohan may have inherited his love of acting as well as his talent from his mother, although he was clearly not the only artistic child in the home. Describing the McGoohan household at that time he writes:

'Odd statues, pieces of sculpture, and a pottery kiln now adorned our garden, all evidence of the scholarship which my first sister Patricia, had won to the Slade School of Art. My second sister, Kathleen, was nearly ready to take her university entrance. Marie and Annette were still at school.'[26]

Little is known about McGoohan's domestic life at the time, though he once remarked that as the eldest and the only male offspring, he frequently found himself in the position of doing the heavy lifting or generally sorting out a problem. At these moments he would mutter, 'Don't worry, "Joe Serf" will do it,' no doubt accompanied by a sarcastic tug of the forelock. 'Joseph Serf' was a name he would later use as a pseudonym when directing certain episodes of *The Prisoner* and despite the potential meanings ascribed to this, its use may have just been due to this family in-joke.

His family remained incredibly important to McGoohan throughout his life. Apart from his personal belief in its value, the significance of the family unit was emphasised always in Catholic doctrine. In austere times it was also vital that one family member could support another either emotionally or financially, bringing individual families and their communities closer together, bonded in the adversity that the mid to late 1940s brought to the people of England.

First Break

It is often assumed the theatre would be regarded with suspicion and an underlying contempt in a late 40s Northern industrial town, but quite the reverse was in fact the case. Sheffield had a thriving professional and amateur theatrical tradition and was a lynchpin of mainstream entertainment, sharing the duties of keeping the exhausted, demoralised and financially drained populace entertained. The demand for new material and new performers was huge and it was inevitable that once accepted into the ranks of the Sheffield Rep, a performer with McGoohan's talent and drive to succeed would make swift progress. Finally, McGoohan had taken the first decisive step on his journey towards becoming an actor, a star and eventually a cult figure.

McGoohan started out by fulfilling his pledge to Geoffrey Ost and sweeping the stage, clearing up, making tea and generally being a useful and extremely keen dogsbody. Ost was noted for his perfectionism with sets and dressings and McGoohan was able to develop the stagecraft skills he had learnt at St Vincent's. He was promoted to the job of assistant stage manager, an elevated dogsbody who was still nominally responsible for the provision of tea and coffee. However, his new role meant he also had extended responsibilities for finding and maintaining props, cueing technicians, estimating the size of the audience and generally carrying out the commands of the stage manager, acting as backup to that person in case of illness. This was an excellent position for any aspiring actor to develop a wider understanding of the holistic process of theatre, of which the actor is the final and most visible (and vulnerable) link in the chain. Under Ost's guidance, McGoohan was able to gain experience in every discipline of the theatre during this period. By the time he was given the job of prompter, he earned enough money to no longer need financial support from his parents, though they remained enthusiastic and attended regular performances:

> 'They came to the theatre every fortnight and praised my progress in ascending order: first, the clean stage, then the assistant stage management, the building of the sets, the scenery, the wardrobe, the lighting, and the prompting, all of which finally earned me £4 10s. a week.'[27]

While the prompter usually spends their time nervously clutching a script and following the actor's every word, McGoohan, being McGoohan, committed every line to memory. He seems to have had a remarkable memory for lines, bordering on photographic, once intimating that he could glance at a page for thirty seconds and have the lines memorised. He always attributed this skill to his training in rep, where the demands of learning a new play every fortnight exercised and strengthened the memory as one would strengthen a muscle. Though he had already done a great deal of amateur work, he had yet to make a professional appearance on stage, something he now yearned for. McGoohan's patience was about to pay off and he was not the type to miss a chance.

> 'Inevitably came the night when one of the actors had appendicitis. As prompter, I knew his lines, and went on. Next day I was in Geoffrey Ost's office, ready to fight for my big break.

Not a Number

"I'm not coming back till you make me an actor," I began.

There was no fight.

"Welcome back," he said, "at six pounds a week."

I was twenty-two and an actor at last.[28]

CHAPTER 2
Rising Star, New Romance

Patrick McGoohan was finally a professional actor, and this would remain the main focus of his career. He had always written and, according to many friends and contemporaries, would continue to write new ideas, new material and new poems every day for the rest of his life. He would later branch out into directing and production (and, it might be argued, every other production discipline on *The Prisoner*). But it is as an actor that he will be remembered and this was a profession that suited him well. McGoohan had chosen wisely when he made his financially dangerous leap from the security of the bank to the Sheffield Rep. His belief in his own talent had been validated by Geoffrey Ost's acceptance and his non-conformist nature was no doubt satisfied by the ever-changing work, the feeling of doing something different from the norm. In a word: escape.

A Visible Intensity

I was introduced to McGoohan's work, like many, through *The Prisoner*. When I remember watching the first episode *Arrival* on video, I recall being struck not just by the concepts, the storyline and the astonishing sight of the location, the Welsh village Portmeirion in all its glory, filled with brightly-coloured idiots. It was the commanding performance of McGoohan that really demanded my attention; McGoohan playing the part of a man who is ripped from his comfort zone and put on the defensive from the moment he wakes in his new home.

For anyone who is not familiar with the series, the basic premise of *The Prisoner* is as follows: the main character Number 6, is kidnapped the very morning he resigns from his job (perhaps in national security though we are never quite sure), and wakes up from the drugs his kidnappers have administered to find himself trapped in an intensely peculiar place called 'The Village' apparently far away from his familiar environment, Westminster, London.

In the role McGoohan portrays confusion, fear and anger in quick succession, each arising naturally from the other, replaced finally by a steely defiance. When Number 6 warns the authorities of The Village that they will not hold him, despite the evidence against his assertion, the viewer believes him and immediately sides with him.

What struck me most on my first viewing, was how strongly individualistic and distinctive I found McGoohan's acting to be. Sometimes completely naturalistic, at other times highly-mannered with facial expressions as twisted and sliding as his vocal scale, yet without ever feeling contrived or distracting from the character he was portraying. Like many that are considered to be amongst 'the greats', his style of performance was considered to be quite unique and few could match his passion or presence.

So where did McGoohan find this power? What inner emotion allowed him to project such immensity on stage? In the Arnold Hano interview mentioned earlier, McGoohan referred to a definite driving force in his performance style. When recounting how he had been promoted from mere prompter and 'shoved' on stage, he explained:

'It felt good. But nerve-wracking. Scary. I'm always scared. It's a scary world. You have to be nervous. I don't want to be placid about my work.'[1]

That McGoohan should derive some of his on stage energy from fear is also fascinating. Fear is certainly a powerful emotion, causing actual physical changes as the adrenalin response kicks in, and many actors refer to the 'rush' that they get from appearing in front of a live audience. For McGoohan, however, rather than triggering a positive rush, his fear seems to have been quite genuine and he used this to make himself sharp, determined never to put a foot wrong or expose himself to ridicule.

The best way this can be judged now is from his surviving live television work. Due to the nature of the production, actors were frequently seen to fluff lines, as often as cameras bumped into scenery, boom mics appeared in shot and 'off-camera' noises shattered the calm. These mishaps were all accepted by the viewing public of the time as part of the fabric of the medium, as much as a loudly coughing audience member or stumbled dialogue were accepted in the theatre. Though the results can seem almost absurdly amateur to modern sensibilities, there is a sense of intimacy with these live productions that has been lost with the advance of technology, facilitating frame-by-frame control over the finished edit. It's somehow heartening to see well-respected actors fudging their words and recovering fast with the instincts born of a stage career. All except the virtual machine that is Patrick McGoohan, a man who never once appears to have forgotten what he is doing, why he is doing it and who he is supposed to 'be' at the time.

During my recent correspondence with Roger Goodman, a life-long McGoohan fan who has both met and interviewed the actor, I asked him about McGoohan's acting style. His impression was that:

> 'It's not just what Patrick says and the accent with which he says it or what he does and the way that he does it with every fibre of his body, from the drumming fingertips to the angled ankle, but the interaction of the whole personality with the camera or a theatre audience that makes him irresistibly watchable. He seems to be living out a tense and tortured section of his life, everyman's life, in public. The watchful distrust and sense of resisted inevitability is projected with great technical skill. And at no point does he ever telegraph what he's going to do next until the instant of the eruption.'[2]

When interviewed about McGoohan's performance, colleagues, particularly actors, often mention the word 'danger' and 'a feeling of unpredictability'. As Goodman observes this comes from the fact that he never announces what he is about to do. Actors commonly find it hard to suppress micro-expressions or movements that suggest what their next action may be. The most obvious examples include instances of performers acting nervously around an area which has been primed for a special effects explosion. Though the performer knows that they are safe, they are also aware that there is a potentially harmful event about to happen and must work to not betray that fear and thus step outside the artifice. McGoohan was incredibly controlled in his performances, both mentally and physically, and it is this that helped add to the sense of danger. The viewer would be given no hints as to where the character might turn next. There was always a genuine sense that anything might happen (within the boundaries of the character obviously) and McGoohan knew exactly when to accentuate this for maximum dramatic effect. His technical skill was an ideal counterpoint to his intuitive talent, though he was by no means a 'method' actor. As he recounted many years later:

> 'I never let any part that I play sort of take over. I think that that's nonsense when that happens. I think you should be able to go in and do it, learn your lines and do it. Some are more fatiguing than others, some are more emotionally exhausting than others. I mean, you can't play Hamlet without being drained or King Lear without being drained but to say that you lived through the day playing Lear or playing Hamlet before you go out the next night and go on to the stage, I think that's ludicrous.'[3]

Work Ethic Upheld

McGoohan was a very down-to-earth individual and his attitude to acting was that it was a job. It may be a job that he was very good at and immensely privileged to have, but nonetheless a job. His commodity was his performances and he churned them out as he had once churned out bales of steel rope. His work ethic had not changed. When later he was taken on by the Rank organisation, as a new star name to be groomed, he found that because of his disinterest in jumping through the media hoops he was sidelined. However, he nevertheless made a point of coming to the studios frequently and taking mediocre parts in films that he thought were 'rubbish' simply because he was on a contract and therefore received a regular salary from the film company. Many other actors in the same position have been content to enjoy a well-paid holiday but for McGoohan, payment meant that there had to be the due amount of work. This was an old-fashioned and extremely admirable attitude, which he retained even through his years of stardom in the 1960s.

However, it cannot be denied that McGoohan brought more than just a technical mastery to his work. As Roger Goodman noted in the interview mentioned above:

'He seems to be living out a tense and tortured section of his life, everyman's life, in public.'

Though McGoohan claimed to leave each part behind when not at work, his performances suggest he must have put a great deal of himself into the roles that he played. Drawing on his own experiences to inform his reactions, as all actors do, he would throw his whole being at the part. With the level of intensity he achieved at each show, it's surprising that he managed to hold anything back in reserve for the next night and the next. It was noted by popular character actor Peter Sallis that while playing the title role in *Brand* on stage in 1956 for the BBC, McGoohan was best left alone after the show, being withdrawn and exhausted. Watching the raw emotion that he pours into the performance on the BBC recording, it's easy to see why. McGoohan had fire in his belly that he would use to tremendous effect in his acting.

On Stage, On Screen

As his career advanced, McGoohan also learned the importance and techniques of acting according to the medium. Television, stage and film all required different disciplines and McGoohan did his time in the 1950s working extensively in all three, absorbing information and adapting his performances. A case in point, McGoohan would appear in an ABC Armchair Theatre production of *The Man Out There* in 1960. The role demanded that he play a Russian cosmonaut who, due to a technical failure, was shot into a decaying orbit with no means of avoiding burning-up during re-entry. The play takes place in three locations: the panicked Russian control centre, a snowed-in trapper's hut in Canada and the tiny confines of the space capsule itself. While the actors in the other sets are able to use the full range of their skills, McGoohan is largely constrained to close-ups and the occasional mid-shot. With little recourse to technical wizardry, the directors of the time used the close-up a great deal more than it generally appears today, focusing closely on the actors and allowing them to do the work rather than the visuals. Demonstrating that he was equally skilled with both the expansiveness required for stage and the tiny nuanced performance required by the intimate TV camera, he pitches his performance perfectly, it seems almost on a shot-by-shot basis, and commands the entire production. It wouldn't surprise me if he had memorised the entire camera script – an annotated document showing each piece of dialogue or action against the shot type, number and camera that would be taking it – and therefore knew exactly what was required of him in every shot.

Many have compared these comparatively early and primitive broadcasts, often transmitted live from the studio or theatre with cameras, and there are persuasive similarities, certainly, but the craft of performance is very different between the media. Though there was a definite and frequently-voiced snobbery towards television from the more theatrically-minded performers, many actors learned to relish the different challenges brought by the new medium. They could build upon the filmmaking experiences they had so far garnered which, although affording the same flexibility and opportunities for close-ups and subtlety, were inevitably shot piecemeal giving less continuity of performance from shot-to-shot. Live television gave the best of both worlds and McGoohan instantly understood and embraced the possibilities of the ever-evolving medium.

Comparing his performance a few years later in the Disney family classic *The Three Lives of Thomasina* (1964), McGoohan is certainly the main focus of attention in every scene in which he appears. But the performance is heavily reined-in, he does not dominate, he is more than happy to and capable of fitting into an ensemble piece and realises that the histrionics that might be acceptable in the extreme close-up of the television will simply be ridiculous in a movie of this genre. The shooting is stylish but ultimately merely a storytelling device and McGoohan knows his place in every shot. He knows precisely what he has to do to serve the story and how to do it, with such on screen ease that he clearly thought about this role in as great a depth as any other he was approaching. He finds his position, whether as lead and focus, member of an ensemble or simply as background facilitator.

He had an innate understanding of technique, much developed during the period of his life that he was now embarking upon: a career in Repertory Theatre. Local and national Rep companies devoured plays and constantly needed new actors to replace those who had moved on – to either better things or simply London. Once accepted, the career possibilities for a young actor were greatly broadened. Now that McGoohan had taken the formative step of dedicating himself to a career as an actor, the Sheffield Rep was a great company to start with. It was already a veritable crucible of talent, with familiar names like Paul Eddington, Peter Sallis and Peter Barkworth having been schooled and influenced during their time there. In an interview published on the British Library's website, Elizabeth Ewing recalls McGoohan's departure from the bank where she had been a co-worker:

'He worked at the high street branch and I worked at George St. We used to have to meet up each day at the local clearing house to do our cheques and he used to help me, the little junior, do my sums. And he left … the story is he went to Geoffrey Ost, he wanted to act, and he said, "I will sweep the stage if I can just come," and he ended up as leading man.'[4]

Second Mentor

Just like James Lodge, Geoffrey Ost proved to be another extremely formative figure in McGoohan's life. An unassuming-looking, middle-aged, balding man he was to many actors a greatly empowering figure, now looked upon as being a great influence and a stalwart of the theatre. The Sheffield Rep had a fortnightly turnaround of plays meaning that actors in the company were usually performing one play while rehearsing the next and often learning a third; still trying to clear their heads of the previous. Rep has long been acknowledged as one of the greatest practical training grounds an actor or actress can have, enabling them to gain experience in a huge variety of parts in anything from high drama to low comedy. Ost had a great faith in his company and in himself. In general, apart from dress rehearsals, his team of thespians never worked in the afternoons, returning to the theatre in the evening for that night's performance. Such faith instilled a great self-belief into his charges, enabling them to spread their wings. The flexibility that his working methods allowed gave many young actors a much needed boost of confidence in themselves and their abilities.

Ost provided a broadly populist collection of plays for his audiences every season, his reasoning being that he should not dictate what the audience 'ought' to like. This ensured that the Sheffield Rep gained maximum exposure and indeed maximum box office takings. However, he shrewdly scheduled more highbrow or controversial pieces in between his diet of comedies and melodrama, feeling that although these pieces shouldn't be excluded from popular culture, their appearances needed to be balanced to avoid losing his audience.

The local theatre in those post war years, before the sudden and explosive development and spread of television, was an important social event for the relatively impoverished population. In the UK, people were still suffering through the tail end of rationing. They were slowly rebuilding a shattered country – both physically, in the case of many towns and cities, and economically. Britain was a country whose status as a world power had been dramatically reduced by the events of the century and whose sense of national pride had been shaken.

Ost and others built on the sense of a shared community experience by giving a personal face to proceedings. A stage manager would generally greet punters on the door and after the performance would take to the stage to introduce the next week's play, exhorting them to come back to witness the new production; in effect a verbal trailer. It proved to be a remarkably successful combination of salesmanship, marketing, talent and creativity, with theatres every night usually filled to eighty per cent of capacity.

His management style aside, Ost was also fascinated by stagecraft. Having trained as an architect he took a particular interest in design and his sets were always noted as exemplary, which would have appealed to McGoohan's sense that excellence should come as standard. He was the typical actor-manager, with a hand in all aspects of the production.

However, Ost took a light-handed approach to his supervision of the performances themselves, as recalled by actor Peter Sallis, now famous for his role as Clegg in *Last of the Summer Wine* and for being the voice of *Wallace and Gromit*. A contemporary of McGoohan's, in his autobiography Sallis explains that according to Ost the craft of acting was the actor's job, not the director's.[5] Sallis saw Ost as not so much a teacher but 'an enabler' and McGoohan, never one for being told what to do, would have responded well to such tutelage. (Of course, when the time came for McGoohan to be the one directing performances, such a free rein wasn't always granted to the actors...)

In 1948, a note in the minutes of the Committee of the Sheffield Rep mentions the possible acceptance of McGoohan as a student under Ost; his first. Like Sallis, Ost saw his role as a facilitator, one who would create and provide the productions in which the actors could learn their craft in their own way. During his Rep career, McGoohan's eye was always on the goal of appearing in London, because that provides the greatest exposure for a stage actor within the UK and he was determined to make this career work financially. (Partly to further this end, he would later show great interest in the medium of television which many stage actors regarded with a great disdain.)

McGoohan was extremely appreciative of the rigorous theatrical training of Rep, gaining experience in a wide diversity of roles, leading and supporting. He remembered:

> 'When Geoffrey decided who would get the parts, he never told anybody, never had a discussion with any of the actors. The list would just go up on the bulletin board on Saturday afternoon. I know because I was the stage manager, and I would nail it up.'[5]

McGoohan no doubt thrived on the challenge of ingesting and performing so much new material in a comparatively short time frame. He would later directly attribute his great ability to learn lines to his Rep training, which would stand him in good stead for the rest of his life, allowing him time to concentrate on the performance rather than the tedious learning of the material, the volume and diversity of which seems astonishing. A typical year-long season could see twenty plays or more being rehearsed, produced, performed and replaced by others. Under Ost's direction, material ranged from popular Shakespeare plays to Greek tragedies, interspersed with modern classics from JB Priestly and Noel Coward and first run productions fresh from the London stage by challenging new playwrights. There was an endless treadmill of comedy, drama and tragedy, terrific amounts of material to be digested and a behind-the-scenes workload to contend with as well. This consisted in supplying the sets, props and costumes for each new show, reusing old pieces, creating new ones and scrounging whatever else was needed. With Ost taking a particular delight in scenic perfection, it's a wonder McGoohan managed to learn lines at all.

McGoohan's remarkable faculty with memory may have come from his father, as the actor recalled in an interview to publicise the film *Jamaica Inn* (1983):

> 'My father couldn't read or write, but he played the violin like an angel and he had total recall. We would read to him, he'd ask us what page we were on and days later he'd refer to the material on that page number.'[6]

Enter Joan

Now settled into a satisfying working life at the Sheffield Rep, McGoohan was absorbing all the information he would need to successfully further his career. He was also making friends and contacts and expanding his social group, though the few memories of his contemporaries still have him as being somewhat introverted, considered and thoughtful. I have no doubt personally that this was down to his fantastic ability to concentrate on the work in hand. To improve his stagecraft, he was determined to wring every last nuance out of the text that he could, though his previous shyness was still with him. But his levels of concentration were about to take a body blow, as while working on a performance of *Taming of the Shrew*, McGoohan met a young actress named Joan Drummond. He describes this first meeting:

'They had a new actress in the company too. Very new. Straight from RADA in London, called Joan Drummond. We were both cast in the next play. She was "Mavis Pink", a marvellous comic character. I was "Jack Bannerman" a dull, straight nothing. Next morning there was I, sitting on a stool in the middle of the empty stage, trying to get into this dull character part, while over in the wings with customary ease, the "Tall, Blond and Handsome" of the company was turning his charm on the new girl.'[7]

That Joan was a RADA trained actress must have been intimidating to McGoohan, who had received no formal drama education. At this time, there was a distinct bias towards actors with formal training; an unfair judgement against the skills of performers who hadn't, as McGoohan demonstrated. Rep theatre, though respected as a source of quality entertainment, was still compartmentalised as being 'semi-amateur' in some quarters. There was concern about the growing breed of untrained but talented and experienced actors entering into the professional arena (though 'professional' could often be replaced by 'London' in many of the objections raised in the national press at the time). Amongst many in the business, the prevailing attitude was that Rep was a valuable local resource, but there were enough trained actors in London to fulfil all the requirements of the stage.

However, this restrictive attitude was being shaken by the growth of the film industry, with its voracious appetite for new performers and attractive star names, where formal training was of less importance than good looks or raw talent. Though many theatrical actors had successfully made the transition from the stage into film and indeed radio, a significant and loud minority regarded both with great suspicion. Despite the fact that McGoohan had already started to carve a reputation as a serious actor, he would have felt the stigma of the lack of recognised dramatic education.

Though McGoohan had a great belief in his abilities as a performer, there is an underlying feeling that runs through his life that he was not particularly contented with himself as a man, something which many years later director David Cronenberg would characterise as a quite extreme and destructive self-hatred.

Not a Number

McGoohan's reminiscence of the moment he met the love of his life continues with his description of an image that had been etched onto his mind, his first sight of Joan:

'Up came this glowing sunburnt-to-mahogany girl with black hair and dark eyes and she promptly enveloped me in a snowstorm of words:

"I'm sure this play's going to be really good, aren't you? Do you feel nervous, too? Are you living in Sheffield? Where did you go for your holidays? ..."

All my ponderous plans for long and serious study of my first, two-page professional part seemed in imminent peril of being drowned in a cascade of chatter. She was eighteen, and bent on making me feel at home in a theatre where I'd worked for two years and where she had worked for barely two weeks! I took advantage of my superior knowledge of the building to seek peace and quiet in every corner I knew and she didn't – yet.'[8]

In the face of this confident, self-possessed and attractive young woman McGoohan buried himself in the work. In a later interview he recalled that he was shaking for two days solid after their initial encounter. In his later relationships with women, particularly actresses or journalists, he would treat the confident women with respect and interest, while the nervous or shy would receive a less favourable reaction. Many times, as with his relationships with men, it appeared that a woman had to 'stand up' to McGoohan and, having done so, had passed the test. Well, the initial test...

Though at first it seems McGoohan found Joan slightly irritating, taking himself away from her 'chatter' so that he could apply himself to the serious business of being an actor with his usual single-mindedness, it wasn't long before McGoohan found himself in the state of blissful confusion that often accompanies falling in love.

'Soon Miss Drummond began to make my life a series of contradictions. I found her overwhelming, but fascinating. I wanted to get to know her but, if I saw her coming down the street, I would hastily cross over to the other side.'[9]

'Overwhelming but fascinating' seems to be several people's first impression of Joan Drummond, a figure who could be quite as powerful as her husband. Hailing from London, at the age of eighteen she already seemed to him to possess a sophistication and worldliness that was beyond his limited experience. No doubt Joan was doing her best to make a good impression, joining a new company in a world quite removed from that to which she was accustomed. She may well have overdone the act a little, becoming overwhelming to some in the process. McGoohan's words conjure up a whole Ealing Comedy about missed romance and shyness: him in his macintosh, observing at a distance, never able to bring himself to get too close while Joan twirls in the spotlight. It was certainly a meeting of very different worlds in terms of their background. Joan was used to the bright lights and fast pace of London, McGoohan was a rural lad at heart, coming from a much less progressive part of the world. No wonder he was confused by her, but at the same time attracted.

The lovestruck actor was to get a chance to become better acquainted with Joan when she began to bring a puppy with her to rehearsals. He was christened 'Noah' because of his propensity for producing floods at inappropriate moments. Drummond had impulsively acquired the dog to combat a feeling of homesickness, without necessarily thinking through the responsibilities of pet ownership, and her landlord at the pub where she rented a room in Sheffield had rapidly run out of patience with Noah and his Biblical bladder. Knowing that McGoohan was more than amenable with animals, she decided to approach him with the problem, though he wasn't above making the occasional acidic jibe about her behaviour:

'All I knew about Noah, then, was that Miss Drummond hadn't trained him properly and was now complaining to me that she wasn't allowed to keep him in her digs.

"You live on a farm, Pat. Could you take him for me?"

Thus started her daily inquiries: "How's Noah?" and the usual reply from me: "All right, considering the way he's been brought up."

Then the sparks would fly and she would toss that black hair and march off. I always invited this, and didn't know whether or not to like it when I got it. Once or twice we managed to have a brief conversation without arguing. I even got around to inviting her to egg and chips, twice, between matinee and evening performances.

Asking her out was, for me, like going back to Square One – and the youth club dance. Once again, the whole idea was impossible, and I wanted to do it.'[10]

Arguing seems to have become a way of life for the couple, McGoohan describing much later how he would frequently return home and vent spleen about his working day at his wife who would promptly hit back twice as hard, without ever damaging the relationship. Despite their connection via Noah, McGoohan was still too shy to properly act on his growing feelings for Joan, crippled by both his nervousness and her expansive confidence. McGoohan describes several fumbled meetings in a local café, him always trying to stay as inconspicuous as possible, her energetic and voluble. Her vivacity was infectious to the shy young man, himself unable to project such a trait without the shield of performance as an excuse. He no doubt found her as frustrating and challenging as he did beguiling, and if there was one thing guaranteed to interest McGoohan, it was a challenge. Joan herself was also falling for the actor, claiming later that she was always impressed by his magnetism and individuality, mentioning in an interview published in *The Palisadian Post*, the couple's local newspaper, that:

'He was an independent thinker. He followed all world happenings, the Middle East. He was a brilliant mind. All sorts of people, when they met him, they listened. Where it came from, I have no idea.'[11]

She was also consistently impressed with McGoohan's acting ability and the power that he could summon. The pair had a mutual professional attraction as well as a growing emotional bond. However, McGoohan was still unable to move on to the next stage with Joan and as with his eventual conquest of the terrifying doors leading to the youth club dance floor he would require an external influence to progress his plans.

'Mrs Wood, as the wife of one of the directors of the Playhouse, gave an annual party for the company at her house in Fulwood. Though never much of a party-goer I went to this one. So did Joan. So, of course, did "Tall, Blond and Handsome", a little of whose poise and technique I could have found useful just then. While sitting in my corner, watching Joan dancing with him, the realisation dawned that, so far as I was concerned, the only person she had any right to be as close to as that, was me. I had two clear thoughts in my head for once.'[12]

Thus seized by this sudden revelatory bout of jealousy, McGoohan was finally spurred into activity. As he describes it, the story of his father's spontaneous proposal to his mother comes to mind at just the right moment. It's a very neatly written story and difficult to say how much McGoohan has embroidered it to that end. He was, after all, apt to fudge the details of his own life, as I'm sure anyone would be tempted to. Motivated by the moment, he finally makes the leap and again, achieves the impossible:

'As Joan danced by I reached out and pulled her down on the seat beside me:

"I'm taking you back to your digs. On the tram. Now. Go and get your coat."

It was a vivid green coat, with a hood, I remember, and she was still arguing about fetching it even when she had it on and we were rattling back on the tram to Sheffield. That was when I had my third brilliant thought that evening. As we reached the small pub where she had her digs. I asked her to marry me.

"No," she said, and shut the door.

"Why not?" I asked, opening it again.

"They don't like the door open, after they've closed," she said, and shut it again.

I opened it, "Why won't you marry me?"

"Shut the door," she said, and shut it herself.

"Open the door," I demanded and opened it, "Why won't you marry me?"

"Because I'm too young," she said, primly.

I didn't open the door again; she did.

"See you tomorrow," she said.

"Yes," I said, "Good night." And this time, I closed the door for her, gently.'[13]

Undeterred, McGoohan wasn't about to let her get away that easily. With characteristic single-mindedness he continued to pursue Joan, eventually receiving the answer he required.

'A few months later, I asked her to marry me again. This time she said "Yes," but added anxiously: "I'm still only nineteen; we'll have to ask my parents."

"Of course we will," I said, feeling ten feet tall and a veritable rock of confidence. "Of course, we must, but don't worry, everything will be all right."'[14]

Having finally conquered the shyness barrier, McGoohan's actions became incredibly impulsive if the above account is to be believed. This trait reappears several times throughout his life, strange in a man who, especially in his work, favoured meticulous planning. As with everyone, there are many aspects to McGoohan's personality, but few exhibit such opposing characteristics.

His tendency to swing between emotional extremes would be later demonstrated in the making of *The Prisoner*. Even at this stage, though, the veritable rock of confidence that characterised McGoohan's self-belief in his talent had now transferred across to the man. The two major factors of his life had fallen into place and Joan was to become the most important person in his life for the next fifty years, empowering him as well as loving him very deeply.

Joan was to give so much of herself that McGoohan would later express great guilt that she should abandon her own acting career to bring up the children. However, her acceptance was only the first tiny step, the correct protocols now required that McGoohan should consult and receive approval from Joan's parents before anything else could happen. Without such consent it was entirely possible for the parents to either block the wedding or make it far more difficult to achieve. When an acting career was considered by many to be extremely perilous, one can imagine that Joan's parents might well be hoping for a more financially sound suitor; someone who could support their daughter's career by bringing in a regular salary. This merely served to energise McGoohan, however, who had become determined that he and Joan should be together. He was prepared to work himself into the ground to make it possible. He describes how his fertile mind was already working on the problem:

'Though I'd never met Joan's father, who was a lawyer, wedding bells were already ringing in my ears as I walked home, rehearsing the words with which I would ask his permission to cherish and support his daughter for the rest of my life.'[15]

McGoohan was an incurable romantic, writing love letters to his sweetheart every day, a practice which he apparently kept up until the end of his life. The couple were able to see a lot of each other as their work brought them together. According to first-hand accounts, McGoohan missed Joan's presence tremendously when they were apart. With his usual precision, he started to arrange the night that could change their lives, already figuring out what he thought would be the best approach to impress her father, no doubt cross-questioning his intended in the process of gleaning every vital fact that may work in his favour. McGoohan would have approached the problem the same way he approached everything else in his life, with 100 per cent commitment and dedication. By his own account:

'In the front row, left-hand side, centre circle of the Sheffield Playhouse, sat the father of Joan Drummond, the nineteen–year-old actress I wanted to marry. I knew exactly where his seat was. I had booked it, with great care, myself.

We had never met. When the curtain rose he was going to see me for the first time, as an actor. Afterwards, Joan and I were going to his hotel where I would ask his permission for our marriage. She was apprehensive: "I'm sure he will say I'm too young."

"Don't worry," I kept telling her.'[16]

McGoohan had already thought through his plan in some detail, right down to arranging where his quarry should be placed to best advantage. His attention to detail in evidence, McGoohan had absorbed all the relevant information about his prospective father-in-law and had plotted accordingly. He desperately wanted to make an impression both as an actor and suitor, proving that he could deliver the goods on stage. In effect, he was a tradesman demonstrating that he was skilled enough at his craft to earn a living. If his marriage to Joan was going to work, her parents would have to be supportive of her suitors' career as much as they were of their daughter's. So McGoohan was going to make his first impression on stage.

> 'For weeks I had been trying to put myself in her father's position: "London lawyer, specialising in divorce; parent of one attractive, impulsive daughter who, after only seven months in provincial repertory, now wanted to marry a twenty-two-year-old actor in the company, earning the same salary as she did – by now – £8 a week."
>
> The main disadvantage, as I envisaged it from that point of view, would be the insecurity of a livelihood in the theatre. However, if I could prove to him that he had a potential Irving-cum-Olivier as a future son-in-law the rest, I thought, should not be too difficult."[17]

That McGoohan should unconsciously choose not only recognised icons of 'great acting' but also notable actor managers (particularly in the case of Irving), suggests that his ambitions already lay beyond the confinement of the stage. He had maintained his interest in the wider aspects of production. Besides demonstrating that he was capable of doing more than just act to his prospective father-in-law, it would also show that he was a man to be trusted with the responsibility of running his own theatrical troupe. A prodigious writer, McGoohan must by now have also been considering the possibilities of penning a play himself, and for artistic reasons would want to keep control of his own material. It would, however, be a while before such ambitions were fulfilled.

McGoohan's plan was one of contrasts. He planned that his adversary should see him first on stage in a part as far removed from his own persona and appearance as possible; the part of a lunatic, a violent horror. He would then follow up this first impression by introducing his real persona: a sober and respectable ex-bank clerk, a man used to handling money, someone who was perfectly capable of looking after this precious and wilful daughter. He applied himself 100 per cent to make the on stage character as convincing as possible, intending that it would be in stark contrast to the second persona who would therefore surely be granted an overwhelmingly favourable reaction. To his delight, he was given a part that would allow him to take this contrast as far as possible.

> 'That fortnight we were doing *Bonaventure*. The setting was a convent, I played the odd job man. A sinister loon who had already attacked someone with an axe and in his worst moments, was ready to lay his hands on any woman.
>
> Joan, in the part of a young nurse, was the target of these moments. As I chased her round the stage she had to scream out her terror that I would lay my filthy paws on her.
>
> I had spent a fortune on make-up to reproduce the most repellent characteristics of a half-demented simpleton with heavy, lowering brows, hair powdered to look straw-coloured and lifeless and combed to stand on end.'[18]

Looking at a photograph of McGoohan in character that was taken on the night, it is a frankly horrifying sight. He looks almost completely unrecognisable, his mouth contorted and drooping, eyes wild yet somehow lifeless, and the aforementioned combed-up hair creates a disturbing frame for the face. It's a tremendous piece of physical acting and simple make-up combining to produce a thoroughly distorted vision of stupidity. In retrospect, one is almost inclined to reach into the past and pat McGoohan on the head in sympathy for thinking that this approach was in any way a good idea to introduce himself to a career lawyer. Perhaps he had for once underestimated his talents. The play opened on November 20th 1950 and the fateful day came when McGoohan would have his one and only chance to make a favourable first impression.

'As the lines moved towards my cue I focused my eyes in a vacant stare, let my face fall into the slack droop of stupidity, my hands dangling at my sides. The cue came and I lurched forward to make my shambling entrance. Joan shrank, ready to run and scream.

Then it happened. The spotlight picked me up but before I could lunge towards her there broke across the pin-quiet theatre one low, anguished clearly audible comment: "Oh – my – God!" There was no mistaking it. The voice came from the front row. Left hand aisle, centre circle.'[19]

Not presumably, the ideal reaction. McGoohan continued his performance undaunted, though no doubt laying his 'filthy paws' with considerably more care than on most evenings. The Ealing comedy of their early relationship continues with this performance. One can imagine McGoohan playing the comedic awkwardness of the situation in a screen adaptation of his life-story. Having squirmed through the performance, aware that his carefully-judged plan might have hurtled off the rails, McGoohan hurried back to his dressing room and divested himself of every shred of the lunatic who had elicited such a negative exclamation, donning his now seldom-used bank clerk's suit of conformity.

'After the curtain, as I scrubbed my face, bashed my hair down and changed into my dark suit, instinct told me that ex-bank clerk McGoohan, now shiningly-reflected in the dressing room mirror, was not going to erase that first, idiot impression easily.

Instinct was right.

Among the depressing regimentation of hard chairs and small glass-topped tables in the hotel lounge I made my second 'entrance' of the disastrous evening and faced Joan's father. Our preliminary conversation did not include any congratulations on my performance, and soon I plunged into my carefully planned speech: "I would like your permission, sir…"

He let me do the talking. I ploughed on doggedly, but with the distinct feeling that I was being heard more as a petitioner for divorce than as an applicant for marriage. When at last, he did speak, he was brief and discouraging. I heard something about "being cautious... prudent... only earning eight pounds a week."[20]

McGoohan's temper rapidly manifested itself as he characteristically refused to simply take what was being said by his elder and the petitioner became the accuser: a typical position for the opinionated actor and one that he would adopt time and time again in *The Prisoner*. McGoohan had already decided that he was going to marry Joan and nothing was going to get in the way of that union.

> "'That's not important,' I contested hotly, "eight pounds or eighty pounds a week. Joan wants to marry me. I will always be able to earn enough to support her. If I can't find work as an actor I can do anything – even dig ditches!"
>
> He let that somewhat unoriginal protestation pass without comment.
>
> I knew there would have to be a fight, and it wasn't my night for winning. I asked if I could see him again in the morning.
>
> Again he let me do most of the talking, countering my arguments with "the advantages of waiting" and other, justifiable parental doubts. The night before I had been nervous. Now I was outraged. With sustained composure he let me lose my temper. Gaining momentum in my purifying performance of righteous indignation, I finally succeeded in arriving at the beautiful irrelevancy that it was suspicious, over-cautious minds like his that caused world wars!'[21]

McGoohan's handling of the all-important meeting of the parents (well, the father at least) could not, it seems from this account, have been more supremely mishandled. But against all odds, with his temper and no doubt his nostrils flaring, his passionate rebuttal of his prospective father-in-law's concerns was finally putting him on the right track. The elder responded well to his demonstrative and sincerely felt outburst.

> 'At the end of my tirade he told me, among other things, that he had seen more of marriage – and divorce – than I.
>
> "You may become engaged. We'll review the question of marriage in six months' time."

We then shook hands in mutual acknowledgement that, from our opposing standpoints, we were both right. Suddenly his face relaxed. "Now let's go and meet your parents," he said.

There was never any looking back. The ground was cleared for all time for a relationship between father and son-in-law that could not be bettered. Even in the times when I was virtually on the brink of having to fulfil my promise to "dig ditches" for a living, he never questioned either my ability, or my intention to see things through.'[22]

McGoohan had found himself a second father, another supporter. The actor had demonstrated that he did not make idle promises and went on to prove that he had not only the talent but the drive to make his acting career a successful one, enabling him to look after his wife in the approved manner of the day. McGoohan related in an interview with Lisa Reynolds for *Photoplay* magazine that the couple were quite prepared to wait until Joan was 'of age' to marry.

'We waited two years to marry … because she was underage, I suppose her parents would have given their consent for us to marry sooner, but there was no hurry. We were together and we knew everything was going to be all right.'[23]

Such propriety would have also pleased his own Catholic parents, as well as Joan's, and the couple dutifully waited, spending as much time together as they could. They would meet outside work in Sheffield, a place to which McGoohan would later bring Joan several times as they reminisced about their courtship, though amusingly, the actor did once have to point out to his wife the significance of one particular spot, where he had made his eventually-accepted proposal to her.

The venue for the eventual wedding was St Williams' Church in Sheffield and it would take place on May 19th 1951. The lovers sneaked away from work to have a small family ceremony, then returned to the theatre to continue rehearsals. What either of them thought of the fact that their meeting, romance and marriage was framed by the Sheffield Rep's production of *The Taming of the Shrew* has to be left to conjecture, but I imagine they would have been amused.

McGoohan had found and married his life partner, the woman to whom he devoted all of his energies outside work. Theirs was to become something of a fairytale romance, according to other members of the industry; a rock solid relationship that never wavered and did not suffer from the usual tribulations resulting from one of the partners being a 'major star'. This was largely due to McGoohan's attitude to his private life and the importance he was to place on family. It can be speculated that the actor's much discussed distance from women on set, many of them startlingly attractive young actresses, was his way of removing himself from temptation. He greatly disliked being away from Joan, and later his daughters, for any great length of time and would take pains to ensure that his wife and family were able to accompany him on long location shoots. With such a supportive partner, McGoohan also now had a firm foundation upon which to build the rest of his life and together they would start to shape their individual careers.

CHAPTER 3
Not a Brand

McGoohan was now a married man and like all good Catholics had every intention of starting a family with his new bride. If anything, this intensified his desire to succeed as an actor, always mindful of the early promise he had made to Joan's father that he would go and dig ditches if things didn't work out. (Both Patrick and Joan McGoohan were now major players in the company and *The Rivals*, the Sheridan play they had been rehearsing on the day they were married, was now on stage at the Theatre Royal in Bath. This gave both performers valuable exposure and experience outside Sheffield.)

Cause and effect followed intention and around September 1951, Joan became pregnant with their first child. The pressure was now greater than ever for McGoohan to earn a decent wage out of his chosen career. It did not require much speculation for him to realise that to make the breakthroughs required to achieve success as an actor, he would have to seek a career in London: the heart of the theatre and media just as much then as it is today. McGoohan had served his time in Sheffield Rep, had gained a great deal of experience and had honed the mechanics of his art to complement his natural talent. At the beginning of 1952, he left the company with a great deal of gratitude and warmth. In his mini-memoir for *Woman*, McGoohan recalled the time:

'Between us we were now earning £18 a week and felt immensely rich but when we knew we were starting a family, that was the end of our joint, princely salary. The time had come for me to earn more than Rep. could pay and that meant London.

Joan went to stay with her parents in Hampstead. I auditioned success-fully for a part in my first West End production, scheduled for a month's tour and a London opening. "The Closing Notices" went up on the second week out and left me unemployed.'[1]

McGoohan remembered looking for a flat for the two young performers, eventually finding a 'self-contained rabbit warren with a communal staircase'[2] and always looking for the next role. He spent the next few months flitting between several different acting companies, all of whom would have been delighted to have a performer of his calibre as part of their group. McGoohan had begun to attract attention – even while mostly confined to Sheffield – and word of mouth is a powerful tool in the industry. He secured a part in *Cupid and Psyche* starring Alexander Knot and Peggy Cummings, a comedy that was planned to tour the country before arriving in the West End. However, for reasons unknown the play did not make it to London, ending its run instead at the Liverpool Royal Court.

This was a prestigious enough location for a young actor from the Sheffield Rep to be treading the boards but hardly what McGoohan had been hoping for with his need for London exposure. With the early collapse of the play, he was out of work again and so auditioned for a play at the prestigious Arts Theatre Club in Soho, London. This hallowed establishment was a private members club and was therefore less bound by censorship rules than its public contemporaries, leading to a wider variety of new and challenging material being presented. McGoohan got a part in *Hobson's Choice* starring Donald Pleasance, who had recently returned from a stint on stage on America and was becoming something of a star name. However, the money he was earning was insufficient and with Joan now nearing the end of her nine months' pregnancy, the need for employment drove him to return to the life of a labourer.

'Eventually I got another part, at the Arts Theatre, which paid £10 a week, but nothing during rehearsals, so I went along to see what suggestions the Labour Exchange could offer. Next night, after rehearsals, I was standing at a factory conveyor belt wrapping choc-ices by the thousand – and the next night.'[3]

However, life had changed for McGoohan since he had last worked in a menial position and he found that he had developed an unexpected problem with the repetitive business of coating confection in paper.

'The third night I quit. At rehearsals all the lines on my script had shot past my eyes like choc-ices too.'[4]

Despite the fact that his wife was about to deliver their child, he had enough confidence in his abilities to know that he would be able to provide for them somehow. He immediately took another job as a waiter, work he remembered as being harder on the feet but much easier on the eyes, and which left him enough free time during the day for rehearsals. His hours were 7 pm to 6 am, meaning that he must have averaged about four hours sleep per night during this time. Fortunately, McGoohan seems to have been able to survive with little sleep and, as he pointed out in the same interview, there was enough black coffee on offer to keep him going through the night.

'The other advantage of night work was that I was around on the Saturday when the baby advised Joan it was time to phone the ambulance and hospital. By three-thirty that afternoon we had a daughter.'[5]

On May 31st, Catherine McGoohan made her way into the world. The effect this birth had on McGoohan must have been profound. The birth of a child is a highly emotive event for any parent but for McGoohan, who had once taken such wondering joy in watching the birth of a chick from an egg back in his farming days, the birth of his daughter would no doubt have been loaded with symbolism and meaning beyond the norm. What is very clear is that he loved her with all his heart and became the dedicated family man. Nothing was going to prevent him from achieving excellence as a parent any more than in his professional life.

From the Boards to the Screen

Unfortunately for McGoohan and his family, the pressures of work were to keep him away from his new brood. Sharing the stage with Donald Pleasance at the Arts Club in June 1951, his performance was noted by a talent spotter for the Midland Rep and he took advantage of his new address to write to two BBC Drama producers, Fred O'Donovan and Campbell Logan. Both letters received the standard BBC 'brush-off' replies and McGoohan concentrated on his theatrical work, winning a role in *A Priest In The Family* at the Theatre Royal in Windsor which had just migrated from the West End where it had garnered good reviews. Though he claimed to never have a particular career path in mind, aside from making enough money to be able to support his family, McGoohan made a shrewd choice in accepting this part. During the class-conscious 1950s the cachet of acting in Windsor, the home of the Royal Family, was huge and potentially influential.

The play itself seems like typical McGoohan material, with themes of repression and choice set against a backdrop of religion. Kate Murphy is a publican who insists that her son abandon his dreams of joining the priesthood to labour on the farm which she also owns. His ambition thwarted, her son becomes a drunkard but once she is financially secure, Kate forces him into sobriety and sets him back on his original course. With his easy familiarity with Ireland and ability to produce a convincing accent, McGoohan fitted the part beautifully and it appears that the Windsor Rep made a special effort to win the young 'up and coming' into their ranks for the duration. His stock was growing in the theatre and McGoohan was desperate to capitalise on that. After all, he had a promise to his father-in-law to fulfil.

Soulmates Severed

The successful run in Windsor paid dividends for McGoohan as he was now invited by the Midland Rep to join their ranks, having first been noticed by them during the arts club run a few months earlier. McGoohan took temporary accommodation in Coventry and while there he finally found a name for their daughter:

> 'Three weeks later she was still "the baby". We couldn't make up our minds what to call her. I'd applied for a job with the Midland Repertory Company in Coventry and. while waiting for an interview, strolled round a local churchyard. Carefully, I read the names on every tombstone. That evening I phoned home: "I've got the job – and a name – Catherine."[6]

Not a Number

The Midland Rep played in theatres in Coventry, Nuneaton, Loughborough and Netherton with the usual pattern of performing one play while rehearsing the next. McGoohan was by now quite used to the demands of Rep but unhappy at being so far from his family. He made hundreds of appearances for the Midland Rep, including an apparently stunning interpretation of *Macbeth* (one can imagine the young McGoohan glowering from the towers of Cawdor while wrestling with an invisible knife). Since both the local cities which the company visited and the Arts Council had decided to offer financial assistance to the company, the work was financially secure at a time when the couple needed security more than ever. McGoohan had successfully managed to avoid returning to the stultifying boredom and confinement of factory work and was providing for his family once more – just. Despite their overworked and impoverished existence, the family would at least be together for Christmas.

> 'Catherine was six months old before I found an attic room I could afford to rent in Coventry for the three of us. We were now so broke that Joan persuaded the lorry driver to include her and the baby as part of our "part-load" he was bringing in his removal van from London. When the time at Coventry ended, we thought ourselves lucky if we managed to be together as long as a week.'[7]

Their enforced absence had served only to bring them closer together. They truly cherished the little time they could spend as a couple.

In terms of geographical obstacles, the situation worsened when in June 1953, McGoohan and Joan split up once again. Having taken time away from the Midland Rep in April to once again play at Windsor, McGoohan had been noticed and snapped up by the Bristol Old Vic. Joan meanwhile, a classically-trained actress and therefore in many snobbish circles much more of a draw than her husband, was lured to the West End, McGoohan's holy grail. She was to appear as 'Chief Wife' in *The King and I* at Drury Lane. In the *Woman* article McGoohan explained how, at that time, they 'met on Sundays and parted on Mondays'. Joan presumably once again took up residence at her parents' house where Catherine could also be cared for, leaving Joan free to pursue her career. This would have been an ideal situation for her, but not for Patrick, who was living alone in his Bristol digs. His stint with the Old Vic was to last only until Christmas, largely one suspects due to his overwhelming desire to be once more with his family.

During my research it has become abundantly clear that as well as loving Joan immensely, Patrick McGoohan also profoundly needed her. In correspondence, Roger Goodman remarked about her that:

'She reminds me of Catherine Zeta Jones, you know, full-on attractive female but seemingly mild, not pushy or aggressive. She appeared very supportive of Patrick, inserting into my conversation with him tit-bits that backed up whatever he may just have said, especially if he was countering a critical remark … Where she did influence Patrick was that he was definitely different talking in her company than when not. He was more relaxed, sociable, lightweight, mischievous.'[8]

A clear pattern emerges throughout the course of McGoohan's life which, when simplified considerably, boils down to the fact that he was at his happiest and most stable when with or close to the woman he loved – and at his most unstable, unpredictable and unpleasant when deprived of her companionship for any length of time, whether by pressures of time or distance. That he found his soulmate in Joan is undeniable, but what he also found was an anchor, someone who could stand up to him. While such fiery temperaments can often be destructive in a relationship, it seems that the genuine bond of love between these two individuals was enough to keep them from being torn apart emotionally. McGoohan once described their relationship with obvious delight:

'When I'm under pressure or displeased with things, I go home and roar at my wife. If something's wrong at the studio or I've had an all round bad day, I go home and just rage at her … She roars right back. Oh, we have some great fights. She calls me a "stupid idiot" and things like that. It's wonderful! When it's over, nobody apologises but we cuddle a bit and it's fine. I roar at my wife, but I couldn't kick the cat – the cat wouldn't understand. Joan does understand. At our house, fighting is a very important part of marriage, because we love each other."[9]

That Joan 'understood' Patrick must have been singularly important to him. That she was prepared to not only tolerate his moods, but presumably also had the ability to sympathise with what drove them, would have been of immense value to such a highly strung individual. He undoubtedly felt indebted to Joan for her unflinchingly strong support and repaid it by fulfilling his promise to provide for the family and by his devotion and loyalty.

The brief run with the Bristol Old Vic did yield dividends. McGoohan was given the chance to once again perform in London in *Henry V*, as part of an exchange programme run between the parent company and its Bristol spin off, and for this performance he received a mention in reviews. By this time he had an agent, Eric Glass, who was pursuing his client's interests with the BBC and was starting to receive encouraging responses from, in particular, senior BBC producer Michael Barry. Barry had seen the young actor at Windsor and had been duly impressed, consequently he was recommending McGoohan to his colleagues. McGoohan continued to 'do his time' away from Joan in Bristol but by now was already making plans to move to London in time for Christmas to be with her. *The King And I* had been hugely successful on Broadway and its future and therefore Joan's employment was secure for at least a year, so it made both financial and professional sense for McGoohan to move full time to the capital. Intriguingly, his work for The Old Vic at this point included musicals, something for which McGoohan was never well-renowned. His stint ended with a production of an entirely new play by the BBC's theatre critic TC Worstey; a prestigious enough name to attract a large contingent of press and producers to its opening night, therefore bringing McGoohan invaluable exposure.

The close of 1953 must have been a buoyant time for the McGoohans. They were reunited in London, Patrick had taken great career strides over the year and Joan had now secured employment in a successful and high profile West End musical. Many men in a similar position might feel a pang of jealousy at their spouse's success but I believe that McGoohan would have positively revelled in Joan's success.

TV Debut

By 1954, television had progressed from being a curiosity to a nationwide obsession. New transmitters were being constructed to allow TV programmes to be received outside the confines of London with the Sutton Coldfield transmitter launched in 1949 opening up the Midlands to the new craze. The program of construction had been continuing since then and now over two thirds of the country were capable of experiencing the new wave of the communications revolution. The medium had been given a terrific boost in popularity and national interest by Queen Elizabeth II, who allowed her coronation to be televised the year before. Against the recommendation of her advisors, she was sufficiently forward-looking to realise the potential of such a broadcast. Sales of sets rocketed as the public clamoured to be part of the 'first big television event'; a shared experience that would resonate in the national and global consciousness with telerecordings of the live event being made for posterity and being flown out to British colonies. Television was rapidly progressing from being seen as the silly, little, complicated invention that had been the exclusive reserve of the affluent in the mid to late 1930s, to becoming a unifying force for the entire nation and an astonishingly powerful tool for politicians.

1954 also saw the passing of the Broadcasting Act that would allow the BBC's monopoly over the new medium to be broken and would provide for the creation of a new independent television service, all made up of distinctive regional companies contributing their programmes to the network. While many actors and indeed their agents were incredibly dismissive of television, others such as McGoohan saw the huge potential, not just for employment but also because it offered the chance to bring their work to a mass audience. He jumped at the opportunities it offered. The BBC, realising the potential competition, began to up its ante, looking for more and more original drama which was starting to prove tremendously popular in a variety of slots. The potential for work for jobbing actors, particularly those who were making a name for themselves and lived within the metropolis, was now considerably expanded and it seems that McGoohan's letter writing of the previous year, to BBC producers who wielded more influence than they might have known, finally bore fruit.

His television debut was in an episode of the BBC drama-documentary series *You Are There*, produced by Michael Mills who had been persuaded to look at McGoohan by Michael Barry and who had been impressed by what he saw. The series itself was a concept which had been leased from the network CBS in the States and took the form of an anthology retelling historical events in dramatic form. McGoohan first appeared in an episode called 'The Charge of the Light Brigade' in which he played the pivotal figure of Captain Nolan. A second booking soon followed for an episode dealing with Charles Stewart Parnell, an Irish reactionary from the 19th century, for which McGoohan would have been ideally suited.

It would be fascinating to be able to view McGoohan's first steps into live television. Although his Rep training would have stood him in good stead for the arduous business of remembering the lines and blocking the moves, the craft of making live television was very different from that of theatre. Every filmed movement has to be much smaller and more precise to accommodate the lumbering and insensitive cameras of the day whose moves, out of necessity, always took precedence over those of the actors. However, like the vast majority of the BBC's output at the time, no recording was ever made of the performance and if there had been it would have only been retained for a few weeks.

What does survive is footage from McGoohan's next foray into television on the filmed series *The Vise*, made for the American TV market in England by the Danziger brothers: legendary film producers with a reputation for working fast and cheap. This experience would have introduced McGoohan to an entirely different way of making programmes, inherited by the cinema. Instead of the theatricality of the complete performance being run through live as if on stage, while the director cut between the varying pictures being offered by his four cameras on the studio floor, filmed series like *The Vise* used only one or at most two cameras to capture each shot as an individual entity. Many directors vastly preferred the extra control and therefore quality that this approach gave over live production, not to mention the comparative lack of angst involved. In live television, a mistake was seen by the entire audience. When filming, the director simply has to call for a retake. This gave filmed series a slickness and speed that quickly left their live counterparts behind; though live and later videotaped multi-camera drama found its own voice and made some extraordinary achievements in the decade.

The filming approach was preferred by directors. However, actors – whose only experience had been the smooth continuity of stage work – found it much easier to adapt to live broadcasting than they did to the disjointed stop-and-start nature of filmmaking, where one scene may be followed by another set on a completely different day or even year. McGoohan learned the new technique with his customary fascinated zeal. His work on *The Vise* shows that he quickly found a natural affinity with the camera as he turns in a performance as at ease and accomplished as any other on screen with him playing con man Tony Mason. The 35 mm film format that the Danzigers used was flexible enough to allow for sales to both cinema chains and TV stations. McGoohan's appearances must have raised his profile and he was soon enjoying the benefits of steady employment. Moving to London had been one of the best decisions he could have made. He and Joan could now share the babysitting duties with their parents and both were within easy geographical reach of the main centres of theatrical, filmed and televised entertainment production.

Film, Theatre and TV

In May 1954, McGoohan secured a part in *Burning Bright* at the Q Theatre in Kew, followed by *Spring Model* at the same venue in which, according to reviews, he displayed a flair for comedy. The third show of the summer season was *Grace and Favour*, a new work by Ronald Jeans, which McGoohan produced and directed. He was finally fulfilling his desire to exercise some control behind the scenes and to present his own artistic interpretation using the talents he had honed under Geoffrey Ost's stewardship at Sheffield Rep. This would have been a big leap forward for McGoohan, whose ambitions had never been confined to just appearing on stage or in front of the camera. He was already a prodigious writer, always scribbling notes, ideas, stories and daily love poems to Joan. In addition, he now had two new forms of media to explore technically, learning the basics as well as finding new ways of using and stretching these techniques now opening up to him.

During his time at the Q Theatre, it appears that McGoohan was talent-spotted once again. This time a film producer offered him a role in the Roy Ward Baker directed feature *Passage Home* (1955) for the imaginatively named Group Film Productions Ltd. This small role saw McGoohan's character acting as spokesman for his workmates, alerting the Captain to the fact that their rations are hardly fit for human consumption. He makes a definite on screen impression in the role despite having only a few lines during the course of the film and effortlessly commands the scene, demonstrating once again his easy mastery of the acting techniques required for filming.

It seems that McGoohan also filmed his two roles in the Errol Flynn flick *Dark Avenger* (1955) around the same time, though that would not be released until the following year. This movie gave McGoohan a particular insight into the detached world of movie-making, often criticised (rightly) by laypersons as placing too much emphasis on the status of its 'stars'. McGoohan described his experiences with characteristic dry humour:

'As the knight "Sir Oswald", with two lines to say, I was entitled to Rolls Royce transport between home and studio and a place in the restaurant with the hierarchy and stars – on a peasant's pay. Another actor, as the "Leader of the Peasants" had a huge part. But because he was a "peasant" he had to eat with the peasants and come to work under his own steam – on a knight's salary. The whole thing was ridiculous and I didn't take it seriously. Perhaps I should have done. It was the first glimpse of the topsy-turvy standards and protocols of the film business – Hollywood style – that later were going to involve me. But at that point, filming meant just a temporary way of earning money: film stars a curious breed of people to be watched with detached interest and amusement.'[10]

Evidently McGoohan would take this experience to heart. On any production in which he was the star, particularly *Danger Man* and later

The Prisoner, McGoohan never separated himself or placed himself socially above any other member of the cast or crew, refusing to be pampered as his status would have allowed. Despite often being obtuse in his thinking he is frequently referred to as being 'down to earth' and 'one of us'. Always questioning and always searching for truth, or at least a truth that he could relate to, McGoohan was unimpressed by the veneers of privilege granted to those who were succeeding at the fame game and maintained a genuine contempt for the artifice throughout his life.

In between branching out into these new areas, McGoohan was still appearing on stage at the Q. He then moved to The Embassy Theatre towards the end of the year, geographically on the very edge of the West End and therefore bringing him closer to his goal. Joan's run with *The King And I* had now concluded and she was appearing in Rep at The Strand Theatre. Once again, the McGoohans were able to celebrate an increasingly secure future together as the year drew to a close with them both still regularly in work and with McGoohan's star particularly in the ascendant.

West End Debut

It was McGoohan who, in March 1955 was the first to finally make it in a staring role in a West End play. He was offered the lead in *Serious Charge*, a play by Philip King dealing with the experiences of a young vicar, newly arrived in his parish. Having accused a teenage thug of being involved in the death of a young girl, the vicar is in turn accused of sexually molesting a teenager, as an act of revenge on the part of the thug and his associates.

It was an unusual subject for the stage at the time, sensitively dealt with in the play, and the part no doubt appealed to the socially conscious McGoohan. He was returning to once more play a man of God on stage – an ironic echo of the vocation that his family had originally intended for him. McGoohan was clearly impressed by the script, recounting that:

> 'I got a West End chance of a really strong leading part, as a Protestant priest in the play *Serious Charge*, with Frank Lawton and Olga Lindo.

We opened at the Garrick Theatre and next morning the critics gave us good reviews. Studio casting offices began to take some notice.'[11]

Theatre World described his performance as 'outstanding' while *Plays and Players* also singled him out for special praise:

'The acting throughout is of a high quality. Patrick McGoohan makes a most refreshing vicar with a performance remarkable for the amount of light and shade it introduces.'

McGoohan had finally made his big leap and had made a huge success out of it. His talent and persistence had paid off and from now on, he need never have to worry about returning to manual work again. It was something of a triumph for any young actor, but this was only the start for him. McGoohan was now being recognised as a significant talent on the London stage, audiences and critics both noting a remarkable quality in his art, born out of sheer dedication. Featuring his performance in their 'Tomorrow's Lead' series, *Plays and Players* magazine were of the opinion that:

'The role of Howard Phillips may not have great depth, but it demands an actor with a wide range, capable of bringing out many facets of character. Patrick McGoohan skilfully makes him an upright man of high Christian ideals without once making him appear priggish, and he exploits the moments of comedy to the full with his excellent timing.'[12]

The Influence of Orson Welles

In the audience for *Serious Charge* was a man who would come to be extremely influential on McGoohan. An actor, writer, and film director who had, many argued, redefined the language of cinema with his groundbreaking film *Citizen Kane* in 1941. Orson Welles was so struck by the power of McGoohan's performance that he later admitted to feeling 'intimidated' by the young actor.

Due to unforeseen circumstances involved with the booking ahead of theatres, *Serious Charge* was forced to close early and McGoohan took full advantage of his early release to take a prestigious part launching a primetime BBC anthology series of thirty minute plays all set around a railway terminus. He would star as James Hartley in the opening play *No Margin for Error.* It would have taken up a full week of his time, rehearsals ran for five days before the live performance on Saturday, and the exposure of this starring role would be worth every second of it.

It was now June 1955 and the individualistic movie genius Welles was in England for an extended period. He had been in talks with both the BBC and various film studios on a variety of projects, notably a close-set talk show for the BBC who were mindful yet disdainful of the imminent birth of Independent Television and who therefore were starting to look for such transatlantic stars. With his typical flair for juggling several projects at once, Welles had decided to also form a theatre troupe to perform his own adaptation of Herman Melville's *Moby Dick.* As with the Mercury Theatre, his first 'media troupe', Welles wanted to recruit actors who had done enough work to be competent but who had not yet received major exposure. Impressed by McGoohan's performance in *Serious Charge* and maybe reminded of the actor from the BBC series *Terminus*, he arranged for an invitation to audition to be sent out to the rising star of the West End. McGoohan recalled in the aforementioned interview given to Arnold Hano in the *TV Time*s 1977 that:

> 'I came in to audition. All the lights were on the stage, the rest of the theatre was a black abyss with Welles out there, listening. I started to read then I heard two voices. Welles and somebody next to him, discussing production costs. So I stopped and Welles immediately boomed out, "Why did you stop?". I said, "I thought you might like to listen to me." Welles snapped, "I can listen and talk at the same time. Keep reading." I started in again and again he kept talking and again I stopped and Welles said, "I told you to keep reading."

After a few more instances of this behaviour, McGoohan reverted to type. He reportedly threw down his script, told the great Mr Welles precisely what he could do with *Moby Dick* and began to storm off the stage. Whereupon Welles called him back (either shamefacedly or with a roar of laughter depending on accounts, both from McGoohan) and offered him the part of Starbuck on the spot. McGoohan would later observe that the play's three week run was 'one of the most exciting moments of my career'[13] and that while compressing the scope of the novel for stage was undoubtedly a challenge, it was nothing compared to the challenge of working with Welles himself. However, it seems that the feeling was mutual.

Confidence or Ego? The Auteur

The above quote is further evidence of a tremendous self-belief within the man that speaks of an equally tremendous egotism. Interviews provide us with a portrait of a highly emotional man who simply did not know how to control his temper. This was a person who, when he felt he wasn't being given the attention that he felt he deserved, would very quickly explode with anger. McGoohan was, I believe, perfectly aware of this failing and his penchant for initially challenging a new colleague might have been a way of gauging their reactions, seeing how far he could push them in both performance and, I suspect, their personal relationship.

In any case, Welles cast McGoohan as Starbuck. The character was a sincere Quaker, with deeply held beliefs and convictions, significantly the first character to stand up and question Captain Ahab's relentless and insane pursuit of the Sperm Whale. Starbuck remains the lone voice of reason throughout the novel and it's feasible that Welles realised there was something in McGoohan's character akin to these traits at that very first audition. As a side note, it is worth commenting that Starbuck was as devoted to his family as McGoohan himself, though I doubt Welles made that connection upon their first meeting.

Also cast by Welles, was a young Joan Plowright, who recalled her first impressions of the piece:

> 'He was going to do this extraordinary version, his own, of *Moby Dick* where I played the cabin boy, Pip. Because – it sounds extraordinary – but the conception was of a travelling theatre company rehearsing a play

that's just come in a pile of scripts, which is *Moby Dick*, but originally they were there to rehearse *King Lear* and I was playing Cordelia. So I was in ... it was kind of eighteen-something or other, this company was supposed to be, so I was in, you know a long skirt and a bustle.'[14]

The premise of Welles' version, titled '*Moby Dick: Rehearsed*', is that a company of actors and their director are rehearsing an upcoming production of *King Lear*. However, their background project, *Moby Dick*, which is notoriously difficult to bring to the stage, becomes the focal point of the story and the actors slip in and out of character, offering their contemporary perspectives and experiences into the original narrative. Written in blank verse and skilfully edited by Welles to focus on the heart of the story, this was never going to be anything less than extremely impressionistic.

Joan Plowright's assertion that the production was very much the vision of one man gives weight to the theory that McGoohan learned his auteurship from the great film auteur of the 20th century. Eleven years later, McGoohan would go on to take total authorial control of *The Prisoner*. At the time the two men worked together, Welles had already made the remarkable *Citizen Kane* with total artistic control (provided he did not exceed a certain budget – which he proceeded to do). His single-minded pursuit of his artistic vision had alienated friends and colleagues but had, in the end, triumphed.

Welles' film was a thinly-veiled assault on media magnate William Randolph Hearst, the Rupert Murdoch of his day and a man who Welles felt exerted far too much influence on the American people, distorting and shaping their thinking by controlling and spinning the information given to them. He had been warned of the inevitable backlash and the damage that it could do to his career, but he shrugged off such fears. He the story that he wished to tell, taking the inevitable fall-out with a wry smile, secure in the knowledge that to have provoked such a reaction, his point must have been heard *and* taken seriously. Subsequent years vindicated Welles and such hyperbolic epithets as 'the greatest film ever made' have been applied to his movie masterpiece.

Welles' creative control of *Moby Dick* had, of course, included the casting as Joan Plowright recalled:

'So when he gave out parts there was Peter Sallis and Patrick McGoohan and Kenneth Williams, all in this production. And everybody was given a script when these new scripts arrived, and Orson said, "Well you play that, and you do that, and Miss Jenkins is … we don't have a negro cabin boy, so you play Pip, and if you can also play the harmonium that would be helpful."[15]

McGoohan would be hugely impressed by Welles' willingness and eagerness to collaborate, as recounted in *Woman*:

'He had chosen his cast from repertory and character actors. There were no "star" names among us. We worked as a team, and Orson drove us to find the exact force of the play much as Captain Ahab drove his crew to find the white whale which had taken off his leg.

Larger than life, blasting directions through his megaphone, he bullied, persuaded, encouraged and led us through rehearsals. We sweated, tried, failed and triumphed.

Though he had a dozen different, creative ideas a minute, he wanted ours, too. Anyone could make a suggestion, from the electrician to the leading actor – "Good! That's a better idea than mine. Come on, let's try it."'[16]

I believe that McGoohan's experience of working with Welles absolutely distilled the aspect of his personality that needed to be the auteur. He was learning how he might present a creative vision that would be entirely his, via the mechanism of film or television, with its literally hundreds of collaborators and services. To an extent, Welles had circumvented this from the start. He had taken it upon himself to adapt the novel and produce a script that was an unmistakably different and original interpretation of the text, stamping his personality on the project and then 'driving' his cast in rehearsals. Welles was just as capable of designing costumes or lighting plots as he was of fine-tuning a performance. McGoohan had kept his fascination with the behind-the scenes mechanics of production from his time at Rep and would have noted that Welles' control extended even to these areas, one shaping hand ensuring complete continuity of vision.

Another important facet to Welles was his fierce dedication to whichever project he was engaged upon. The work was everything to him and it had to be equally consuming for his band of collaborators. His was the final responsibility and he took that responsibility seriously. McGoohan recounted that although the cast and crew were more than willing to give their all for their inspiring leader, there was one night where Welles' drive for perfection was enough to drive even the most dedicated of performers to revolt:

> 'One three-line sequence defeated us. We had begun rehearsals at ten that morning. By quarter to eleven that night even Orson's devoted crew were near mutiny. We looked at each other and by common, unspoken consent we all walked out across to the pub, So far as we were concerned, that was it for that night. We underestimated Mr Welles. It took him one-and-a-half minutes to realise what had happened. Before we had time to order our drinks he was among us, ordering them himself and turning on such force of personality that, actors as we were, we became a captive audience, helpless with laughter at his anecdotes and stories. Then, without mentioning the play, he led us back to the theatre like a flock of lambs, and kept us there until 5 am on the same three-line sequence.'[17]

McGoohan uses the word 'force' twice in the above quotes. Once to describe Welles' personality, but more interestingly in his account of how the director drove his team to find the 'force of the play'. My inference is that, above all, Welles wanted his actors to find and portray the truth of the characters and their emotions. What can be gleaned of the staging reinforces the theory that Welles was interested in symbolism through performance. A contemporary account from *Hammer Horror* favourite Christopher Lee, who was involved in a filmed version of the play runs as follows:

> 'It was a version of his stage play, which I wasn't in, but it was mostly done in mime, drinking from non-existent cups, throwing non-existent harpoons. The notion was that of a play within a play, where the actors step in and out of their roles, in the story of *Moby Dick*. I remember one

of the first lines in the film. Orson came up to me and said, "If we touch land, Mr. Flask, for God's sake, no fornication!"[18]

The use of mime over props further reinforces the impressionistic feeling of Welles' vision. Lee recounted also that the director developed a peculiar foible during the shooting of the film, one that it is hoped he controlled on stage:

'He'd also talk all through your scenes, so of course they would have to be looped. We did *Moby Dick* at two theatres in London, The Hackney-Empire and The Scala. Another time, there was a scene where I had to say to Patrick McGoohan, "There's bad news from that ship," when The Pequod is approaching The Rachel. Suddenly, Orson's voice came from behind the camera, "There's bad news from that ship – mark my words." Well, I looked at Patrick, and Patrick looked at me, because we didn't quite know what was going on. We both wondered why Orson was repeating our lines. Then, on another occasion, Orson came down the centre aisle of the theatre while the cast and crew were all waiting on the stage, turned to the cameraman and said "action" and the cameraman said, "Mr. Welles, I haven't got a set-up yet," and Orson said to him, "Find one and surprise me."[19]

It's intriguing that McGoohan and Welles are described using very similar terms by their contemporaries and colleagues. Words like 'size' and 'force' are frequently used to describe both their personalities and performances. While both men were of above average size (though Welles considerably more so due to his substantial girth), it is nevertheless unusual that both are often described as managing to fill the available space. No doubt this was due to force of personality coupled with an actor's innate understanding of how to use their body, even unconsciously, to dominate and therefore effectively control those with whom they are working or socialising.

Opening in June 1955, Welles' production of *Moby Dick* ran for three weeks to rave reviews, before being forced to close early. McGoohan was once again singled out for praise, with critic Kenneth Tynan writing that:

'Patrick McGoohan as Starbuck, the mate who dares to oppose Ahab's will, is Melville's long, earnest man to the file, whittled out of immemorial teak. His is the greatest performance.'[20]

The New York Post claimed McGoohan's performance had been more finely honed than that of Welles himself; a fact that is not difficult to believe considering the workload that Welles had placed upon himself, coupled also with McGoohan's fanatical dedication to his craft. In the audience was a freelance film director, Pat Jackson, who remembered on the DVD commentary for an episode of *The Prisoner* he later directed that:

'I'd never heard of him. And within a few minutes he had the audience absolutely spellbound, including me. Not only had I seen a great actor but I had also found a leading man.'[21]

Jackson arranged to meet with McGoohan and invited him to come to the studio to shoot a test reel but found that the young actor was very nervous, largely, it seems, because of the fact that he was not well-versed in the mechanics of filmmaking.

'He looked very pale and worried and he came up to me and said "Pat, I think I've changed my mind because I know nothing about filming and I'm very frightened that I'm going to waste an awful lot of your film. So I said Pat, my dear fellow, we look on a thousand feet of film as no more important than a roll of lavatory paper. You have nothing to lose and everything to gain … I know you'll do brilliantly. And of course he did brilliantly and was put under contract.'

Unfortunately for McGoohan the film did not quite happen in the way it was planned and both Pats departed the project. As, according to Jackson, it managed to empty the cinemas and was withdrawn after about two days, perhaps this 'misfortune' was a blessing.

On-screen Exposure

McGoohan was now keen to explore his career in film and particularly television. The latter offered greater creative opportunities, he felt, especially as, because of its unique system of funding, the BBC was able to offer highbrow programming from a diverse variety of sources. At that time, the corporation was considering anything from adaptations of the classics and Shakespeare to new material written especially for the medium.

However, the big money was in film and McGoohan was now keen to reinforce the stability that he had at home with Joan and Catherine. Television was rarely exported to Hollywood but, at that time, the British film industry had a vibrant export trade. He made bit part appearances in a few films, notably as a Swedish water therapist of all things in *I Am A Camera* (1955) before landing a substantial role as Moor Larkin in the Victor Mature vehicle *Zarak* (1956). McGoohan had to endure three weeks away from Joan in Africa, shooting for the movie, though fortunately he was home in time to spend Christmas with his family once again.

Zarak would be released to largely negative reviews, but once again McGoohan emerged shining. He was singled out in one review from Margaret Hinxman in *Picturegoer*:

> 'In the fantastic hodge podge of *Zarak*, there's only one acting performance worthy of the name – from Patrick McGoohan. He plays that invariably thankless role of the doom-predicting second-in-command to the British Army hero (Michael Wilding).
>
> Yet McGoohan, an Irish-American newcomer to the British screen, gives his stupid character a stature and strength. In a half-way decent role, McGoohan will be really something!'[22]

The reviewer had clearly missed *Serious Charge* and *Moby Dick* that year, in which McGoohan had already proved he could be 'something', but it is yet another testament to his drive for excellence that he should manage to bring such depth to a largely one dimensional character in a supporting role.

No 'Voice Only'

Surprisingly, McGoohan very rarely took on voice-only work. Radio was still a much bigger employer of acting talent in the 1950s than television and required even less work for the money, as the script did not have to be memorised before the performance. However, McGoohan steered resolutely clear of radio work and potentially lucrative voice-over work also. It seems he had a problem with vocal-only acting. Eric Mival, music editor on *The Prisoner*, recalled that McGoohan was nervous whenever voice work was required and did his best to avoid it at all costs. The reasons for this fear are unknown. Perhaps McGoohan was so conscious of his physicality as an actor that it was indivisible from the vocal performance for him. Being unable to express himself visually on radio might have caused him to feel somehow exposed. In any case, this was an endearing quirk for a man whose voice alone carried a tremendous power and richness in performance. In 1956, he made his one and only radio appearance in a dramatic operetta called *Travelling Companions*. Apparently he did not have to sing but was so traumatised by the appearance that he was scared off radio for life.

McGoohan spent 1956 gradually building up his TV and film portfolio. For the first time in a long while, he was also able to take a part that enabled him to share the stage with his wife. *Ring for Catty* was a play that McGoohan had previously performed in at the Q Theatre and now he returned to it on the West End stage with Joan, amusingly, playing his character's girlfriend.

The cast also featured Mary Mackenzie, Andrew Ray and William Hartnell, with whom McGoohan would be reunited in the Rank film *Hell Drivers* (1957). *Theatre World* noted that both Hartnell and McGoohan 'immobilised in beds, give impressive demonstrations of horizontal acting'. McGoohan clearly had a flair for comedy, citing it as a favourite form in theatre because of the immediacy of the response of the audience, allowing the performer an instant judgement on what was working and what was not. Clearly McGoohan's thoughtful stagecraft extended into the performance itself, with the actor always looking to refine, improve and fine-tune, even when on stage. This was rare, as for many actors, once the performance is laid down it is locked and they rarely deviate; if nothing else to avoid confusing their fellow actors.

Patrick and Joan no doubt revelled in the chance to work together for the first time since their Sheffield Rep days, and were now able to juggle their home and work commitments to the detriment of neither. But McGoohan still had his eye on bigger things. He yearned for greater financial security and so not long after the conclusion of *Ring for Catty*, he decided to devote more time to progressing his film career. With several high profile and well-received TV appearances behind him now, not to mention the successes of *Serious Charge*, *Moby Dick* and indeed *Ring For Catty* – all of which showed his flexibility as an actor – he was in a better position than ever before to break into the lucrative world of movies. Recounting the story of how he got his break, McGoohan explains:

> 'Some time after, more than able to do with one day's money for one day's work, I went along to the film studios again. A young actress was being given a test for a part opposite Dirk Bogarde, and I volunteered to act as his stand-in. In the haphazard luck of films, when the Rank casting office saw the rushes, it was to me they offered a contract, for five years, starting at £4,000 a year. This eclipsed any guarantees my bank clerk days had offered and, for the second and last time in my life, financial security tempted me.
>
> I saw it providing us with all the things we had never been able to enjoy as a family: a home of our own. Time together, a chance to see more of Catherine growing up.'[23]

At the time, £4,000 a year was considered a considerable sum, certainly well above the average. McGoohan had become a minor star, a valuable and saleable commodity, a resource to be packaged and exported. That he had the talent to match his good looks was no doubt a bonus to the Rank execs. He was immediately put to work in a film called *High Tide At Noon* playing a womanising tough guy, Simon Breck; one of three potential lovers vying for the attentions of a seventeen-year-old girl. The movie was sufficiently well written, the end product was of decent quality and it was entered into the Cannes film festival which gave McGoohan the chance to attend and, reportedly, meet Jean Cocteau.

Though little is known about this meeting, it seems that Cocteau and McGoohan, in the presence also of veteran blowhard actor James Robertson Justice, met on the roof of the festival cinema, taking in the views over Cannes, talking and no doubt exchanging ideas. Though almost a piece of apocrypha in McGoohan's history, I suspect that this meeting had a great effect on the actor in ascension and auteur-in-the-making. McGoohan was always open to new ideas and no doubt knew of Cocteau's work. A multi-talented polymath, Cocteau had been an early exponent of surrealism and carried the dreamlike unreality of that artistic movement into his movies, producing extraordinary works such as *Le Belle et la Bête* (1946) and *Orphée* (1950). Cocteau saw himself foremost as a poet and approached all his works from that perspective. McGoohan was to create a similar effect in episodes of *The Prisoner* later, an allegorical series laced with surrealism and symbolism, and I cannot imagine that he wasted his time with Cocteau by discussing showbiz gossip.

One immediate consequence of McGoohan's new contract was the much longed-for financial freedom. A piece in *The Bulletin* from April 13th 1957 reports that:

> 'Off to Portugal with his attractive Scots wife Joan and his five-year-old daughter Catherine, is a film star who plans to spend a month writing a highly technical book on theology. A queer sort of subject for a film actor to busy himself with? Not at all. And anyway, Patrick McGoohan – "the man with a mind of his own" who has a key role in the new film *High Tide At Noon*, a love story set in a Lobster fishing community off the coast of Canada's Nova Scotia – won't talk about it."

Aside from including the bizarre fact that apparently McGoohan had by now taken up Scottish country dancing and liked nothing better than to 'dance to the radiogram at home'(!), as an early piece of Rank-related publicity the text above is revealing. Rank had clearly already decided that McGoohan was to be sold as a rebel, a free thinker, a dangerous figure. He would be cast accordingly in subsequent roles. However, fresh from his experiences at Cannes, which had even been described by his co-star as 'phoney' in one interview, McGoohan was already starting to detest the restrictions placed upon him along with the media-friendly hoops he was now expected to jump through. Speaking in *Woman* magazine in 1965, the actor recounted his experiences as a rising star:

> 'I soon began to discover, in a bank, or a film studio, the basic price demanded for security remains the same: conformity. At nineteen I'd been unable to settle for the 9 am to 5 pm daily routine with a pension as the golden carrot at the end of forty years, At twenty-nine it became equally difficult to submit to the ideas the Studio had then for "grooming a potential star".
>
> I fitted into the conventionalities of their glossy publicity schemes with about as much ease as I had embarked on my first dancing lessons at the Sheffield Youth Club – and certainly with less enthusiasm.
>
> Getting me to take part in The Parade of Stars at the Cannes Film Festival, or cultivate a smooth line in cocktail party talk was an un-rewarding task. They must have felt that, in me, they'd netted an oyster with more sand than pearl.
>
> They compensated for this by deciding to project a public image of me as a "rebel" In fact, I had never been less rebellious. I passively accepted it all, as disinterested in the kind of films I was having to make as in the round of publicity "celebrations" I was expected to attend.'[24]

Hell Drivers

Swallowing his objections, McGoohan moved onto his next Rank project, *Hell Drivers* (1957), a kitchen sink drama filmed ten years before the term was coined, set in an austere post war landscape of constant rebuilding and new construction. McGoohan played Red, the foreman of a firm of truckers run by Cartley; a splendidly dour performance by William Hartnell contrasting McGoohan's smouldering intensity. Red is a violent bullying thug and McGoohan brings real tangible danger to the part. Later commentators have mentioned it was often difficult to tell whether McGoohan would 'shake your hand or thump you' and his portrayal of Red gives a square on insight into that side of his personality. *Hell Drivers* was well received for what it was, a standard Rank drama, but it became something of a cult film in later years. This is largely because of its astonishing cast which counts amongst its number Sid James, David McCallum, Herbert Lom, Sean Connery and the unfairly forgotten Stanley Baker in the lead role.

In an interview reproduced on a DVD release of *Hell Drivers*, Stanley Baker recalled that the fight scene between him and McGoohan had been one of the best he had ever achieved on screen, but that the intensity of it had left both men with bruises and loosened teeth. This is entirely in character for McGoohan, who gave as much dedicated energy to the physicality of his roles as to every other aspect.

McGoohan won further plaudits for *Hell Drivers* but again he had to go through the round of self-congratulatory ceremonies that accompanied the release and publicising of the movie. In *Woman*, McGoohan reminisces:

'At one such party, when the champagne was flowing to launch a new picture, I found myself thinking back to my first real success in the West End. *Serious Charge*.

That play had earned me a fraction of the money I was now receiving. But the work had been challenging and absorbing, and I knew that in the two hours of the first performance alone I had gained more personal satisfaction than I would in five years of contract film-making.

On that First Night, still unaccustomed to the accepted publicity ballyhoo of "celebrating", Joan and I had shared a quiet drink in my dressing-room. Afterwards we had gone home talking all the way about the thoughts and hopes we had put into reaching this goal, and all the things to which it could lead.'

From such a hopeful perspective, McGoohan then described how he had moved from a position of active anticipation to one of blind resignation. After only a short period, the price of financial security was proving to be too high and it was inevitable that he should start looking for a way out. McGoohan continues in the same piece:

'Now, when I came home after some publicity stunt, there was little to tell her about except my growing dislike of all the things I regarded as phoney nonsense and the studio called "glamour". I felt I was becoming not only a puppet actor but, to some extent, a puppet human being, too. I should have had the honesty to break the contract. Instead I thought I could see it out comfortably for five years.'

Tough Guy Image

Rank was not making a great deal of use of its star name, finding him difficult to place in films as McGoohan resolutely refused to conform to a saleable ideal. His next venture for the company was as yet another womanising hard man, this time a gypsy named Jess, another amoral character desperate to grab at the money inherited by the sister-in-law of his lover. McGoohan claimed to have accepted the part without even looking at the script. He felt that as he was being paid, he should be doing some work, any work, and he wanted to rebut his 'difficult actor' image. I suspect that he may have bitterly regretted this decision, particularly in light of the fact that for this film he had to perform an on screen kiss. Without any recourse to perfectly valid artistic reasons to avoid this clinch, McGoohan simply did what most actors would do and performed the scene as written and directed; a passionate moment between two lovers. His likely discomfort at this event has never been recorded but, bearing in mind the lengths he went to in later work to avoid such scenes, it seems probable that his reaction was not positive.

McGoohan was by now heartily sick of his Rank contract. During the production of *The Gypsy and the Gentleman* (1958) he had been profiled by Peter Tipthorpe in an article called 'I'm not a tough guy,' for the magazine *Photoplay*.

"'It's all very well playing these tough guy parts," he argued, "but surely what is interesting is why the fellow is tough. In British films characters are either black or white – good or bad. We merely scratch the surface of the story."

There is a lot to like and admire about McGoohan. He is a character. He has ambition and enthusiasm. His main fault, it seems, is that he wants everything to go his way. I don't mean he wants to rule the roost. But he wants to get on in his own particular way and do the things he wants to do. And they don't include playing toughs. He pushed his empty glass away. "I've worked hard in the theatre," he said. "I don't think I have much to be grateful for as far as my career is concerned."[25]

McGoohan was quite clearly happy to acknowledge that he had, as far as he is concerned, done his time in Rep and in the theatre and had mastered his craft. While this could be misconstrued as arrogance, I am inclined to believe that this was simply his 'no nonsense' truthfulness coming to the fore. After some interesting snippets about the fact that McGoohan planned the next year to hire a theatre and present five plays, one of which, a farce, he had written himself, Tipthorpe tells an amusing anecdote concerning McGoohan's reaction when asked by the interviewer his opinion of the Stanislavski method approach to acting:

> "'I heard a story about the late Humphrey Bogart," he replied, "He went to a party and everyone was talking about The Method and how wonderful it was. Someone turned to him and asked him how he tackled his parts. Bogart, who until then hadn't said a word, replied: 'It's easy. I just learn my lines.' That sums up what I think of The Method."
>
> Patrick McGoohan is a man who says what he thinks.
>
> We drank to his future. But I warned him: "Take it easy. Pat. Or you'll be in trouble.'"

McGoohan's 'five plays project' appears never to have come to fruition, like so many other projects thrown up by his fertile mind. Indeed, following through with an idea seems to be a constant problem for the actor which perhaps contributed to his later determination to see *The Prisoner* through to completion at all costs.

McGoohan's final film for Rank as a contract player was *Nor The Moon By Night* (1958), shot on location in South Africa, and it was to prove an unhappy experience not just for the frustrated actor but for the entire production team. As reported in the *Ottowa Citizen* in February 1958, bad weather caused delays from the outset, a continuity girl was taken to hospital with a poisoned leg while the chief cameraman succumbed to a recurrence of pneumonia and his replacement was held in quarantine for a week. Even McGoohan did not escape unscathed:

'I spent Christmas Eve of 1957 sitting on the *stoep* [porch] of a Durban hotel, looking across the Indian Ocean under a sky glittering with stars.

It presented about as much beauty as any part of the world can provide, but I was in no mood to appreciate it. We were in South Africa on location and had two bases there, the main one in Durban, a smaller one in a wild and beautiful place called The Valley of a Thousand Hills. Driving myself back to Durban, after a day's filming, the back axel snapped and the car hit a bridge at sixty miles-per-hour. It was several hours before another car passed, its driver found me and could get me to hospital.

The studio was afraid my injuries might mean they would have to scrap the entire sequences of the picture. But in three weeks, the severe concussion subsided and the healing scars on my face were easily disguised with make-up.'[26]

More important to McGoohan than the physical discomfort, however, was the yawning gulf between him and his family. Never at his best when away from Joan, the frustrations of the ailing production would have only added to his burden. Due to the early setbacks, the schedule was pushed further and further back.

'We should have been home for Christmas. Instead, I had been waiting all day for the telephone call booked to London and when it came, my wife Joan and I had scarcely been able to hear each other. Now the sticky heat of the African evening, the paper hat and crackers provided with "the greetings" of the hotel, were only added reminder that I was 6,000 miles away from her and our five-year-old daughter, Catherine.

"And why?" I kept asking myself. "For what satisfactory or really worthwhile reason?"

Most jobbing actors, delighted to be in thrall to a company that guaranteed them a high income for five years, would offer several responses to that question. But McGoohan felt that he could earn more than enough from his far more rewarding television and theatre work to fulfil his obligations as a husband and father. Besides which, he had great concerns about how his career as a movie actor might come to cause something that he simply could not countenance.

'We were the adult version of the circus coming to town, banging our big drums, waving our biggest cheque books in the world … But, unlike the circus people of childhood, we didn't travel with our families in our caravans, facing the realities of sweating to put up a big top, maintaining the disciplines of practising to perform dangerous skills, anxiously counting the night's takings, working until we were too tired to see.

We travelled alone and the studios provided the planes, hotels and cars, the publicity, the glossy image. When the day's scenes were shot, too often there was nothing to do in an attractive place, thousands of miles from home

Then, boredom and loneliness, damaging in any circumstances, became totally destructive to those who were already unhappy or insecure in their personal lives.'[27]

McGoohan went on to explain that he had seen three marriages break up during the course of the cursed shoot and this had clearly affected him deeply. It seems that he finally made a definite decision to leave his Rank contract as soon as he possibly could and had also come to another more personal conclusion:

'I had seen enough to make up my mind that never again would I go on location without Joan. I came to a few other decisions at the same time, the main one being that I'd had enough of messing around with the financial security of a long contract. I'd learnt my lesson. An actor who wants the freedom to choose his own way of life has to be a gambler. If he isn't prepared to live by the harsh but fair rules of gambling, he should quit.'[28]

It does seem that from this point on, whenever possible, if McGoohan had to leave home for any length of time to attend a shoot, he made sure that Joan and his children are accommodated with him. My opinion on this is divided; while this is an incredibly romantic gesture in some ways, it could also be interpreted as confining and controlling. Did McGoohan want to make sure he could keep an eye on Joan while on location? Was he prey to such jealousies? Or was he perhaps making sure that Joan could keep an eye on him as his lifestyle became ever more star-studded. It's hard to say, but considering his apparent emotional dependence on his wife, I imagine that his motivation was a genuine desire to be with her and his family as much as possible, nothing more sinister.

Strident Rules

'Harsh but fair' is a phrase which characterises much of McGoohan's approach to life. He was not one for taking the easy route, nor for talking on roles he did not believe in. Fortunately, his gamble paid off. He had been used so sparingly by the studios that he had plenty of free time to take on television work. With money in his pocket and free time on his hands, McGoohan reacted typically to his golden imprisonment by Rank. In an interview given to Tom Hutchinson for his regular column 'The Runaround' in *Picturegoer* (which was a precursor to today's celebrity magazines and therefore an unusual source for the otherwise disdainful actor), McGoohan explains why he decided to take himself off to Spain in disgust to make a film of his own on 16 mm:

> 'I am going to make this film to get something out of my system … to enjoy myself creatively. One can't say I've done that with the films I've made for Rank. I know that my name has been made far more important by the three TV plays I've done than by any of the five films I've made at Pinewood. They said I was an awkward customer so to prove that I wasn't I accepted two roles without even reading the scripts.'[29]

He named *The Gypsy and the Gentlemen* and *Nor The Moon By Night* as being the two films, mentioning that he was 'ashamed of the latter'. Angrily, McGoohan continued, no doubt enjoying the chance to finally speak out:

> 'They (Rank) haven't suggested a thing to me. You'd have thought they'd have cashed in on me because I'm told that my plays *All My Sons,*

Disturbance and *This Day in Fear* were very popular. But nothing. Do you know I've been two years under contract to the Rank organization but until the other day, when I called in myself, I hadn't met the casting director for just over a year?'

One can imagine McGoohan delivering his outraged diatribe, his voice rising as he expresses his disbelief at the Rank stupidity. Hutchinson describes how McGoohan caught himself and smiled:

'Maybe you think I'm big-headed. But I'm complaining as loudly as this because there's so much frustration in British films. And there shouldn't be.'

In his summing-up paragraph, Hutchinson describes McGoohan as possessing 'a dominating talent that needs discipline, but which is definitely a talent'. The implication is that Hutchinson feels that if McGoohan doesn't learn to control his outbursts, his temper will adversely affect his career. He was to be proven right a decade later.

As McGoohan mentioned, his recent TV work had indeed brought him yet more positive attention. Of particular note was the BBC teleplay *This Day in Fear*, in which McGoohan took the role of James Coogan, an ex-IRA man who finds that his past has caught up with him. Once again, McGoohan gave a potentially unsympathetic character a twist of honesty and decency in his wish to start again with his wife and to protect her from his terrorist past. The desire to take on more challenging 'out of step' roles can be attributed in part to his current experiences in film. Fortunately, McGoohan was able to find an easy way out of his Rank shackles.

'A few months later, the Rank Organization began an economy drive and when the renewal options on my contract were due, we reached an amicable decision to part.

I was now free to accept a number of plays for television. After several years spent in the hot-house atmosphere of a big studio empire, this was like coming home to the beat of everything I had known and enjoyed in the theatre.'[30]

Rest in Violence

McGoohan's divorce from Rank meant that finally he was able to pursue work that he found to be artistically satisfying and that would meet his high standards. Peter Sallis, as mentioned previously, recalled that McGoohan would only take a part if he found it worthwhile, with no interest in the status of the role. He was only interested in work that challenged or simply fascinated him and now he had the exposure and track record to allow him to pursue roles of his choosing, while commanding high enough fees to support his family. The 'all or nothing' approach had worked.

> 'Now, instead of a publicity luncheon in a Mayfair restaurant, I was meeting TV producer Cliff Owen in a Hammersmith workmen's cafe at 9 am. There, over endless mugs of tea, we thrashed out details of how to interpret dialogue, build a character, before starting rehearsals at 10 am. Sometimes we didn't finish till midnight, but the hours flew. I had forgotten what boredom meant.'[31]

Cliff Owen had bravely decided to team up McGoohan and Richard Harris to perform a live TV play called *Rest in Violence*. Having dismissed the initial script, much to Owen's delight, the three began to craft a new storyline, against the growing deadlines of rehearsals and the immutable transmission date. After the stultifying creative atmosphere of Rank, McGoohan relished this opportunity to enjoy a ferocious and energetic collaboration with two wills as strong as his. For his part, Owen was willing to let the two lead actors have as much creative input as they wanted. His idea for the script was that it should feature two Irish brothers, diametrically opposed. Harris was to play the hot-headed nationalist, McGoohan would play a farmer and family man, concerned only with protecting his own and with the general trait of inflexibility that would inevitably lead to violence. McGoohan recounted the writing process in amusing detail:

> 'In the morning, at 9 am, we all moved into one of Granada's committee rooms and the arguments started. Harris, pacing up and down, began to

invent lines. As he spoke, a typist took them down. Cliff started pacing alongside him, making alterations. The typist took them down. Then they tore the whole thing up and started again. I joined in with my big speech, and the typist took that down. Cliff went to work on it. We scrapped and re-wrote that.'[32]

There is a wonderful similarity here between McGoohan's description and actor Alexis Kanner's reminiscences of the chaotic and exuberant production of 'Fall Out' (the final episode of *The Prisoner* in which he appeared as well as in 'Living in Harmony'). Kanner had described this script as being written on trains and planes, even in the spare minutes before a take. McGoohan had studied at the 'Church of Welles' by now and was ravenously creative; joyously bellowing at Harris and Owen who bellowed right back at him.

'Typist number one vanished, exhausted, and was replaced by typist number two. What she thought of the trio she had come to work for I can't begin to imagine: two far from docile Irishmen thumping the table and pacing the floor with Cliff Owen in the middle, more than dwarfing any slight superiority we may have had in mere inches, with the full power of his lungs. Compelled to out-shout both of us, by this time not only co-author and producer, he was referee as well.

The air was blue, with smoke and language, the floor ankle-deep in paper, and we quickly wore out typist number two. Number three arrived, together with a scriptwriter called in to help.'[33]

McGoohan always took his work home with him, devoting head-space and time to it even when he was at home with his family. This reached extremes during the current creative battle over *Rest in Violence*, with each side determined to ensure that their creative input was heard.

'Joan, grown accustomed to the fact that when I did get home it was only to sit up all night composing pages of dialogue, solely in order to go back to Granada and tear them all up first thing next morning, took to leaving me notes on the kitchen table. More than once I picked up the scribbled replies I intended for her and took them back – to be torn up too. If Cliff Owen needed any proof that inflexibility leads to violence, Harris and I were supplying it. Though I reckon if I'd been really inflexible I would have killed Harris. I've no doubt he had the same thoughts about me.

At the end of fifteen days – and nights – of this, we'd lost count of the number of typists we'd driven mad: the script-writer gave up television for good and took up architecture, and we had four days left to rehearse and go on the air.

It took three months to get over it, and was worth every ounce of the energy, time and effort.'[34]

How typical of McGoohan that last sentence is. The eventual play, *Rest In Violence*, was well-received and McGoohan would go on later in the year to receive a BAFTA for 'Best Television Actor'. His work had now been recognised with a prestigious award, one of the highest honours the industry could bestow, and his fee would have tripled overnight. Having McGoohan on board was now a guarantee of quality and as 1958 gave way to '59, he was about to take his next big career step. He was about to return to his original training ground, the theatre, in a role that many at the time felt would define him forever. It stands testament to McGoohan's skill and strength of will that it did not.

Back to the Boards: Brand

Running all through his life, there is a strongly selfish streak about Patrick McGoohan, a strong desire for events to go his way. When they did not, he could be loud and frequently furious, exhibiting an almost uncomprehending frustration and being entirely dismissive of those who were in opposition to him. These traits can be seen strongly to the forefront of the character of *Brand* in Henrik Ibsen's 1865 play of the same name. This was to be McGoohan's next big role and one that would influence him greatly. *Brand* was a play which he would return to again and again in interviews and one which he later planned to make as a film, entirely his own creative vision, shot on location in Norway.

In early 1959, the 59 Theatre Company leased the Lyric Opera House in Hammersmith for twenty-four weeks, their intention being to produce a series of five plays. Formed by Finnish émigré Casper

Wreade along with James H Lawne, its stated intention was to produce works where the play was the main focus of attention, rather than the players; a style popular in Europe but becoming increasingly scarce in England and the United States. This would have immediately appealed to McGoohan's disdain for a focus on the individual star, though he would come to stand out above all others in the company during the eventual three-play-run. Wreade was a producer of plays for BBC television, now taking a break from that medium, and McGoohan was finding his TV work the most fulfilling of his career at present; so there was a mutual interest in collaborating.

The company featured many actors who would go on to achieve greatness and become household names: Patrick Wymark, Peter Sallis, Fulton Mackay and Michael Gough, to name but four. McGoohan joined the company with enthusiasm, always feeling that being amongst good actors raised the levels of his own performance.

The first work to be presented by the company was *Danton's Death* a play by Georg Büchner set during the French Revolution. Starring Patrick Wymark, the play was performed to generally positive reviews, with many of the cast receiving good notices in the press. This included McGoohan, who was described as being 'Grimly sinister at all times' in his role of St Just. However, McGoohan was focusing most deeply on the play in which he was to take the lead. After a staging of August Strindberg's *Creditors* and appearing within a double bill alongside *The Cheats of Scapin* (which received less than glowing reviews), *Brand* opened on April 8th 1959.

For some time, it had been considered that a direct English translation of *Brand* was unstageable. Peter Sallis, the only performer to take two parts in the 1959 production and who had been a contemporary of McGoohan at the Sheffield Rep, recalled that 'the script would have been two inches thick.'[35] However, Michael Meyer had now crafted an interpretation that could feasibly be mounted and the 59 Theatre Company had taken on the ambitious and challenging production. Wreade had long since been fascinated by the play and was keen to preserve the dramatism of the piece in the English version, finding that Ibsen's work came vary naturally to him because of his Scandinavian upbringing. In McGoohan, he had found an actor who was capable of sustaining the driving remorseless power of the righteous believer, a performer who already embodied the character's 'all or nothing' dictate in his own life. Indeed, the parallels between actor and character are startling.

On the surface, Brand is a priest enslaved to God and apparently shackled by his belief, but there are yet again keynote similarities. Brand sacrifices everything for God, he is an 'all or nothing' supplicant who is absolutely devoted. He is also an obsessive who snarls his anger at those who are less willing to give deeply of themselves. In direct parallel, many actors and crew have mentioned that on any production, but especially those in which he was most deeply committed, McGoohan would tear apart any professional who wasn't showing as great a commitment as he, while lauding, praising and fiercely supporting those who were.

Yet precisely because of his devotion to God, Brand is another rebel, disdaining society's rules for his divine calling and behaving in a manner that would be judged cold and uncompromising to those close to him, particularly his mother.

I submit that Brand crystallised McGoohan. At one point in the play he says, 'It is our time, our generation that is sick and must be cured. All you want to do is flirt and play and laugh.' It's an uncomfortably intense accusation, one that is tempting to dismiss. There is after all, no harm in laughter. However, as an indictment of today's society, where entertainment has become a demand and where consumerism, fed by dream weavers, is a necessity, this utterance wields an undeniable raw power.

The truth, of course, lies somewhere in the middle, but this is Brand's world. What his character fails to take into account is freedom of choice. For though we may live in a society that is drowning in a glut of desire, the final decision to buy or not to buy remains one's own. Many people probably take comfort in the goods that are offered to them, even if this is unconsciously, particularly those leading unfulfilled lives. The denial of pleasure is a lonely and unfulfilling path, perhaps suitable for a man of God who believes he will receive his reward for such abstinence in another life but unsuitable for most. If McGoohan had indeed been as intense as Brand, then as a rule, he would never have worked.

Nevertheless, Brand's persona seems to have become something of a crutch for McGoohan. When faced with those in whom he had little belief, he resorted to the black and white 'for you or against you' mentality that characterised so many of his characters for some time after his breakout performance as Ibsen's tortured priest. His portrayal could not have been better fitted to the complex play. It was a role which McGoohan took on with every fibre of his being. Translator Michael Meyer recalled:

> 'He wasn't good at acting relationships. He was very much like Laurence Olivier in that respect; he couldn't act convincingly a son, a husband or a father. But what Pat was good at was acting loners or people who can't make contact.'[36]

I disagree with Meyer's assertion that McGoohan had difficulty in convincingly showing relationships in his performances. Even Brand himself, cold and harsh though he is, shows flashes of an intense love for his suffering wife, noting at one point that, 'If Agnes were here it would be different. She would banish all my doubts. She would see greatness where I saw only smallness.' The surviving BBC recording of the play shows that McGoohan underplays this with great sensitivity, micro expressions of knowing happiness chasing across his features as he conjures her to mind after her death. It is one of the few softening aspects to Brand's character – his conviction that he and Agnes shall meet again in the afterlife – making him momentarily pitiable. McGoohan showed that he understood the moment perfectly, before once more bursting into righteous rage.

Brand provided a huge leap forward for McGoohan, cementing his reputation as an actor of above average quality and integrity. I would also argue that the play shaped him and strengthened his attitude to work. Casting McGoohan in the role of a dedicated, obsessive and uncompromising man, driven by his belief in what he is doing, was an inspired move and it was the power of this one performance that was most often noted in contemporary accounts of the play's run.

Rosalind Knight, from the British Library's theatre archive project recalled the opening night:

'The first night of *Brand* was something to be seen to be believed. Michael had said to Patrick McGoohan, "Don't push it. Don't force it. Just let it come on the press night." ...And quite a lot of the great and the good were there. And it, you know, started slowly and everything. And finally an actor called Fulton McKay ... he had to pick up a mind stone and throw it at Brand. Now the force and the weight and the viciousness of that mind stone had to be seen to be believed. And Patrick McGoohan received it, and became furious as the character of Brand. And then he piled on the pace, the intensity, the agony, the passion, the fury...'[37]

Peter Sallis, co-starring in the production and interviewed on the BFI's DVD release of the BBC version of *Brand* stated:

'If you imagine an acting performance between A and Z, Pat started at Z, he never went back, Z plus, plus plus, but the astonishing concentration, the total absorption in the character was there for anyone to see on the audience and certainly for those of us there on stage.

Brand is probably the most single-minded character ever written ... In Patrick McGoohan they'd got a man who could do it and get away with it. Well, not get away with it, do it and make it compelling. The point about *Brand* is that it needs application to the *nth* degree, you cannot go on stage to do *Brand* and do the shopping list at the same time. It may not be pure Stanislavski but, boy, do you need concentration and Patrick's concentration, the look in his eyes never wavered from one night to the next. At times he was terrifying on the stage to be with I mean, you saw this look of god going right through you. And he sustains it.'[38]

Sallis noted with good-natured amusement that McGoohan had not responded well to his attempts to introduce a tiny scintilla of levity into the play in his second role as the Provost, testing out the acoustics of his new church by calling for lambs to fill it and be saved.

'With the Provost, there was a bit of naughtiness there which I know Patrick did not approve of, he went from Z 1 to Z 4 when I was doing the Provost.'

Sallis also offered an insight into McGoohan's personal involvement with the role. In interviews and reminiscences from colleagues, the picture is of an actor who puts down his character at the end of the day as easily as he takes off his costume. McGoohan seemed to have taken Brand to heart, unless he was simply exhausted by the emotional exertions of infusing the role with such power night after night.

'I tried not to go round and see him in his dressing room in any of the performances … the first night of the play we had done before *Danton's Death*, I think that he and Joan and Elaine my wife, we all went out for supper. But with *Brand*, he wasn't in that sort of mood, I don't think he wanted to see anybody after the show and you could understand it. Talk about unwinding, I don't think he did unwind. I think from the moment that he did the first performance to the moment he did the last performance he was thinking and breathing Brand. Now that, of course, is a wild exaggeration and probably untrue but that was the sort of feeling you got with Patrick.'

In this age of image sculpture, where the public persona of a star performer is crafted and guided by a skilled team of PR people, publicists and marketing experts, it is amusing to speculate that the character genuinely became, in a way, McGoohan's 'brand' (as opposed to just his *Brand*). One he would use as an avatar to hide behind in interviews, forcefully expounding upon his Catholic doctrine when it came to the pernicious subject of sex (or sometimes even mild affection it seems) on TV. The character gave as much to the actor as he to it though, even at his most extreme, McGoohan never descended to the levels of Brand's unquestioning self-belief and reliance on an undefined external source of guidance and insight. While Brand was yoked to God, McGoohan was a free thinker, able to question beyond dogma.

Brand propelled McGoohan into the stratosphere. By 1959 he was in a position to cherry pick the work he was offered. The reviews and notices that he received for *Brand* had been outstandingly positive. Sallis noted that although the audiences had been very appreciative of the settings, lighting and the work of the other performers, their greatest respect was reserved for the man who had so convincingly embodied Ibsen's tortured priest, a warning against blind obedience and belief:

'At the end of the play the audience stood and they stood to him.'[39]

Or as Rosalind Knight writes about the play:

'Well, I mean it was just a huge success. And people poured into the theatre – Lyric Hammersmith – to see it. The notices were ecstatic and the beginning of Michael Elliott's career was made.'[40]

McGoohan now had the growing desire to become the Victorian 'actor-manager', following in the sizeable footsteps of Orson Welles, who I firmly believe had influenced him more than anyone else in the 1950s. Welles had become McGoohan's latest mentor. He influenced the actor sometimes through argument, sometimes through cajoling, often by sheer force of personality and always by his relentlessly inventive mind and desire to express his own individuality in his work. It was a drive that would stay with McGoohan during his next big career step, which saw him virtually abandon the stage for the lure of television. This was a medium in which McGoohan had a great belief. The British Library's theatre archive project, includes an intriguing comment from Braham Murray:

'Well, he was an extraordinary actor, and it was just awful that that was it! He hardly did any stage after that. He did a disastrous *Iago* at Stratford and then was taken over by television, and although he kept on saying "I'll be back, I'll be back," he wasn't. The money was the thing.'[41]

The Lure of Finance

I certainly believe that money was a major driving force in McGoohan's choice of roles and he would have realised that his TV work gave him a great deal more exposure than his theatre roles. To fulfil his intention of becoming the actor-manager, he would need as much industry power behind him as possible. In May, CBC Folio presented a CBC production of *The Iron Harp* by Joseph O'Connor, concerning an IRA officer blinded in a skirmish. McGoohan flew to Toronto to take part in the production which was presumably a videotaped studio-based piece.

However, his 'next big role' after starring in *Brand* could not have been more different, at least in concept. It would also make him one of the biggest names on British television in the next decade, giving him unprecedented success and the power that comes with it. *The Big Knife* was a TV play adapted from a stage play by Clifford Odetts which had already been made into a Hollywood film in 1955. Concerning Hollywood corruption, McGoohan was unlikely casting, as he himself recounted:

'I was offered another television part, of Charlie Castle in Clifford Odetts' *The Big Knife*. I was doubtful if I could handle this character successfully and asked the producer if he could try to replace me, but there wasn't time.

One man who saw *The Big Knife* was looking for an actor to play a secret agent in a new ATV series. His name was Lew Grade: the series *Danger Man*. What led Lew to decide that my portrayal of a faded Hollywood film star on the wrong side of fifty would make me suitable for the role of John Drake, secret agent, I don't know. Neither, I learned later, did his colleagues.'[42]

Whether it was Lew Grade or Ralph Smart, the creator of this new series, that noticed McGoohan is uncertain, but McGoohan's life was about to change dramatically. His next role would make him the highest paid television actor in the UK and would bring even greater intrusions into his precious privacy than those he had already learned to despise.

CHAPTER 4
Danger Man, Risk Taker

Lew Grade was looking for a new set of filmed half-hour adventures, a package of twenty-six that would screen first on his slice of the ITV network, ATV. Grade had set up ITC to supply programming to ATV and to the rest of the ITV network companies, but crucially, he also had an eye for the biggest single market for television content: the States. With a career starting in theatrical management, Grade had built up an empire, with a roster of star performers on his books and those of Bernie Delfont. The advent of commercial TV had allowed him the chance to create opportunities for new and established talent.

Known for his strongly populist sensibilities, Grade was highly regarded throughout the industry as a man whose instincts were to be trusted and who had the power to act upon them. He had made a big success of churning out filmed action/adventure series, half-hour episodes that sold as well to the incredibly lucrative market of the United States as they did at home in England. Having first been behind the incredibly popular *Robin Hood* series starring Richard Greene, Grade had repeated the formula in a variety of historical and contemporary series. One of his later offerings was a reworking of HG Wells' novel *The Invisible Man*, updated to the present day and with a spy thriller twist. However, although well cast and well made, the series did not do well in America, so Grade pulled the plug on a second series and instead commissioned writer Ralph Smart to devise a new TV series to replace the format.

Smart came up with an idea called 'Lone Wolf', at the time, which would be based around the activities of a single spy, working for NATO. Having apparently had meetings with Ian Fleming to discuss bringing the character of Bond to television, but finding that the rights had already been sold to Eon Productions, Smart took the character as a cue for a new lead: super spy John Drake.

The initial somewhat simplistic concept was of a series following the adventures of a secret agent. This was the type of thing that was fashionable in literature, film and television in the 50s and was about to become one of the defining genres of the decade with the launch of the James Bond film franchise a year later. John Drake would be a typically Bondian spy: an alpha male with a girl waiting at every casino, handy with his gun, a killer devoted to Queen and country, not afraid to do what was necessary to achieve his mission. Smart passed the concept on to fellow *Invisible Man* writer Ian Stuart Black and according to Black, in an interview with DWB, McGoohan was in the frame right from the word go. Apparently, Black had been asked to write four pilot scripts, all with McGoohan in mind as the lead. He even went so far as to suggest that McGoohan's appearance in *Brand* had helped to shape the new character.

'I went to see Pat in *Brand* by Ibsen at the Hammersmith theatre and his performance was excellent. Of course, it's a classical and religious play but the *power* of the man came through and after that I thought that this concept of being a single driving power, not talking to people but all contained within himself, would be ideal for him.'[1]

McGoohan had come to the attention of Ralph Smart (or Grade) during the broadcast of *The Big Knife* in late 1958 and his BAFTA win had done nothing but help his reputation. Having shown that he was equally capable of appearing in light-hearted whimsy, as well as taking on a role as dour and demanding as Brand, the producer knew that he would be well-suited to the new series and, crucially, capable of dealing with the gruelling production schedule. McGoohan readily accepted the part, which came at just the right time for him, professionally and financially, describing his initial feelings towards the show as follows:

'The basic theme, which he described as action-adventure, was interesting and different. I felt this outweighed the misgivings any actor has towards anchoring his identity to a long television series. There were personal reasons, too, which made the prospect of settled work attractive. Joan and I … had just found an old gardener's cottage on the outskirts of London, not far from Elstree Studios … we urgently needed to put the conversion in hand, in order to move in before our second child, Anne, was due to be born early in January 1960.'[2]

Serious Puritan

Even when money was a very pressing concern, with a cottage to rebuild and another child imminent, McGoohan never took the easy route in his work life. In 1960, concurrent with *Danger Man*, he was offered the role of James Bond in *Dr No*, a film which went on to spawn a franchise that is still running and which made a star out of Sean Connery, bringing him financial rewards beyond his dreams. But the role was not for McGoohan. He despised Bond and his attitude to women, his cheapening of life at the end of his Walther PPK. While most men at the time would see Bond as an aspirational figure, to McGoohan, the character was contemptible and simplistic. He therefore insisted on changes to the Bond-like character of John Drake before he would accept the part, removing any salacious element and refusing to carry a gun, surviving instead on his wits and fists. This would bring many of the people he worked with in front and behind the camera to observe that McGoohan had a fiercely puritanical streak. Ian Stuart Black, who has also claimed that the idea for *Danger Man* was his, recalled in the DWB interview:

> 'What I did was write about four pilot scripts. I remember Pat McGoohan being absolutely furious about one of them, absolutely furious because I had him lying on a bed with a girl. They were simply lying on a bed in order to open a safe which was behind the bed, nothing more, but Pat was white-faced with anger at a meal we all had together because of this apparently dishonest sexual implication, because he was very puritanical.'

McGoohan himself dismissed this criticism, explaining in the aforementioned interview with Jeannie Sakol for *Cosmopolita*n:

'Call me prissy Pat. A lot of old horse is being written about my attitude towards TV but it can be summed up in a few simple words. I see TV as the third parent. It doesn't give you bulging muscles to say a four letter word. The love-life planned for John Drake would have made me some sort of sexual crank. Every week a different girl? Served up piping hot for tea? With the children and grannies watching?'[3]

Though his attitude here is commendable and responsible, Black's assertion of McGoohan's fury at being asked to perform a scene devoid of any sexual implication whatsoever does suggest a ridiculously over-the-top response. Time has no doubt distorted the memory, but there are many similar stories of McGoohan's heated objections to performing anything that could even remotely be considered sexual on screen.

His comment that he viewed TV as being 'the third parent' is fascinating. To me it speaks of a deep feeling of social conscience and an awareness of the responsibility of his position, with all the methods of communication offered to him. And he does seem to have had genuine problems with the way that sex was sold in the media, though its portrayal would have been far milder in the 50s than it is now. McGoohan was undoubtedly a fierce romantic, feeling that casual sex cheapened his character in some way.

While undoubtedly good news for his family, his puritanical attitude brought McGoohan into conflict with his co-workers time and time again. An episode of *The Prisoner* entitled 'The Chimes of Big Ben' has Number 6 carrying out a covert conversation with a fellow inmate, Nadia, as they plan a joint escape. The scene was meant to be a staged 'date', with both characters showing a romantic interest in the other as a cover for their real intentions, to beguile the ever vigilant Village authorities. It was explicit and unambiguous that there was no genuine romantic subplot between the two but McGoohan wasn't having any of it. Interviewed for the TV documentary *Don't Knock Yourself Out*, Anthony Skene, who wrote various other episodes, remembered:

'He knows they're being bugged everywhere and doesn't want them to hear so he brings a radio out and gets ever so close to her and gives her a little kiss to make it look as if he's fallen in love with her. It isn't a sexy scene, it's a man being very crafty; a spy doing what a spy would do. But McGoohan wouldn't kiss her and he simpers instead and waves this strange radio about … And it looked ridiculous to me! I was just amazed that a professional actor would not do what a professional actor should do, which is to do the story, this is a man who would do that, you don't let your personal foolishness get in the way but he certainly did.'[4]

McGoohan himself offered a specific explanation: he was a married man and would not want one of his children to see him engaged in a romantic liaison with another woman, even if it be a performance. I don't doubt that this was partly true, his love for Joan appears to have been every bit as true and dedicated as that of Brand for God, but I suspect that the rebel was also making a stand against what was expected from such a character as Drake. Gun-wielding womanising users are the staple of the spy genre, epitomised by Bond, and McGoohan was not one to conform to anyone else's ideals. Consider his response when questioned in *Cosmopolitan* about his attitudes to the pill, the great sexual liberator for women of the 1960s:

'Malcolm Muggeridge said he thought the pill was more dangerous than the bomb. I agree because it hits at the very root of what a human being is. It interferes with the natural function of the body and we don't yet know medically what the repercussions of its long usage will be.'[5]

One senses the 'long range psychological effects' of a Catholic upbringing at play in McGoohan's thought processes here. It was typically paradoxical, therefore, that when the next question in this interview was about the recently-enacted bill legalising homosexuality, McGoohan's response was entirely liberal and advanced for the times: 'Homosexuals are a fact of society. It was a progressive and very humane bill.' That he should have afforded homosexuals the rights they deserved, to practice consensual sex with whoever they choose, is startling when in the previous sentence he condemned the use of an advance that would free literally millions of women from the dangers of unwanted pregnancies, unlicensed and dangerous abortions and a life they might not have opted for given the choice.

One is tempted to question just how far McGoohan's much-vaunted desire for the freedom of the individual actually stretches. Why is there such a blind spot in his otherwise remarkably liberal and humanitarian beliefs?

Roger Parkes, who later wrote the episode 'A Change of Mind' for *The Prisoner*, was certain that McGoohan's moral objection to performing romantic scenes was based largely in the actor's Catholicism. Speaking on the DVD commentary for the episode on the Network release, he explained that McGoohan was notoriously 'coy'. He also states that Joan, who was then working at a convent school in Finchley, coincidentally teaching McGoohan's three daughters, was very aware of the actor's religious beliefs. Yet McGoohan once described himself as a lapsed Catholic. Perhaps, like many who hold strong religious beliefs, McGoohan had adopted what suited him from the Catholic ideology and discarded the rest. Certainly his views on abortion reproduced above read almost like a speech from the Pope. Interviewed in the *TV and Radio Mirror*, discussing in detail his beliefs and why he feels so forcefully resentful of performing anything approaching romance, McGoohan concludes by revealing that:

'I have two guiding lights before me, every second of my working day. The first is my daughters. The second, my Religion. You know, every hero since Jesus Christ has been moral. He wasn't a coward. Like John Drake he fought his battles fiercely but honourably.'[6]

Whatever his more deeply-held beliefs about the subject of sex, McGoohan's desire to keep it out of his professional life does seem to have been genuinely based on his feelings of responsibility as an actor, now about to become more high profile than ever. He reiterated his usual explanation in an interview for *Motion Picture* magazine in the mid-60s, further distancing himself from the kind of hero exemplified by James Bond:

'I think the films are grand entertainment but I think that it's pernicious the way that Bond is becoming a cult. All these Bond raincoats and so on. All this publicity can easily lead young impressionable lads into believing the Bond way of life is the right one which of course it isn't. It has an insidious and powerful influence on children. Would you like your son to grow up like James Bond?'

I imagine that when McGoohan posed that question, many parents would be delighted to see their son grow up to be such a driven and financially-enabled character. Certainly in the 60s, the Bond character was popular across all ages and genders, a popularity helped greatly by the physicality and performance of Sean Connery, as well as a general softening of the character that appeared in the movies from Fleming's original conception. However, nearly half a century later, Daniel Craig's interpretation of Bond is much closer to that of the novels. His Bond is a cold bitter killer, emotionally sterile and borderline psychotic, unable to form any kind of meaningful relationship and taking refuge in the trappings of his business. Although minimised and frequently left open to interpretation, these subtexts were certainly present in Connery's portrayal of Bond, and McGoohan characteristically divined the central truth of the character at once. This intuitive grasp is very much one of his strengths as an actor.

Then there was McGoohan's very Catholic sense of responsibility. In his much-analysed *Woman* interview (conducted by Joan Reader) McGoohan returned to an earlier theme. He was concerned with the pervasive power of television which, as he saw it, was able to influence a far more passive audience than that which has made a choice to leave the home and go to the cinema.

'I didn't like the scripts. I thought there was too much emphasis on sex and violence. My reasons were simple. While you can select what sort of film you or your children will see when you go to the cinema, you have no such control of choice over television programmes. They come right into your home.

When these programmes are unduly concerned with violence, the ugly noises, the impact of brutality, are all intensified in realism because they are happening in your own living-room. As they go into millions of homes each night, you can never guarantee that elderly people, or children, will not see them and be both frightened and offended.

Since I hold these views strongly, as an individual and as a parent, I didn't see how – as an actor – I could contribute to the very things to which I objected.'

The writer Ian Stuart Black, however, found that this was a positive attribute while crafting the character of John Drake, clearly influenced by the actor's own personality:

'It was very good because it fitted in with the character. Everything was suppressed in a sense. Pat was an explosive time bomb, you were always waiting for him to go off, and that fitted in extremely well with the concepts.'

Once the character had been reshaped to his desires, McGoohan typically gave everything to the role, immersing himself in the character and the production of the series. Whatever his real reasons for omitting the expected sexual element, it cannot be denied that as a direct result of his 'interference,' the character of John Drake was unlike any other spy to ever grace either the small or big screens. Drake is a masterful piece of characterisation by both McGoohan and the writers in this first series: young, energetic and fiercely devoted to his work, loyalty and efficiency being his watchwords. In early publicity material for the first series of thirty-minute episodes, McGoohan stated his opinion of John Drake:

'...he is not a thick ear specialist, a puppet muscle man. There is action, plenty of it but no brutal violence. If a man dies it is not just another cherry off the tree. When Drake fights, he flights clean, he abhors bloodshed. He carries a gun but doesn't use it unless absolutely necessary, then he doesn't shoot to kill. He prefers to use his wits. He is a person with a sophisticated background and a philosophy.'

During the location shooting, McGoohan and the team travelled to North Wales, to a grand folly built by architect Clough Williams-Ellis: Portmeirion. This village, often described as being 'Italianate', stood in for a village in Italy for the shoot, since there was no way that the production could afford to actually go abroad for location shooting. McGoohan was immediately enraptured by the place and filed the details away in his mind for future use.

Whilst making the initial batch of episodes, McGoohan also met and struck up a friendship with David Tomblin, then working as an assistant director on the series. The two men found that they had a lot in common, particularly in their socio-political concerns and in their desire to express those feelings in their own work. They began to develop ideas for potential series, Tomblin being inspired to write by his new friend and soon-to-be business partner. McGoohan and Tomblin founded Everyman films on 18th August 1960, according to George Murphy, who now owns the company and runs it as a talent agency. It would be several years before the company actually started shooting but the groundwork had been laid. McGoohan now had a collaborator that he trusted and had a good relationship with; a man who also had the production expertise he needed to help to bring his ideas to the screen.

Production continued on the new revised version of *Danger Man*, now reformatted to McGoohan's satisfaction. The episodes were well-made, fast-paced and dominated by McGoohan. He involved himself with great interest in every aspect of the production, once again soaking up knowledge to later apply to his own projects. He maintained also his domination over the production of the series, encountering resistance from the highest levels to his 'no guns, no girls' policy:

> '...by the time the first six episodes were in the can, all without girls and guns, the front office people were worried. A high-powered sales and publicity executive arrived from New York to meet me for lunch in the studio restaurant ... what the syndication people wanted were the girls and guns re-instated. Without them, they were convinced, the series would be a resounding commercial flop.'[7]

McGoohan explained that, as he saw it, Drake was a character who could not afford any romantic entanglements, with his life potentially in danger every day. It was an extremely reasonable argument that gave away none of McGoohan's real reasons. The actor insisted that to include such plotlines would be 'phoney and ridiculous', persuading the executive that the series should continue along the lines that had been laid down.

'He went off and sold the completed series – minus sex and brutality – to sixty-one countries and they made a fortune.'[8]

International Star

Danger Man became a worldwide hit, catapulting McGoohan to stardom in the UK and, crucially, cracking the notoriously difficult American market. Lew Grade was delighted with the results and McGoohan had found the filming to be a very creatively satisfying process, though he resented the media attention that such a high profile series was to bring to him. He was offered the opportunity to direct an episode late in the run of the series, entitled 'The Vacation', and had made an excellent job of it finding the process as fascinating as he did acting. McGoohan was already a keen amateur filmmaker though, alas, very little is known about these efforts, and he would have relished the opportunity to branch out into directing professionally.

After the success of the initial series of *Danger Man*, McGoohan had gone beyond the point of being able to cherry-pick the best roles offered to him and could now virtually choose whichever part he liked. He immediately launched into a new project, working for director Anthony Asquith in the movie *Two Living, One Dead* (1961). The part was of Erik Berger, a post office clerk who is married, has one young child and whose only ambition is to one day become postmaster.

Berger's comfortable life is shattered when he interrupts an armed robbery and, unlike one of his co-workers, offers no resistance, trembling in panic. After the event, Berger is vilified for his cowardice. Though his family are grateful he did not endanger himself, he becomes increasingly isolated and self-doubting, with the only comfort coming from a stranger named Rogers who is watching over his injured brother. Berger communicates the salient facts to Rogers in the third person, refusing to admit that he is himself the subject of the discussion. At the same time, the heroic co-worker is given the promotion and plaudits.

Berger's marriage collapses when he brings Rogers home, where the guest mistakenly mentions that he has no sympathy for the wife of Berger's imaginary friend.

Rogers eventually reveals the he was one of the robbers and he has returned to make amends for his deeds. He explains that the supposedly heroic co-worker was knocked unconscious when he ran into a door, rather than by any act of violence, and that it was because of his loose tongue that they were able to plan the robbery in the first place. Berger exposes the co-worker's cowardice in a staged hold-up and is able to return to his family having overcome his crucifying self-doubt.

McGoohan dominates the screen in every scene he is in with a typically powerful presence, at odds with the character. In later scenes, where Berger is working under his newly-promoted colleague, it is clear that the real power lies with Berger. Bill Travers gives an excellent performance as the unintelligent, over-promoted Anderson, a weak and ineffective individual but the character is no match for McGoohan's. Fortunately, Alf Kjellin as Rogers is given a character with sufficient fire to stand-up to McGoohan's performance and it is in the scenes shared by the two actors, that McGoohan is at his most effective.

The Odd Play

McGoohan's single play work in the early 60s often saw him taking parts that were out of step with conventional beliefs. In the Armchair Theatre's *The Man Out There* he plays a Russian cosmonaut who has only hours to live after an accident with his space capsule. Through a freak of radio, he is put in touch with a mother in Canada whose child is dying. Being a doctor, the astronaut is able to instruct and guide the woman in performing a life-saving tracheotomy on her daughter, before he perishes as his capsule re-enters the atmosphere. To play a sympathetic Russian in 1960 was a brave move for McGoohan; the Russians were leading the space race and Cold War paranoia was reaching its height. The play, as with his previous outings, received good reviews. At this stage of his career, it seemed that in the eyes of both the public and the critics, McGoohan could do no wrong. He had managed to achieve stardom without really wanting to, simply through the pursuit of excellence in his work, and must have enjoyed the recognition from his contemporaries, if not the attention he was now receiving on the street.

Diversifying on Screen

McGoohan wanted to stretch his wings, however, and decided to take a break from *Danger Man*. Keen to take on a diverse range of parts to ensure that he was not typecast as the suave but unapproachable secret agent, McGoohan took a part in *All Night Long* (1962), in which he played a scheming jazz drummer, trying to start his own band. Loosely based on Shakespeare's *Othello*, McGoohan played the role with a drawling American accent and a sideways smile, as his character Johnny Cousin fast-talks his way through the movie, amorally happy to trample over anyone with little regard for their feelings if it will be to his advantage. Showing his usual determination, McGoohan promptly bought himself a drum kit and spent hours on end practicing so that he could play the role with the verisimilitude he demanded.

Around this time he also appeared as an idealistic doctor in the movie *Life for Ruth* (1962), a morality play concerning religious objections to blood transfusion, resulting in the death of a young girl. McGoohan's character brings charges against the parents in court. It was another film in which important ethical issues are brought to the fore. That the actor felt a great responsibility towards portraying such issues is certainly conveyed by his intensity of performance.

McGoohan's TV work continued with major roles in *Sergeant Musgrave's Dance* and a BBC production of Bridget Boland's stage play *The Prisoner*. Aside from the title, this second play shared many themes with McGoohan's later work and it is likely that the former in some way influenced the latter.

The storyline is that of a cardinal, arrested for treason and taken to prison, where he is psychologically and physically tortured in order that a confession might be extracted from him. The cardinal, a popular and powerful man, succeeds in resisting everything that his tormentor, the interrogator, can throw at him, eventually evincing sympathy from the other man. In the BBC production, McGoohan played the interrogator, but later he would turn the tables on himself. There are obvious theatrical similarities between Boland's play and McGoohan's *Prisoner*, such as the continuously burning lights shining in the prisoner's face in each. However, it is the verbal battles that ensue between the two men in the play that really put one in mind of the later TV series, especially so in the episode 'Once Upon a Time', a similarly intense two-hander between Prisoner and Captor in which the power struggle is turned to the Prisoner's advantage in a similar battle of wills.

No recording survives of the BBC production. But a film made ten years earlier, starring Alec Guinness and Jack Hawkins, suggests what it may have been like. (Coincidentally, Kenneth Griffith who would later become one of McGoohan's collaborators in the final days of *The Prisoner*, also appeared in this film.)

The Quare Fellow (1962) was a film adapted from the play by Brendan Behan. It begins with the appearance of a new young prison warder, Thomas Crimmin, who is inexperienced, with an extremely black and white view of the world and the criminals now under his surveillance. Crimmin realises during the course of the film, that the prisoners are still human beings and is influenced by his elder superior, Regan, before becoming emotionally involved with the wife of one of the prisoners. It is then discovered that new evidence may be calling into question this man's conviction and Crimmins now faces a difficult choice. Despite the fact that he was by now in his mid-thirties, McGoohan was able to successfully convey an impression of greater youth and a wide-eyed innocence, coupled with a very thoughtful side which comes to the fore more and more as Crimmins' assumptions are inevitably questioned.

Able to command increasingly high fees for his work, McGoohan's next on screen appearance was *The Scarecrow of Romney Marsh* (1963), a Disney classic for which he received top billing as the eponymous character. Publicity material displayed an arresting image of McGoohan's face, half-human, half-covered by his scarecrow disguise. That the principled actor, known for highbrow and challenging work, took two parts in Disney films, known then for their sanitised depictions of life and experience, might seem out of character. However, both films were extremely proficient pieces of filmmaking and storytelling, and for the family man to want to be seen in high quality family films was in fact entirely in character. *The Scarecrow of Romney Marsh*, though starting life as a three-part mini-series, was reedited for theatrical release and did extremely well at the box office.

McGoohan's face was everywhere. However, the following year in May 1964 he was arrested on a charge of drunk driving. Though the laws concerning such behaviour were surprisingly lax compared to today's rules, he nevertheless spent six days in jail and was banned from driving for one year. Surprisingly, the press coverage seems to have been minimal, a far cry from today where any high profile actor would have his image splashed across every tabloid in the country for such an offense.

Interestingly, this is another moment in his life that is referenced in the autobiographical episode of *The Prisoner* called 'Once Upon a Time', with Leo McKern's Number 2 taking on the role of judge in a version of a trial. Number 6, like McGoohan pleads guilty and accepts the punishment handed down to him.

Fortunately, the driving ban did not interfere with his work and McGoohan's next high-profile appearance was in a completely different role once again. In his second film for Disney, *The Three Lives of Thomasina* (1964), he played dour vet Andrew McDhui, a widower who has recently moved to the Highlands to take over a veterinary practice there, accompanied by his young daughter. There, his belief in science is put to the test by Lori MacGregor, known to most as a witch but in principle more of a Wiccan. In any case she is a woman who uses her special gift with animals to heal them in her own way, through natural remedies.

McGoohan's character is fiercely opposed to this kind of 'hocus pocus' but in the end he is won round by Lori's extraordinary charm, especially when she helps him to reconnect with his child. Once again, McGoohan plays a man whose beliefs are challenged and changed, as he had in *The Quare Fellow, The Prisoner* and *Two Living, One Dead*. It seems he would always be attracted to parts that allowed him to display the innately conflicting nature of the human condition. His own life was now surely one of conflicts, the shy and quiet family man having to constantly endure the media junket that was expected of him. Susan Hampshire, his co-star from *Thomasina*, recalled that McGoohan's reserve extended well into his working relationship with her in a piece about the actor from the mid 60s, by Peter Howell:

> 'At first he was terribly quiet, but when he got to know me better we would talk quite intensely about all kinds of things. Everything, in fact, except Patrick himself. At the end of the film I still didn't know much more about him than when we started. I think he's shy. After we had finished the film, he bought me a beautiful bunch of flowers – but do you know, he was too shy to give them to me himself and sent a porter round with them. And he doesn't like being photographed – he's rather strict about it. The only ones taken were of scenes we did together. Never anything informal.'[9]

In an interview the actress gave for the movie's DVD release, Hampshire mentioned that in-between takes, the actor would remain reserved, studying his script and rarely indulging in useless conversation. She found the working relationship very satisfying and their collaboration on *Thomasina* a pleasant experience, remarking that McGoohan was a very 'matter of fact' person. He wasn't consistently difficult to work with, as might be imagined. Hampshire's reaction was shared by many actors who worked with him; though by no means all.

Super Spy Revisited

It was at this time that Lew Grade suggested to McGoohan that he should return to *Danger Man*. The series had continued to be a huge commercial success and Grade was keen to build on that, reformatting the series into hour-long episodes that would allow McGoohan more time to explore the character of John Drake, now a few years older. McGoohan took a certain amount of persuading to return to the part, no doubt aware that, this time, he would have greater leverage and a larger degree of creative control – not to mention a vastly increased salary that was to make him the most highly-paid television actor in the UK. McGoohan described how satisfied he was on the *Danger Man* set.

'So probably for the next two years. *Danger Man* will continue to be a way of life for me. It is one which couldn't bring me greater enjoyment or satisfaction. Personally, and professionally, it is the nearest thing to working in Sheffield Repertory again, Sometimes it's extremely demanding, often tiring, but never dull.'[10]

The series had a new producer, Sidney Cole, with Ralph Smart as creative head of the enterprise. So now it was the turn of Sidney Cole to run into McGoohan's puritanical streak, which he attributed to the actor's Catholicism in an interview with the BECTU (Broadcasting, Entertainment, Cinematograph and Theatre Union):

'The thing about Pat was that he was a very fervent Roman Catholic … he had a fervent sense of sin … He always refused in the series – whoever the female character cast in the same episode was – to kiss a woman, even if they were supposed to be in a scene which implied some degree of intimacy between them. I asked him once why this was so and he said he didn't want his children asking their mother why is daddy kissing that strange woman. To which the answer obviously is, or should have been, "Don't be silly dear, that's your bread and butter." As a result of this I used to take a certain amount of pleasure in casting what I thought were the most attractive actresses opposite Pat.'[11]

In the episode 'The Ubiquitous Mr Lovegrove', Sidney Cole had cast Adrienne Corri. McGoohan disapproved of this casting on the grounds that Corri had recently publicly announced that she had two daughters out of wedlock. To the staunch Catholic and family-minded McGoohan this was outrageous enough, but to be proud of it was even worse. Cole continued:

'Anyhow I told Adrienne that Pat seemed to disapprove of that. I wasn't there when it happened but apparently the first morning she was on call she came out of her dressing room the same time as McGoohan did and saw him and called down the corridor, "Hey, McGoohan!" He turned round and she said, "I understand you disapprove of me, well fuck you for a start!" After which they became quite good friends.'

Not a Number

McGoohan was now able to take ever-greater control of the set and exercised his power whenever he could, though he was sometimes frustrated by the fact that he was not in control of the project overall. His demeanour seems to have been extremely variable at this time. He was still averse to being contacted by journalists, despite the fact that publicising the series would surely have been part of his contract. But if caught at the right time, he could be surprisingly helpful and courteous. Keith Farnsworth, a journalist then working for *The Sheffield Star*, was surprised to be granted an interview with McGoohan and was kind enough to relate his memories and impressions of the man to me:

> 'I was, of course, unsure of what kind of reception I would get when I met him, and I made certain I didn't ask anything provocative. (You will judge how far I went from the article.) I was quite a young fellow then, and simply wanted to get a decent piece – I felt it best to let him talk. When he arrived in the room and I met him for the first time, I felt that he was assessing me (weighing me up!), and I felt that he gradually realised that I seemed a decent lad and soon warmed to me. I am certain that the fact that I was so obviously a Sheffielder, and knew many of the places that he knew (such as the Tinsley Wire Industries firm where he had once worked) and names like Geoffrey Ost (such an influence on his very early days in acting). All this helped.
>
> It was entirely his idea to arrange for me to have lunch in the dining room/café used by the actors, but he did say that he had an appointment and wouldn't be able to join me. He arranged for me to be taken to the dining room. Memory plays tricks with me now, but I think that it was after lunch that I went back and watched an episode being filmed. So I did see him again, and he asked if I had been okay at lunch. Before I left he said a formal goodbye. Yes, I think he liked me – and he was, too, so obviously a gentleman.'

Keith went on to say that he was in no doubt that he just happened to catch McGoohan at the right time and in the right mood, and that at any other time he might well have been told to sling his hook, or worse, receive no reply at all. It does seem likely that McGoohan responded to their shared roots, as the actor frequently expressed a great appreciation for Sheffield and kept the city close to his heart. Keith also gave me permission to quote from his article which illustrates a more light-hearted side to McGoohan at this time. By the time of this interview, shooting was well into the second series of *Danger Man* and McGoohan was at the top of his game. The introduction concentrates, understandably on the actor's past:

'Patrick McGoohan, highest-paid actor in television, knows from experience that the shop floor of a wire mill at Tinsley is no place for airs and graces and high-falutin' talk. It's a long time since he last worked in Sheffield, and even longer since he wore the overalls of a steel-industry worker; but, immaculate, expensive suits, a large dose of fame and £2,000 a week haven't stopped him remaining down to earth.

The first thing you notice about the tall, fair-haired ex-Sheffield Rep favourite is the no-nonsense look written right across the handsome face now so synonymous with *Danger Man* John Drake. But he's human, humorous, too. "Come with me and Ah will show thee things of great wonder..." he said in mock seriousness when we met at Shepperton Studios.'

McGoohan goes on to give details of his time in Sheffield, his work at the bank and on the chicken farm and gives Geoffrey Ost a great deal of credit for his own career, remarking that his time in Rep was the best training he could have wished for. He mentions meeting and marrying Joan in the city and remarks that: 'We have three daughters, and, as I have often said, Joan is now playing the best role of her life – and doing it very well.' The conversation turned to *Danger Man* with McGoohan outlining the rigours of the daily shoot, and by far the most telling material comes right at the end of Keith's report:

'He was called back on to the set. When he returned, he said: "I don't think success has made a lot of difference to me. One is very lucky in this business. A man can get a break, but he has to keep both feet on the ground. When an actor has a leading part in a thing like this, it is all the more necessary for him to be more disciplined. Success increases your responsibilities."'

McGoohan's work ethic and sense of responsibility are once more brought to the fore and it is clear from this and other interviews that he did indeed take his elevated position very seriously. However, the Jekyll and Hyde persona that would characterise much of his time spent filming on his next and perhaps best-loved project, *The Prisoner*, were already in evidence, often linked to an overindulgence of alcohol.

Two Steps Too Far

When interviewed by Steven Ricks for his excellent series of in-depth documentaries about the making of *The Prisoner*, actor Gertan Klauber recalled that on occasion McGoohan could take fight scenes a little too far. Appearing as a heavy in the series three episode 'The Man with The Foot', Klauber was at the receiving end of McGoohan's occasionally unrestrained violence.

> 'They were shooting with two different units ... it meant that Patrick McGoohan was going from one set to the other and there was a tremendous preamble. We had done our dialogue sequences a day earlier and this was a scene in a garage where there was a confrontation and I remember while we were waiting while he finished on the "A" unit, his stand-in and double, in fact the stunt coordinator saying to me, "Well you know, the great thing about Pat is that he's absolutely wonderful in a fight. He will move thorough eighteen or nineteen positions and not touch you and I've worked out with him exactly what is going to happen," so I was quite relaxed and quite happy about it.'

Klauber's relaxed frame of mind was sadly misplaced as when the actor showed up on set to enact the fight scene his mood was completely unpredictable.

> 'Lunch had gone on a little too long and he seemed rather brief and cheery and tough-natured. We did a rehearsal of it, unfortunately during which I was struck several times.
>
> I did complain to the stunt arranger and he said, "Don't worry, don't worry, when we actually come to do it, I've had a talk to Pat and nothing is going to happen."

So we did the first take, unfortunately lots of things did happen and I complained bitterly. In fact, after the second take I said to McGoohan, "Please do not hit me because otherwise the whole thing will go into fisticuffs and I will have to hit you back because there's just a certain amount of pain you can take for no possible reason." And in fact it did develop in take three and four into a fighting match and I think we both settled on take five or six when we both of us did the proper thing.'

The implication is that McGoohan had perhaps had one too many at lunchtime. There are several documented examples of the actor being basically a very bad drunk and this would appear to bear those stories out. It's surprising that, as Klauber pointed out, actual blows are far less convincing for camera than staged ones. So where was McGoohan's legendary professionalism in moments like these?

While his conduct was mostly faultless in the outside world (with the notable exception of his drunk-driving conviction), it does seem that whilst working in the protected atmosphere of the set, he was more liable to let his rock solid self-control slip. Perhaps this was because he knew he was in a 'safe' environment, where he would be shielded from any media attention. Indeed, although he is often described as 'difficult' and 'demanding' in contemporary pieces, there is nothing written about his on set behaviour that could be considered remotely scandalous. This is a far cry from the modern age of the almost instantaneous worldwide dissemination of showbiz gossip across the internet and in magazines. I feel that had McGoohan been making such a high profile show at the age of thirty-seven today, he would be unable to escape the glare of the media spotlight, a situation he would have found intolerable.

In the semi-autobiographical *Woman* article mentioned previously, McGoohan himself paints a much more relaxed picture of his average working day on set which also offers a glimpse into his home life at that time and the workload that the actor had taken on.

'I plan a Danger Man working day to begin at 6 am, the time for which I set the alarm, but usually I beat the clock and wake at 5 am.

In summer, I like to spend the first hour walking round the garden making plans for all the landscaping I've never yet had time to do.

It is still a comparatively new garden as when Frances, our youngest daughter, arrived, we out-grew our gardener's cottage and built a larger house nearby … Usually, when I'm standing on the terrace … she and Anne, now five, come padding downstairs in their dressing-gowns to join me. Faithfully followed by the corgi, Honey.

Then it's time for a cup of tea. Mugs of milk and long talks. We try to keep these great palavers as quiet as possible till Joan and our eldest daughter Catherine, now thirteen, join us. At 7 am, the Studio car comes to take me to Shepperton, where we are filming the present series. The drive gives me an hour to go over my lines for the coming day, take a quick look at the papers and see to any mail.'

McGoohan was a legendarily early riser, like Lew Grade. Whilst filming at Portmeirion for *The Prisoner*, he would rise at 6 am for a morning run on the beach, presumably to build up his stamina for the gruelling days ahead. His picture of typical urban domesticity, is changed abruptly by his arrival at the studio and the commencement of the day's work. McGoohan made an effort to respond to his many fans and devoted considerable time to his 'mail', regarding this is as part of the actor's routine. Having described how, at Shepperton, he changes into Drake's costume for the episode and attends make-up, he reports to the studio floor at 8.20 am to begin the day's filming:

'Shooting begins at 8.30 am and goes on till 1 pm. Half the lunch break is spent looking at rushes of the previous day's work. By 2 pm we're back on the floor till 5.45 pm. It's a packed schedule, largely because the scripts are so hinged on John Drake that, apart from the opening shots. I have to be in every scene. At the end of the day, a few of us usually have a couple of beers, and talk shop, I leave to get home by 7.30 pm, when, if possible. I like to get in half-an-hour's squash as a bit of relaxation before having a meal with Joan and Catherine about 8.30 pm.

Then, more often than not, the rest of the evening goes on script work. Each episode takes two weeks to film, the plots change every fortnight, so does most of the cast, so one always has to be thinking ahead.'[12]

Action Man, Stunt Man

As McGoohan himself noted, the experience was not unlike his time in Rep, with a new script to learn every fortnight, and his remarkable memory must have been inordinately useful to him. As noted above, McGoohan had to be present in virtually every scene shot for *Danger Man* and it was a boon to the production to have such a dedicated and energetic lead actor. One aspect of his work ethic that would no doubt have delighted directors, but terrified the insurers, is that McGoohan insisted on doing as many of his own stunts as humanly possible. This wasn't out of a sense of adventure or desire for random risk-taking. It was simply part of his continuing quest for verisimilitude, and one that paid off. Compare an action sequence from *The Prisoner* to a similar sequence in a contemporary TV series which all too often betrays that a stuntman is being used in a fight scene or to dangle over the edge of a cliff. Authenticity and a real tension can be found in the former, that may not be present even if all is technically correct in current action sequences on TV. That McGoohan was willing to put himself to the test in such a way meant that directors could indulge in close-ups of their lead actor, showing John Drake apparently genuinely at risk and helping the suspension of disbelief in the audience. It was little touches like this that helped to make *Danger Man* such a well-produced show. Fifty years later, the episodes can still count amongst our most entertaining programmes on TV and McGoohan was behind many of the ideas, bursting with the enthusiasm to take them through into the production itself.

McGoohan relished the chance that his new deal with Grade gave him to become more involved in the production of the series. Though he had made sure that his ideas were not only heard but acted upon during the production of the half-hour series, he now had the chance to direct episodes of the hour-long show. He approached this task with the same zeal and flair for preparation that characterised all his work. McGoohan proved to be a great talent behind the camera and was by now frequently taking control of the studio floor if he felt that a director was performing inefficiently or if he, McGoohan, felt that a scene could be achieved differently. Angela Browne, one of the actresses to have a very positive relationship with the difficult and nervy star, recalled her initial work with McGoohan on the episode 'The Girl In The Pink Pyjamas', from an interview on The Unmutual website for *Prisoner* fans:

'I remember I had to stagger across a wasteland somewhere up in Elstree in pink pyjamas on a freezing cold day. But when I met Patrick, he wasn't so well known then, he'd done a couple of films.

I wasn't a fan of his at all, but actually I fell in love with him; I just adored him and he was so kind to me. I was a kid, I was twenty-one, and he took over the lighting I remember. There was a scene where I had to be lying there rescued from some terrible situation. I was lying there thinking, "What a lovely man," and between takes he was saying, "Get more light there, get more shadow there." He was actually lighting it – at a time when he wasn't actually in charge of anything; he was just the actor. And I loved him from that moment on. So when I was asked to do *The Prisoner* I said, "Oh, yes please!"'[13]

When the interviewer, Dave Jones, humorously asks if the director got much of a look in with McGoohan taking charge, Browne replied, "Not much, no." The shadow of Orson Welles still loomed, the actor still yearned to be the actor-manager and to exercise complete control over his work. Of course, he was prevented from taking control in this series by the fact that he had no executive producer status and also by the fact that, essentially, it was Ralph Smart who wielded final creative control over the character of Drake, having initially devised the series. Exacerbating the situation further, it would also have been a source of discontent to McGoohan that he was able to spend so little time with his family over such a protracted period. During the production of the series, he gave another revealing multi-part interview to Iain Sproat which went into further detail about his domestic arrangements and highlighted once again his enduring adoration of his wife.

'And he enjoys taking his wife for an occasional extravagant night out, and giving her what he calls "unbirthday presents".

"I don't," he said, "like birthdays or anniversaries." (He keeps no scrapbook of nostalgic memories.) "I mean, if I'm ever going to drink a lot, it won't be on my birthday, or St Patrick's Day!

You know, I forget to give my wife birthday presents, which makes her very angry, but then I give her a present at an odd time, and that makes up for it. It's more romantic somehow that way.'[14]

The work, however, was creative and rewarding enough to sustain McGoohan through these long days of separation and his Mill Hill home was in comfortable driving distance of Shepperton Studios. Describing the pattern of his day to Keith Farnsworth, McGoohan commented that:

'We live twenty-five miles from the studio, twelve miles north west of London, which means I have to get up at 5.45 am every morning to get here for half-past seven. It's a long day. I usually finish on the set at about 5.45 in the evening. But it's usually 6.30 pm when I get away and later if there are shots of previous shows to see, or a script conference.'"[15]

The second and third series vastly eclipsed the success of the first series of half-hour episodes, the new format finding favour with critics and viewers. Watching the episodes today, it remains an extremely well-made and fast-paced series, with McGoohan's John Drake dominating the show, powerful and compelling as ever. The series occasionally gave the actor the chance to explore his comedic potential with the episode 'The Paper Chase' ending in an almost slapstick run around involving Drake driving a miniature Go-Kart and literally running rings around his adversaries. But McGoohan's desire for complete creative freedom was growing steadily and he was beginning to feel that the *Danger Man* format was becoming stale. He and David Tomblin had already started making plans for a new series and were soon to find an ally in the incoming script supervisor on *Danger Man*, George Markstein.

Technicolour Spy

Lew Grade, however, had other plans. With colour television coming to England over the next few years and already becoming the dominant format in the United States, he planned that the next series of *Danger Man* should be made using colour film stock. This would increase its production costs but also 'futureproof' the series. Grade was ahead of the game in the UK in making sure that his series would have a long sales life, having already branched out into colour production in 1964 with the Gerry Anderson puppet series *Stingray*. Now, he wanted to make the same changes to *Danger Man*, but its star had other ideas.

In the event, only two episodes of *Danger Man* would be produced in colour before the series was finally wound down, though most of the crew moved with the star onto his next project. It was this next project that would come to define him for the rest of his life and would prove to be the hardest battle he would ever have to face in his professional career. However, he would always regard his time as the 'Danger Man' with fondness, not least because his success in this role would enable him to finally achieve his dream of the actor-manager, gaining overall control of the series he would work on next:

'I've been asked if, as a trained actor, I should be above a part like John Drake? Not at all. I did a considerable amount of classical work – all the Shakespeare plays. I think Drake is an interesting character. Admittedly, he hasn't got as many facets as Hamlet, but I find the part stimulating. I hope it has some sort of reasonable influence in that we don't perpetuate evil, we destroy evil.'[16]

McGoohan in playful mode as a young boy

Wild-eyed as 'a sinister loon' at the Sheffield Rep

'Pat and Joan' on their wedding day

Day I met Danger Man

Bowled over: Heap cartoons of Patrick McGoohan from The Star in the early 1950s

THE death of Patrick McGoohan reminds me that, in the mid-1960s while on the reporting staff of The Star, I had the good fortune to interview the former Sheffield Playhouse favourite, who by then was the hero of Danger Man and said to be TV's highest-paid star.

Having contacted McGoohan by letter and had an enthusiastic response, I persuaded the then news editor, Colin Brannigan, to let me visit Shepperton Studios to meet him, and, contrary to reports that he could be difficult and 'doesn't like journalists', he proved friendly and receptive, and the interview was successful – I think that being from Sheffield helped, for he had great affection for his old home city.

He talked with genuine nostalgia of his time in industry at Tinsley Wire, and of his years at the Playhouse, a theatre that he said would always have a special place in his heart and the heart of his wife Joan Drummond.

Before I left, he took me on to the Danger Man set to watch the shooting of an episode and, saying I couldn't make the long journey home on an empty stomach, arranged for me to have lunch in the Studio restaurant – diners at an adjoining table included Sir Donald Wolfit and Laurence Harvey!

A week or two later, McGoohan sent me a note thanking me for the piece I had written, and my only regret is that more than 40 years later I have long since lost that souvenir of a personal link with a fine actor who, as a youngster, told Playhouse boss Geoffrey Ost that he would work for nothing just to get the chance to prove he could make the grade in the theatre. He made the grade all right!

Keith Farnsworth, Sheffield 35

Interview and cartoons from *The Sheffield Star*

McGoohan charms the world as *Danger Man* in 1960

McGoohan stuntman on the set of *Danger Man*

The Prisoner arrives

McGoohan in command: directing *The Prisoner*

Portmeirion: an inspired choice of location for *The Prisoner*

Number 6 runs in The Village elections

In Disney's *Dr Syn Alias The Scarecrow* (1963)

In *Ice Station Zebra* (1968)

McGoohan in *The Man in the Iron Mask* (1977)

Looking typically intense in *Jamaica Inn* (1983)

Images used for the Howard Foy interview in the 1990s

McGoohan with Larry Green in 2008

CHAPTER 5
The Prisoner Arrives

Genesis

In January 1966 George Markstein was hired as script consultant on *Danger Man*. Markstein was a German émigré whose parents had come to England when he was a boy to escape from the rise of the Nazis. He had initially worked in journalism before moving into television. Working first on the factual side, he then took a position as story consultant on the ITC series *Court Martial* before moving onto the same post on *Danger Man*. Markstein oversaw the first two episodes of the new colour season of *Danger Man* but found that he suddenly had a major and possibly insurmountable problem to overcome with the leading man.

McGoohan, towards the end of his time with the show, had an altercation with producer Sidney Cole, in which he had questioned the fact that Cole always had final say in an artistic dispute. Cole had responded that it was because he was the producer, simple as that. Obviously this comment had an effect on McGoohan who had wanted to be master of his own ship for a while, having set up Everyman films with Tomblin in 1960 to achieve precisely this. He felt that the *Danger Man* formula was becoming over-stretched and the stories repetitive though he never ceased to give anything less than his all in the role. Now, however, McGoohan wanted to be free.

So he made *The Prisoner*. This was, Markstein says, motivated by the desire to repeat his theatrical success in some way:

'...my feeling is that McGoohan wasn't really very keen on doing any other series. What he really wanted to do I think was to play Brand. He'd had an enormous success some years previously on the stage with Ibsen's *Brand* and Brand personifies everything I think McGoohan would like to be: God! He was very good as God, so he wanted to play Brand … again. He was very keen to set up *Brand* as a film and I think that was really what he wanted to do.'[1]

McGoohan is Number 6

I think the above is very revealing. Having been thwarted for whatever reason in making a film of *Brand* – the character with which he seemed to most identify and which he had played with the skill and passion of a man born to the role – McGoohan resorted to creating his own version. Number 6 is McGoohan's character, one he imagined, shaped and personified from the outset. John Drake, on the other hand, was initially conceived by Ralph Smart; though McGoohan clearly had a huge influence in that character's eventual direction. Far from wanting to be some sort of all-powerful and controlling God, as Markstein suggested (no doubt due to his own bad experiences of the controlling force of McGoohan's personality), the actor was strongly for the individual, for freedom and choice.

That his defining role should be No 6, one man pitted against a system vastly more powerful than he, a confining society which seeks to control his destiny and take everything from him that he holds most precious, reveals much about the mind of his architect. No 6 is, in effect, an avatar of McGoohan.

McGoohan had clearly identified greatly with the character of Brand, enabling his initial deep connection with the part. When an actor has that level of understanding, they are able to give a more nuanced performance, that is sensitive to the material. How deeply he studied the text is unknown, but there are definite parallels between Brand, McGoohan and indeed Number 6.

It's difficult to pin down the genesis of what was to become McGoohan's defining work. Stories differ widely as to when the concept came to him and indeed how much was unique to the actor. *Danger Man* writer Ian Stuart Black recalled McGoohan discussing an idea which he took as being *The Prisoner* with some colleagues. However, it came largely as a surprise to the production team when, two episodes into the fourth series, McGoohan announced his resignation from the role of John Drake.

Without him, production collapsed. McGoohan had made the series his own from the start, taking some control of the character and redefining the format to suit his desires. Ultimately though, Drake had been devised by Ralph Smart who had final say and, importantly, a slice of the royalties. Though I suspect that control over the character was more important to McGoohan than the money, he did once mention half-jokingly that he had devised Number 6 to avoid paying royalties to Smart.

Portmeirion: The Village

It is possible to pin down the inspiration for using Portmeirion as the setting for his new fantasy show. As mentioned in the previous chapter, McGoohan was first introduced to the location in 1961, when cast and crew of the first season of *Danger Man* spent some time filming at the resort. It had been used for the episode 'A View from the Villa', to stand in for Italy. Taking a mental note of the location for future reference, it had obviously inspired the strange candy-coloured setting for his next idea, contrasting beautifully with the themes of oppression and repression that would characterise the series.

> 'I thought it was a miraculous sort of place ... beautiful. And already in my head I was astonished that I'd never seen this in a film.
>
> This is a setting which could be beautiful enough, mysterious enough and confining enough to be the base for our man in isolation.'[2]

In Portmeirion, 'The Village', as it would soon become, had been constructed over a period of forty years by renowned architect Clough Williams-Ellis and was made up of buildings and frontages that he had rescued from destruction at various places across the globe and transported to his chosen location on the coast of North Wales, near Porthmadoc. It's often rather lazily described at 'Italianate' but this fails to do justice to the huge variety of influences from all over the world that make up this beautiful hodge-podge of buildings.

McGoohan developed an excellent relationship with Williams-Ellis who was delighted that the star had chosen to film his series in the architect's paradise. The themes of *The Prisoner* had immediately captured Ellis' imagination and he was impressed by the way McGoohan used the series to deliver his message.

Themes and Motivation

It is likely that there was a possible cross-pollination of ideas between McGoohan and the aforementioned Ian Stuart Black, one of the architects of *Danger Man*. In December 1966, while production of *The Prisoner* was in full swing, Black had been commissioned by the script editor of *Doctor Who*, Gerry Davis, to write a four-part story initially called *The Spidermen* and later re-titled *The Macra Terror*. The story has themes of control, repression and exploitation as a race of giant alien crabs are surreptitiously controlling a human colony for their own parasitic purposes, using the humans to mine the gas they live on. The colony itself resembles a sinister holiday camp, with huge Orwellian images of the colony's leader staring down from giant screens and sickly-sweet jingles constantly bursting from speakers, exhorting the colonists to work harder and building the idea of loyalty to the colony. This was, of course, not a million miles away from Fenella Fielding's syrupy tones assaulting denizens of The Village.

Though Black did not specifically recall having conversations with McGoohan about his vague ideas for *The Prisoner*, the thematic similarity is startling. Moreover, in the narrative, the Doctor plays very much the same function as Number 6, that of the rebel and reactionary, the disharmonious member who contrives to bring down the oppressive regime and free the inhabitants of the colony. He is the one who refuses to blindly accept and who questions everything.

One of the very few influences that McGoohan admitted to was Orwell's seminal novel *1984* and it's not difficult to see the same themes of control and repression of the individual in both.

The series centred around the abduction and imprisonment of one man. His name was never revealed to us (unless one counts the pseudonym 'Peter Smith' in 'Many Happy Returns') and he was to be known only as 'Number 6'. McGoohan stated in later interviews that he was concerned by the dehumanisation of society, the fact that people were increasingly being referred to by ID numbers and bureaucratic jargon. Indeed, he had been quoted in a 1965 edition of *TV Times*, the listings magazine for the ITV network in the UK, as saying that:

'I fear by AD 2000 we'll all have numbers, no names.'[3]

It has been speculated that the US theme music for *Danger Man* (re-titled *Secret Agent Man* on its release there) may have been one of the inspirations for *The Prisoner*. Performed by Johnny Rivers, this song contains the lines: 'They've given you a number and taken away your name.' I doubt that it impinged greatly on McGoohan's conceptual process but it seems likely that he would at least have been aware of the piece of music and that he might have filed that line away also as being of particular interest. In the same *TV Times* interview, he expressed his dislike of having his privacy invaded:

'I don't like people who obtrude on my privacy or anyone else's. I don't like the trend of being able to go up to anyone in the street and demand a public answer from them on for example, "What do you think of Harold Wilson?"'

Number 6's recurring fury at how The Village authorities had invaded and destroyed his life and at their constant demands for 'information' was apparently a very direct and very personal comment from McGoohan himself. The line between actor and character becomes blurred, especially considering his well-publicised dislike of the media circus that his celebrity status required him to face. Ironically, despite his desire for privacy and peace, McGoohan was in the process of creating a series that would provoke more discussion and bring him more attention than anything else that he had done.

Another motivation was his fear that the lone voice could no longer be heard as society put pressure on the individual to conform more and more. He felt someone in his position should make a stand on this issue and it recurs throughout *The Prisoner*, specifically in 'Free For All' and 'Fall Out', both authored by McGoohan himself.

A Team to be Trusted

McGoohan had already begun to assemble his team. His producer, the man who would be responsible for the mechanics of making much of the series happen, was David Tomblin. The pair had a good rapport and a great mutual respect which would be tested to its limit by the demands of the production. Again echoing the character of Brand, Number 6 was to be a loner, one man against the system, fighting for his beliefs in a world determined to tear him down and remake him in its image.

McGoohan wanted Number 6 to represent the everyman and, having previously named his production company Everyman Films, it seems this idea had been developing since the 1960s when he founded the company. Yet McGoohan saw the character as a hero, once dismissing an entire script which had him studying the migration patterns of birds in order to determine the whereabouts of The Village. His response to this suggestion was the curt yet revealing criticism: 'Heroes don't birdwatch.'[4] Far from being 'an everyman', the character is an idealised version of McGoohan: protector of the weak, accomplished fighter, defender of distressed damsels.

Some may argue that this third trait is underpinned by a streak of apparent misogyny that runs through certain episodes. In one, Number 6 blatantly spells it out. 'Never trust a woman,' he mutters in an episode featuring a mostly-female cast. However, the fact that Number 6 is talking to a cat when he utters this, suggests that McGoohan was probably poking fun at the misogyny of the typical Bond-esque spy movies of the time rather than supporting it. There is also a striking performance from Mary Morris as Number 2 in this episode, a dominant female figure who is one step ahead of Number 6 throughout. Moreover, considering his immense respect for his mother and for Joan, it seems unlikely that McGoohan would want Number 6 to be seen as a misogynist. Distrust, paranoia and suspicion were his dominant concerns.

Whose Creation?

Alexis Kanner, an actor who took two critical roles towards the end of the series, noted that:

'If you spent five minutes in the company of George Markstein (the series' original script editor who left under a cloud after the first production block) and five minutes in the company of Patrick McGoohan, you would be in no doubt as to whose personality you are watching when you watch *The Prisoner*.'[5]

Director Pat Jackson, on the audio commentary for 'The Schizoid Man' told an interesting version of the genesis. I haven't found this recollection in any other account and Jackson admits the story may be apocryphal, but it's certainly remarkable if true.

I asked him once, "Pat, what gave you the idea for this series?" He said, "Ah, it's a strange coincidence. Lew Grade called me in one afternoon and said, "Pat have you got an idea for a series because I've booked space for about three months and the series I was going to make has gone down so have you got an idea to fill the space? Otherwise I shall be paying for the space for nothing." So Pat said, "Well, Lew, not at the moment but you never know I might come up with a flash in a few days. Give me a few days.'[6]

Jackson continues in the commentary to explain that that very night Joan ruefully informed her husband that she had accepted an invite to a cocktail party, which McGoohan loathed. (He claimed he always ended up being trapped with the most boring person in the room, who was always impressed with his much detested 'star' status). However, McGoohan dutifully attended the event and exactly as he predicted was cornered by a civil servant. Several versions of this story have been told by McGoohan to various cast and crew members, all of which are broadly similar and can therefore be assumed to be a reasonably accurate rendition of the true events.

McGoohan's recollection was that he was having a conversation with a high-ranking official who asked him, upon the conclusion of *Danger Man*: what happens to a spy who resigns? The official was speaking in jest but the actor took him seriously and turned the question back to him. The answer he received was that retired spies were 'looked after'; given money, a home, a car. Some sources have this party as being the final wrap for *Danger Man*. In any case, McGoohan was fascinated by this notion of a retiring spy, as such a character might give him a platform to express his own strong opinions on conformity and individuality.

George Markstein, however, claims the basic premise of the show was his idea:

> 'I had been doing some research into the Special Operations Executive and I had come across a curious establishment that existed in Scotland during the War into which they put recalcitrant agents – and who was more recalcitrant than McGoohan! – I thought it was an excellent idea to play around with.
>
> One of the things I didn't know was what to call it, so I ended up calling it *"The Prisoner"*. Simple! The man was a prisoner – call it *The Prisoner*. And McGoohan went for it. He was very curious about the historical or shall we say the factual side of it. For instance, could a secret agent disappear? ...how could someone disappear in our society and be put away somewhere? And so I waffled on about "D" notices, how the authorities can ask the news media not to reveal something … He was very interested, he'd never heard of "D" notices in his life and that convinced him that this fantasy horror story had – as it does in fact have – a certain foundation in fact.'[7]

The true extent of Markstein's influence in shaping the series will probably never be known, but it cannot be denied that many of the initial ideas and the broad themes of the series came from McGoohan. The series had his unmistakable stamp all over it.

> 'What a lot of the people in the studio wanted was to keep their jobs! They hoped he'd go on doing a series and so I sat down at the typewriter one day – you know, any port in a storm – and typed a couple of pages. They were about a secret agent – and after all Drake had been a secret agent – who suddenly quits without any apparent reason, as McGoohan had quit without any apparent reason, and who is put away!'[8]

The two men had a good working relationship on *Danger Man* and had begun to talk about what was to become *The Prisoner* some time before the conclusion of filming. McGoohan also claimed, as part of the interview material for the Channel 4 documentary *Six Into One* (1985), that having become close friends with David Tomblin, the pair 'used to knock around ideas for all sorts of things around a *Prisoner*-type theme,' admitting also, 'so I suppose he was my closest associate.'[9]

Markstein most certainly developed the concept, bringing his own knowledge into play, and it is entirely possible that he also named the series. My personal opinion, however, is that it was McGoohan who devised the theme of one man being imprisoned and that Markstein found a plot which took account of McGoohan's desire to set a series in Portmeirion. Along with Tomblin (whose importance to the project cannot be overstressed as he had discussed it many times over the years with McGoohan), the two began preparing a pitch document for ITC's owner. Lew Grade was shown designs, story ideas and images of Portmeirion. McGoohan was mad keen for the project to happen and was really going for it with his typical zeal and flair for preparation.

Both McGoohan and Lew Grade recalled the meeting well. At six in the morning (their preferred meeting time), McGoohan walked into Grade's office and started showing him the collection of ideas, scripts and designs. Grade asked McGoohan to describe his new show while he studied pictures of Portmeirion, where McGoohan had decided to shoot the series. McGoohan, in an interview for a BBC documentary about Grade, takes up the story:

> 'I think he became somewhat alarmed as he saw all these pages going by and he said, "Pat, why don't you just tell me about it for a while?" So I did that, I closed up the script or whatever it was and started to wander around the office and started to talk and he listened until I'd finished, I sat down, then he got up, puffed on his cigar, marched around a little bit and then he turned on me and he said, "Pat, you know it's so crazy … it might work."[10]

The Making of an Icon: No 6 the Rebel

The money to make the series *The Prisoner*, one of the highest-budgeted British TV shows to that date, was in the Everyman Film's account the following Monday and work began in earnest. McGoohan is rumoured to have initially favoured casting another actor in the lead role but very quickly it was decided that he should star as Number 6. Grade's desire for the actor to feature in another series for him no doubt was a deciding factor in this decision, though to my mind it's doubtful that there was ever really anyone but McGoohan in the frame. This was to be a very personal series, one that would allow the actor to speak with passion about his belief in the necessity of freedom for the individual.

Clearly McGoohan saw Number 6 as a rebel, mirroring his own personality. He had done his time with *Danger Man*. *The Prisoner* saw him striking out from under the blanket of fame that John Drake had brought him and consciously making a series that broke the boundaries of television, decrying the conformity of both the medium itself and of society. McGoohan wasn't a rebel without a cause. Like many contemporary television writers, he had grown up during the Second World War and his work showed that he was fiercely opposed to what he perceived as the uniformity of the Nazi mind. As he said in *Six Into One*, regarding the furore surrounding the broadcast of the final episode:

'As long as people feel something, that's the great thing. It's when they're walking around not thinking and not feeling, that's tough, that's where all the dangerous stuff is, 'cause when you get a mob like that, you can turn them into the sort of mob that Hitler had. We don't want that, we want people who'll turn around and say, "Hey wait a minute, you daren't do that to me, I'm gonna call Lord Grade about that."'[11]

Is it possible that he had experienced a similar mob mentality after his rise to fame in *Danger Man* and that *The Prisoner* was his kick back against that? After three series, he had 'been there and done that' and knew exactly what he wanted to shout about. Indeed, the process of rebellion for McGoohan's TV incarnations seems to have begun during the production of the hour-long episodes of *Danger Man* – four years after the initial season had aired. In ITC publicity material McGoohan was quoted as saying:

'Drake now finds himself more emotionally involved with the other characters. Maturity has given him a greater depth of understanding. He rebels against some of his assignments. He doesn't really want to do them because he sympathises with the under-dog.'

This theme is developed in several of the longer episodes of *Danger Man,* which show the previously more compliant Drake having direct confrontations with his superiors; particularly when the innocent or weak have been exploited or even killed. It was an entirely natural development to create a role which took that rebellion further, since such traits defined McGoohan and his work.

The theme of rebellion was a defining characteristic of the man. In a 1977 interview with Warner Troyer for TV Ontario, McGoohan expounded that even having to sign in to the hotel in which he was staying had been a source of infuriation:

'Pass-keys and, you know, let's go down to the basement and all this. That's Prisonership as far as I'm concerned, and that makes me mad! And that makes me rebel! And that's what *The Prisoner* was doing, was rebelling against that type of thing!'[12]

Aside from the surface similarities, John Drake, Number 6 and Patrick McGoohan shared a fundamental desire to be allowed their individuality, freedom of expression and of movement.

Though McGoohan and Markstein both claimed to have devised the series, the truth is most likely somewhere in between. While Markstein did a great deal of the groundwork, co-writing the opening episode, shaping the narrative and bringing his own experiences into the equation, the basic themes of the show seem to have been very much McGoohan's. In the revealing and detailed interview the actor gave for *Six Into One*, he stated that:

'It had been in my head since the very early days, since I was about seven years old. The idea of the individual against the establishment, the individual against bureaucracy, the individual against so many laws that were all confining, the church for instance, it is almost impossible to do anything which is not some form of sin.'

In an interview for an issue of the *TV Times* that covered February 10th to the 16th in 1968, to promote the screening of the final episode that week, McGoohan claimed that he had also had the finale in his head before any other work on the series had begun.

'I envisaged it from the beginning. In a series like this, you have to know from the outset what you're aiming at. You have got to know the ending before you can begin. So I had the idea for the final episode first of all and took it from there.'

By the time that production came to the final episode, Markstein had long since departed and the actor/auteur had taken complete control of the direction in which his brainchild would play out (greatly to Markstein's disgust). How much of the finale was genuinely in McGoohan's head from the outset is unclear, as we will see later, but for now he and his team were deeply involved in shaping the new venture. Uppermost in McGoohan's mind must have been the characterisation of Number 6 himself.

Number 6: In Close-up

To Markstein, Number 6 was John Drake. Interviewed in the Channel 4 documentary *Six Into one*, Markstein was quoted as saying: 'There's no mystery, he was a secret agent called Drake who quit.' But while Drake had been a character that the actor slipped in and out of as needed, Number 6 was much more than that to McGoohan. Number 6 was himself writ large. There was briefly the intention that Drake would be the spy who resigned from his top secret position and to be hauled away to The Village, but McGoohan rapidly nixed this. This was partly because of the royalties issue that he joked about (saying he didn't want Ralph Smart to cash in on royalties) but also because he wanted to move away from the confines of this character.

McGoohan had already stated that he had become bored with *Danger Man,* feeling that the series had started to run out of ideas, and that therefore it was best to get out before it ran into the ground. There is also the matter of the personal freedom that Number 6 brought to McGoohan: here was a part that the actor was in charge of, created and devised to reflect his own concerns. While some fans of the series still believe that Number 6 is simply Drake, looking at the characterisation in each series, I personally cannot accept this. Drake is a far more relaxed character, more in control, though he faces life-threatening situations far more frequently than Number 6. Number 6, despite his best intentions, wears his heart on his sleeve, becoming almost histrionic on occasions. Sound familiar? This was a pretty accurate description of McGoohan himself.

Perhaps the final word on the Number 6/Drake matter should come from Lew Grade, who gave the following quote to a New Zealand listings magazine in August 1966:

> 'Pat hates publicity and he tells me that he is not yet letting anyone in the British or overseas press know the secrets of the new character he is creating except that it is far removed from John Drake.'[13]

That McGoohan identified very heavily with Number 6 is well-illustrated by comments from stuntman Frank Maher. Amongst the earliest material to be shot at Portmeirion, when the series commenced production in September 1966, was footage for the opening montage to take place after Number 6 has been abducted from his London home and takes his first exploratory steps into The Village. Combining footage from 'Arrival' with new material shot especially, this sequence was used with minor variations in all but four episodes. It culminates in the iconic shot of *The Prisoner* running away from The Village on the beach at sunset, silhouetted by the setting sun as he defiantly punches the air shouting: 'I am not a number, I am a free man!'.

As the stuntman Frank Maher explains:

> 'You know on the opening credits, that's me where I run out and go: "I'm not a number, I'm a free man!". The reason was this. He was sitting on a wall in the square there – remember I'd done all of *Danger Man* with him – and he said, "I'm gonna do that run on the [sand]."

I said, "Now Pat, don't do it unless you are really super fit; sand is a terrible thing to run on. It pulls muscles, it slides, don't do it." He said, "I'm fed up with you doing everything in *Danger Man*." And I said, "You look good don't you?" (laughter). He said, "That's not the point." I said, "Well, it is. I'm telling you, don't do it." Five minutes later, he came back and he looked at me and said, "Alright, you do it." So that's me on the opening credits.'[14]

Most actors and most executive producers, concerned with a potential injury to their leading man, might feel that using a trained stuntman for potentially hazardous scenes is in the interests of the production. But not McGoohan. To my mind, when he explained to Maher that, 'That's not the point,' his meaning is that it is he, McGoohan, who *should* be in the sequence because McGoohan IS Number 6 and this is, after all, the character's defining and best-remembered line.

Frank Maher worked extremely closely with McGoohan throughout the project. The stuntman once mentioned in an interview that:

'We lived out of each other's pockets. Like I said before, it was good for both of us. I could literally change into his gear, same size everything. I think I was one of the few people who actually knew Patrick a little bit. I was with him all the time.'[15]

Perhaps more than any other crew member, Maher had an insight into McGoohan's mind during the making of *The Prisoner*. At the same convention interview, he was subsequently asked how much of McGoohan's character he brought to Number 6. The response is clear:

'I think probably all of it. Patrick was a slightly mixed-up person. Very straight about everything he did and remember this was his baby. I don't give a damn what people say, it was Patrick that made it work. People around, we all did what he said. The whole thing for me screams Patrick McGoohan – having worked with him closely. Unfortunately, nobody's worked that closely with him. I'm very honoured to have done so because I learned an awful lot from him.'[16]

Executive Producer, No 1

Whilst David Tomblin collaborated with Markstein on the script for the first episode, to be called 'The Arrival' (later shortened to 'Arrival'), McGoohan was working on a storyline for a later episode. This was a political satire that would go before the cameras as 'Free For All'. McGoohan was relishing the opportunity to work behind the cameras on his new show, having long held an ambition to be more involved in the production side of *Danger Man*. In an interview with *New Video* he stated that, 'I would much rather write and direct than act. As a director I'm totally objective.'[17] Lew Grade had backed a hunch with *The Prisoner* and had given his star an unprecedented level of control. McGoohan was going to take full advantage of that. His influence would be felt in every department. He gave himself the title of 'Executive Producer', the one who is in complete artistic control of the project, finally achieving his stated ambition of being the actor-manager: Number 1.

I'm not suggesting that McGoohan was a control freak. He was a born collaborator and liked nothing more than working with his colleagues to shape his vision. He did, however, have very strong opinions about what was right or wrong for his series and as production continued, he would become ever more hands-on as he started to feel that certain members of the team were not supportive of his vision. When that happened, McGoohan simply replaced them with himself, taking on a deeper and more exhausting set of responsibilities each time. Several co-workers, most notably Markstein, were of the opinion that McGoohan's ego made him take on these extra responsibilities. However, all research into the production tells a different story. McGoohan was simply putting in tremendous effort to ensure that *The Prisoner* would achieve excellence in every department.

McGoohan vs Markstein

From the word 'go' there was trouble brewing. McGoohan and Markstein immediately differed over the direction that the series should take, with the script-editor refusing to give up the notion that it should be a continuation of *Danger Man*. The script for 'Arrival' dropped several hints to reinforce this theory, suggesting that Number 6 had a top secret background and that the information in his head could be priceless to a foreign power. Markstein disliked what he saw as the series' more whimsical elements, but McGoohan remained firm in his conviction that the new show was to be an allegory, and that therefore the more 'way out' sci-fi elements should be preserved. According to Tomblin, after two months of writing the first episode with Markstein, McGoohan took the finished script away and added his own embellishments. Unfortunately, the rewrite didn't go quite as planned, with McGoohan remarking that:

> 'The first one I re-wrote … came out … not the way I wanted.'[18]

The tensions between the two were to increase during the making of the show. Lewis Griefer, who wrote an episode of *The Prisoner* called 'The General' recalled that:

> 'I wasn't privy to this but it was pretty well known that there was a slight tension going on between George on the one side and Pat on the other. Pat kept introducing things like massive balloons and all sorts of gimmicks which I thought were great, frankly. And if you look on it with retrospect I think that's what made the series quite memorable.'[19]

Considering his insider's viewpoint, albeit for only the duration of his involvement writing one episode, Griefer's assessment would seem to be accurate. Griefer went on to explain that:

> 'It could have been, if George had had his way, a good – a very good – adventure series. I think what Pat did was make it more than that, much more than that.'[20]

The Penny-farthing: Symbol of Progress

To symbolise The Village, McGoohan settled on the image of a penny-farthing bicycle. He regarded this as being 'an ironic symbol of progress', noting that the striped canopy attached to the top made the bike impossible to ride. Such symbolism was unusual in a TV show of that time but this was to be a very unusual show. Art director Jack Shampan created several versions of the symbol which adorned everything in The Village from the mini-moke taxis to tins of baked beans. Speaking again to Troyer, McGoohan confirmed that he was concerned about the speed of progress: 'I think we're progressing too fast. I think that we should pull back and consolidate the things that we've discovered.'[21]

On another occasion, McGoohan suggested that the idea of including the penny-farthing had come to him when trapped in a traffic jam. It had suddenly struck him that the outdated mode of transport would be able to weave quite easily between the gridlocked cars. The fear, or at least the distrust of progress, is a peculiarly 1960s psychosis (as is the fear of depersonalisation and numeralisation) and it is interesting to look back on the concerns expressed in the series from a modern perspective. My personal view is that technological progress like the advent of the internet can only be a good thing, enabling global collaborations and communication which would otherwise be impossible. Though there is obviously a downside to the internet it is a fantastically powerful facilitator. For McGoohan, who seemed for the most part to be a very forward-looking individual, to be so concerned about progress seems out of character to a modern sensibility. But his views must be placed in context.

As with most science fiction/fantasy series of the time, *The Prisoner* places a heavy emphasis on the distrust of technology. Several denizens of The Village are subjected to brainwashing and mind-control techniques, usually accompanied by the typical spinning tape reels and flashing lights that had come to characterise the futuristic machines at the time. Most notably, the episode called 'The General' revolves around a huge supercomputer that is reportedly able to answer any question. The building, maintenance and operation of this machine has completely consumed its human creator and it threatens to make normal methods of teaching obsolete: machine replacing man. Socially and culturally, there was widespread fear about the speed with which computers were evolving. Many predicted, usually without any strong evidence, that before long the human race would become subservient to these increasingly powerful and completely logical minds; devices that, uncluttered with emotion, would be able to think more speedily and effectively than any organic brain. With the benefit of hindsight, this seems completely ridiculous. I view my PC as a tool and nothing more, an effective way of facilitating my work and communications with my friends and colleagues. Yet it is a philosophical trope that recurs again and again in the popular culture of the 60s.

Several of the feared scenarios that McGoohan highlighted in *The Prisoner* have indeed come to pass. For example, to some extent we are all now defined by numbers; from social security to bank accounts. On the other hand, as this has not led to any great dehumanisation, nor, I would argue, the repression of the individual, his fears were arguably a little extreme. Somewhat more sinister is the fact that CCTV cameras now cover every other street in the UK and more of the planet than McGoohan could have imagined when he decided such cameras would cover every area of The Village (again, surely influenced by Orwell's *1984.)* It is said that there is no urban area of the UK that is not now filmed by these surveillance devices and opinion is strongly polarised about their use. One feels that McGoohan would have despised the intrusion, and the rhetoric of the cameras being put in place for our safety frequently sounds like the misinformation of The Village.

Ideas in the Making

Whilst McGoohan was having the time of his life working out the overreaching themes, symbols and concepts for the show, Markstein meanwhile was recruiting writers. In the *Six Into One* documentary, McGoohan had noted that he would rather use writers who had not worked extensively on *Danger Man*, remarking that both he and Markstein were looking for people with a particular 'bent of mind' to handle the offbeat surrealistic and allegorical qualities of the new show.

As the first scripts neared completion, McGoohan and Tomblin started to recruit the rest of their film crew, mostly *Danger Man* co-workers many of whom had been patiently waiting for the call. (McGoohan didn't seem to have a problem with the crew he had worked with, in the way that he wanted to avoid *Danger Man* writers.)

The crew were delighted to be working with the actor again, typical comments include this from stuntman and McGoohan's double Frank Maher, related during a convention and reproduced with permission from The Unmutual website:

'It was a job that I wanted to do because I was given a choice when we finished *Danger Man*.

Patrick came to me and said, "There are two series being made. One is called *Man In A Suitcase* and the other one is with me." I said, "There's no contest, I'm with you." And he said, "OK."'[22]

The Right Director and Producer

Another key recruit was the man who was to bring McGoohan's vision to the screens: director Don Chaffey. Chaffey was an extremely experienced film and TV director, having recently helmed Hammer's *One Million Years BC* (1966) starring Raquel Welch and her ever-decreasing fur bikini. Chaffey explained that he was due to go to Ireland to shoot another movie when McGoohan approached him with the first scripts.

'Pat suddenly came along with this idea and I said, "Great, good, that's fine, do what you like with it," and he said, "No, I'd like you to direct the first episodes to sort of set a style," … and I just refused point blank and I went off over to Ireland … Pat and my late wife and daughter were all good friends at that time and er… we still are … and he grabbed my daughter and gave her these scripts and said, "Get your father to read these." Finally she read them herself and … "You've got to read these," she said, "they're going to be compulsive viewing, I reckon you'll have eleven million people loving to hate you every Sunday night if you make these."'[23]

McGoohan was never one to take no for an answer and his inventive way of getting Chaffey to read the scripts paid dividends. So intrigued was the director by his daughter's comments that he arranged to meet

McGoohan in Ireland and agreed to helm the opening instalments of his friend's new show.

At around this time, experienced producer Leslie Gilliat was brought on board the project by ITC's head of production Bernard Kingham. Gillian was impressed by the initial scripts and joined the project, much to McGoohan's chagrin, who felt that there was no need for another figure that he himself had not approved being on the team, there to ask questions and get in the way. Gilliat, it should be noted was an extremely well-respected industry figure who might, had McGoohan not been so intransigent, been of great help to the project. As it transpired, his role and indeed his association with the show, were to be very limited. Production manager Bernie Williams remembered on *Don't Knock Yourself Out*:

> 'Patrick was challenging the whole television industry by going beyond the norm … so on *The Prisoner*, they brought in Leslie Gilliat. Leslie Gilliat wanted to go down to Portmeirion where Patrick had shot before on the *Danger Man* series. Well, you know, when I was down there with him I sensed immediately that this was not going to work with him and Pat. Because he was too cynical, he was sceptical about the whole show and as a producer, you can't be that.' [24]

This was true of any series, but especially so on a show with such a dedicated and forceful Executive Producer as McGoohan. Bernie Williams' instincts were to prove absolutely correct. He continued in the same interview to explain McGoohan's frustration. McGoohan had devised the idea and had also taken financial responsibility. Indeed, he was indeed risking his career by going out on such a limb. To be saddled with a person who did not believe in the project was to him intolerable and pointless.

In the same documentary, second unit camera operator Bob Monks stated that:

> 'One morning, Leslie was there, that afternoon he was gone … and it was only when I went to Folkestone to work with Don Chaffey and we were chatting away and I said, "Do you know why Leslie Gilliat left?",

and he said, "Leslie pointed out a lot of the problems that have now become apparent. And this was not received too favourably and he was off.'"

Leslie Gilliat remembered the events as follows:

'I felt that it could easily go off the rails and I had a reputation of bringing out films on budget or under budget and on schedule. I didn't really want to get involved with something that was going off the rails … and Patrick McGoohan … he had certain ideas, I didn't even know how the thing was going to end, we hadn't the scripts that far. I asked him several times, "How are you going to finish this series?" and he said, "Well, I'm thinking about it," and you could never get it out of him but it was very difficult because he was acting… he really… it was a one man show as far as he was concerned and I think he wanted a free hand and I just couldn't see any future really, so I wished him the best of luck and retired gracefully."[25]

Filming Begins

Principal photography had begun on McGoohan's new venture on August 28th 1966, with the initial work being the filming of the opening titles. George Markstein decided that he would play the cameo role of the man behind the desk to whom Number 6 angrily hands his resignation. Believing himself to be the creator of the show, he felt that he should be the one at the 'centre of the web'.

Vincent Tilsley, who worked as a writer on *The Prisoner*, describes the Markstein-McGoohan conflict:

'It really presaged the relationship as it was going to be between them because there's George Markstein sitting behind the desk and McGoohan come in and starts banging and the cup going up like that, that was George and Patrick…'[26]

Not wishing to repeat his African experience when filming *Zarak* a decade earlier, the star had arranged for his family to accompany him and stay in Portmeirion for the duration of the shoot. Filming commenced at Portmeirion on September 5th 1966 and was planned to run for a month while key scenes from the first two completed scripts were captured, plus a variety of stock shots that would be used throughout the run of the show. The atmosphere on set was generally positive and McGoohan can be seen enjoying himself in a reel of 8 mm behind the scenes material. However, the production was hardly problem-free.

McGoohan claimed he created the character of 'Rover' as The Village's guardian, a machine which had been designed and built at considerable expense to travel over land and sea with equal ease. When the prop arrived at Portmeirion, McGoohan and his team were horrified and embarrassed by the result: an extremely unthreatening foam rubber cake on wheels. Bernie Williams, the production manager attempted to drive the machine which was mounted on a Go-Kart *chassis* and nearly gassed himself from the fumes. According to some, the machine was then driven into the water for its first test and refused to come out, never to be seen again.

Feeling the weight of this failure on his own shoulders and acutely aware that the clock was ticking, McGoohan was apparently distracted by the sight of a white object floating in the sky, a semi-amorphous sphere which Williams identified as a weather balloon. Making a snap decision, according to his version of the story, he immediately redesigned Rover and sent Williams off to buy up as many of the balloons as he could lay his hands upon. The spheres would become iconic symbols of the show, even though many viewers found the idea of Village residents being smothered by a large balloon laughable rather than frightening.

Director Don Chaffey found the menace to be very effective, symbolising to him the facelessness of bureaucracy. He relates a different story of the prop's genesis, claiming it was him who was struck with the inspiration. Williams' recollection, however, backs up McGoohan's version of the story, and as he was the production manager I'm inclined to take his word for it.

McGoohan drove himself to the limit from the outset on *The Prisoner*, determined that the series was going to be his masterpiece and something with a great deal more depth than the programmes usually made for TV. Reportedly, he even disallowed the use of the word 'television' on set, feeling that TV shows were often compromised in quality over theatrical films. Determined that standards should not slip, McGoohan was working a punishing 16-hours-a-day and his workload only increased when location-filming on 'Arrival' was completed. The crew moved immediately on to film the exteriors for the next episode in production, McGoohan's own 'Free for All'. In the fan publication *In the Village*, Jack Lowin, camera operator, commented that the star would generally get to bed at midnight, then be up again by 3 am to deal with his correspondence and be at the studio once more by 7 am.

Man in Charge

McGoohan's technique for maximising the amount of material in the can at the end of the day was to simply bark, 'Get it done!' to his team, all of whom rose to the challenge magnificently. The actor did not tolerate anyone who was not putting as much work into the series as he himself. In an interview reproduced on The Unmutual *Prisoner* website, extra Gaye Eastwood recalled that:

> 'He was great, but he was so busy and had a lot on his mind so he didn't chat much. Mind you, we did as we were told! He was always pushing everyone to get the best out of them, even the extras!'[27]

Yet he was at times immensely considerate with his fellow performers and extras, in a way that many stars are not. Eastwood remembered that McGoohan 'gave you a lot of confidence' and he is frequently praised by other supporting artists that have been interviewed about their time on the series. McGoohan was not one to segregate himself from the extras as some stars are wont to do and had ensured that the wages paid to the artistes were above average. Projectionist Bob Piercey, who ran the previous day's rushes every evening in the local Coliseum cinema, described McGoohan as being 'one of us' happy to be seen drinking in the evenings with the rank and file. Interviewed in *The Daily Post*, another co-worker, *Prisoner* extra Brenda Owen stated that:

'McGoohan was so ordinary, I remember him queuing up with the local people at the fish and chip shop in Porthmadoc. He was so down to earth and hated people calling him sir.'[28]

McGoohan was also found to be extremely empowering by an actor who would become close to him through the making of the series, appearing in nearly every episode, the diminutive Angelo Muscat playing the mysterious silent Butler. In ITC publicity material, Muscat was quoted as saying:

'I always feel lonely, I feel that people don't want to know me. Girls don't fancy me, I'm tiny and nearly bald but I'm only in my 30s. That's why I'm so grateful to Patrick McGoohan. He has given me responsibility for the first time in my life. I am playing an important part in a big series. I AM something, for the first time ever.'

McGoohan took Muscat under his wing, delighting in his fellow actor's company and personally looking after him. Though tinged with a definite streak of ruthlessness in his work life, McGoohan still sympathised with the underdog. He practically adopted Muscat throughout the creation of the series.

'Arrival' had out of necessity been concerned with setting up the situation, introducing us to Number 6 and the workings of The Village. The second episode that was shot – 'Free For All' – was a chance for a more in-depth examination of one of McGoohan's concerns: politics and the manipulation of both the politicians and the electorate by the media. This episode was entirely McGoohan's own, though Markstein no doubt had a hand in producing the shooting script. Written under the pseudonym 'Paddy Fitz', the story is of Number 6 being convinced to run for the office of Number 2 in a rigged election. It sees him being drugged repeatedly, viciously beaten, swallowed by Rover and finally being left humiliated by the revelation that the maid assigned to him through the course of the election run-up was in fact the next Number 2, waiting to spring her trap. This was an episode where The Village convincingly wins, outwitting Number 6 at every turn and underlining the inescapability of the situation. Nevertheless, the everyman does manage to keep his secrets to himself.

The levels of violence inflicted on *The Prisoner* during the course of this episode are surprising and their depictions often graphic, particularly for television of the time. (Indeed, the original screening of 'Free For All' had the violent scene cut out.) McGoohan seems to be implying that the fight for freedom is a hard battle, that nothing really worthwhile is achieved easily.

Shooting for this episode began immediately, with Chaffey once more taking the director's chair. McGoohan went to particular lengths to welcome guest star Rachel Herbert to the show, phoning her room in Portmeirion to check that she had arrived safely and to ask if there was anything she required. For the most part, he was always charming to any woman on the team though this was to change as he was placed under increasing stress.

Continuity lady Doris Martin recalled in an interview for BECTU that during *Danger Man*, '...he was charming. I liked him very much then.' However, this didn't last.

> 'I did *The Prisoner* later and he had gone a little strange ... it wasn't so bad at the start, he was writing it. He couldn't work out what these awful things were going to be and in the end he finished up with big rubber balloon things. Oh it was stupid, it was beyond him. He tried to do everything himself and he couldn't.'[29]

McGoohan had worked with Herbert before on an episode of *Danger Man* in which she had played a Swedish lady. He was aware therefore that she had a good command of accents which would be necessary for the part of Number 58: a maid who spoke in an incomprehensible tongue devised by McGoohan. Considering the fact that for most of the episode she speaks complete gibberish, she puts in a remarkably believable performance, managing to convey meaning and emotion. McGoohan would have been delighted by her performance and impressed by her professionalism. However, it seems that he was unhappy with Chaffey's handling of the location work for the episode. While Chaffey moved on to shoot the material at Portmeirion for

'Dance of the Dead', McGoohan made up his mind that he would take control of 'Free for All' when it arrived on the soundstages.

McGoohan was very close to this episode, always including it in one of his seven that make up the definitive *Prisoner* oeuvre. When he later directed the studio material, he decided to take full directorial credit on the finished episode. Chaffey's feelings about this are unrecorded. However, perhaps out of a sense of fairness, McGoohan gave Chaffey full credit for helming the episode 'Checkmate' even though this also had the directorial split of Chaffey on location and McGoohan in the studio.

Free for All : Full Directorial Credit

A possible explanation for his feelings about 'Free for All' may lie in McGoohan's ego. Every actor, it could be claimed, has a sizeable ego. The desire to stand up on stage and say 'look at me' isn't for the vast majority. Although many people yearn in some abstract way for fame and the perceived social and financial riches it brings, few are sufficiently self-driven to put up with the hardships that most performers face in their careers. This was McGoohan's big chance to say what *he* wanted and nothing was going to get in the way of that. So when McGoohan's vision for his script differed from Chaffey's view as director, there were bound to be problems. McGoohan had probably formulated his own directorial intentions for it during the thirty-six hour writing process.

No one knows what McGoohan may have had in mind for the story but Chaffey's direction on location is every bit as assured as his handling of 'Arrival'. Did McGoohan perhaps feel that Chaffey was missing the point or failing to bring out some nuance that only he could guess at? McGoohan and Chaffey had collaborated heavily during the planning and the shoot in Portmeirion, talking every night about the plans for the next day, so it seems likely that if McGoohan had an issue with Chaffey's work, he would have brought it up in conversation. Chaffey remembered that there had certainly been creative friction between the two men which was to escalate when the production moved into the studio.

With the first block of location filming concluding on October 1st, with pick-up shots and comparatively sparse material for 'The Chimes of Big Ben' ending the first big shooting block, the crew returned to London to work on the studio sequences. It was already apparent, however, that the series was severely in need of completed scripts.

Script Crisis: Markstein vs McGoohan Again

The problem appears to lie with George Markstein. As script supervisor, it was his duty to ensure that appropriate scripts were ready to meet production deadlines. However, despite his background as a journalist, he was inexperienced at the art of script editing and his vision of the series was beginning to deviate from McGoohan's more strongly than before. In later interviews, Markstein was dismissive of McGoohan's vision for the show. In spite of being an action adventure series, *Danger Man* had essentially been based in a believable reality. Drake's gadgets were more realistic and used more sparingly than those of Bond and other fictional spies. Drake was not permitted to extricate himself from a situation by any other means than wit or fighting prowess.

Markstein would not budge from his conviction that *The Prisoner* was a continuation of *Danger Man*, that Number 6 *was* Drake. McGoohan, in contrast, was far more interested in pursuing the allegorical angle, that freed the storytelling from the constraints of reality and allowed elements of sci-fi such as Rover, mind-swaps and identical doubles to exist within its parameters.

Roger Parks, who wrote 'A Change of Mind' and worked extensively with Markstein after their time on *The Prisoner*, said the script editor was a 'compulsive plotter' obsessed with formulating storylines that worked in traditional narrative terms. When confronted with elements that appeared wilfully nonsensical, his frustration is perhaps understandable. Despite Markstein's claims in later years that McGoohan's ego had taken over the show, there is perhaps also a hint of self-importance about Markstein himself. Interviewed for *Six Into One*, Markstein claimed to have been more than just a script editor.

'I wasn't a script editor, I was a story editor really … pedantic point but it's important. "Script editor" suggests someone who blue-pencils scripts, a story editor's a man who creates and thinks up stories. A story editor is the key man in any series, he is the man in whose hands is the ethos of the series, the spirit of the series, and it is his job to cast the writers and the authors the way a director casts the actors and the stars. It is his job to convey the meaning of the series to those writers and to, hopefully, make sure they write the kind of scripts that are required – to ride shotgun on the whole thing. He is the series on the writing side, just as the star – just as McGoohan – is the series on the acting side.'[30]

For McGoohan to wilfully override Markstein's decisions, while steering the series in his own preferred allegorical direction, was to snub Markstein's creativity. It's perhaps unsurprising that Markstein felt less and less inclined to involve himself in his duties though this does not excuse unprofessionalism.

Several crew members were interviewed by the *TV Times* for a December 1967 edition and revealed a great deal in a few words about their working relationships with the star. Jack Shampan recalled that:

'He has everything clearly in his mind down to the smallest detail. For one episode he told me what props were needed and just where he wanted them.'

Shampan went on to describe how, when devising the elaborate set for Number 2's residence:

'Pat outlined what he had in mind and left me to work it out. I couldn't see at first how some of the things could be done.'

McGoohan was clearly a man who could pick a good team and trust them, despite his iron grip on the production of the series. In the same piece, casting director Rose Tobias Shaw supports this 'team-player' aspect of McGoohan's character:

'We've had a lot of battles. Pat has positive ideas about actors and he's knowledgeable about them. But he will listen to arguments and he's always willing to see players who don't usually appear in television films. So there's a lot of off-beat casting. He has had his way most of the time because, after all, he's the executive producer. And it has worked.'

It certainly seems from these contemporary reports from those closely associated with the production of *The Prisoner* that in the minds of the crew at least, there is no doubt as to whose unifying vision was leading the way on the show. There has been an extensive programme of interviewing those connected with the series since its initial broadcast, from a worldwide fan base as well as professional researchers. Judging from these accounts, McGoohan's presence dominated the experiences of the actors and artisans who worked alongside him, while Markstein is seen as the less important contributor.

Even in the accounts from writers, it seems to be McGoohan's voice which is foremost, though one would usually expect the writer to have stronger memories of the script editor. Markstein's approach to briefing his writers also seems to have been extremely vague. The script editor is usually heavily involved in drafting the 'writer's bible' for a show, a frequently in-depth document giving the background to the settings and characters in a series, ensuring continuity of vision from the start whilst allowing the writer the freedom to place their own interpretation of the scenario in their own episodes.

In an interview conducted in 1984,[31] McGoohan had stated that there was a problem with finding suitable writers who had the right 'bent of mind' for *The Prisoner*. Too often the story ideas they received read like episodes from any other action adventure ITC series. In his series, McGoohan wanted each episode to have something to say, a strong concept and defining message.

The young Alexis Kanner was in no doubt as to who was in the driving seat creatively. It's worth bearing in mind that his experience of working on the show came entirely from the post-Markstein period:

'...the thing about *The Prisoner* really was the absolute driving rebellious persuasive trailblazing force of McGoohan enabled us to do things that were many years ahead of their time on television.'[32]

It's interesting that Kanner uses the word 'enabled'. It's a variation on a sentiment that crops up again and again from McGoohan's co-workers. McGoohan was a great collaborator, provided that he knew he had the final word and was working with actors whom he respected. One of Kanner's co-actors in the final episode was Kenneth Griffith, who, in one of mega-fan Steven Ricks' documentaries about *The Prisoner*, recalled that:

> 'Patrick is a very free improviser. I think he wouldn't be afraid to shift from a formula if he wished to say something slightly different.'[33]

Aesthetic Sensibility

In discussion with David Tomblin, Jack Shampan, who was art director on *The Prisoner*, remembered that McGoohan took as great an interest in the visual side of the show as he did in the scripts.

> 'Everything was stylised and symbolic. For example, the living space, all those lines going upward which symbolised a cage … And then, in the control room, the eye going round, you know, Big Brother watching all the time. Every bit of mechanism I suppose came from me, except for the symbol of the penny-farthing, which was the brainchild of you [Tomblin], or Pat.'

Tomblin responded to Shampan's comments saying that, as far as he was concerned, McGoohan was responsible more than anybody for the style of the series. McGoohan's visual sense was of extreme significance to him, as was observed by other co-workers. On the DVD commentary for the network release of 'Fall Out', Eric Mival, music editor on *The Prisoner* commented that McGoohan was always slightly on edge when only sound recording was required. The interviewer surmises that this was because McGoohan needed to visualise a scene. This is a revealing observation. Many writers are very visual people and McGoohan had clearly taken an extremely keen interest in the realisation of the visual aspects of *The Prisoner*. The inspiration that brought together the diverse ideas that would shape the series was, after all, most likely his first visit to Portmeirion.

McGoohan's desire to direct was no mere ego trip, or just a way of making more money, as is often the case when stars are handed the reigns. He had already proved that he could be a superb TV director when he helmed several episodes of *Danger Man*. Since he was so heavily involved with, and emotionally attached to, *The Prisoner* it's unsurprising that he wanted to take such an active part in the visualisation of his brainchild.

McGoohan was as natural behind the camera as in front of it and, unusually for him, was more than willing to have operator Jack Lowin have the final word on *The Prisoner*. McGoohan was well used to working with Lowin and obviously trusted the operator implicitly

'In some ways it was easier because you can't blame anyone else if it goes wrong ... The danger of it is that one always has to be extra self-critical and it is essential to have someone behind the camera that you can rely on. In my case, it was always the first assistant or the operator, Jack Lowin, who I had worked with for many years. I would ask ... "Was it alright?" and if they said it was okay we'd print it. Quite often they said, "Maybe you should have one more go at it?". In film-making, no one man can do it all.'[34]

McGoohan got a much-needed break with the next script in production. Written by a long-established TV writer, Gerald Kelsey, 'Checkmate' was at this point called 'The Queen's Pawn'. Both Markstein and McGoohan considered the script excellent – a rare moment of concord for the warring creatives. Again under Chaffey's direction the episode went before the cameras in late October. Though production was still severely behind schedule, there appear to have been no major hitches. This would ease the burden on McGoohan, though the staging of the famous human chess game in this episode certainly caused the continuity team a few headaches.

It seems that by the time production started, Markstein had already lost faith in the project. Though he would not leave the show until the thirteenth episode was in production, he was already behind in supplying scripts to the production. Writer Anthony Skene, whose first contribution to the show was 'Dance of the Dead', complained in later interviews about the lack of any direction from the script supervisor. According to him, there were no series notes, no 'writer's bible': 'I saw not one piece of paper. The show was a cosmic void … They sat there waiting for ideas…'[35]

Oddly though, there is contemporary evidence that there *was* a writer's bible, prepared by McGoohan, Tomblin and Markstein, so for Skene to have been deprived of information shows a complete lack of professionalism. When discussing the early script problems, McGoohan had stated:

> 'It was very difficult because they were also prisoners of conditioning, and they were used to writing for *The Saint* series or the *Secret Agent* series and it was very difficult to explain, and we lost a few by the wayside. I had sat down and I wrote a forty-page, sort of, history of The Village, the sort of telephones they used, the sewerage system, what they ate, the transport, the boundaries, a description of the Village, every aspect of it; and they were all given copies of this and then, naturally, we talked to them about it, sent them away and hoped they would come up with an idea that was feasible.'[36]

One hesitates to suggest it, but it almost seems that Markstein was trying to sabotage the series, maybe even subconsciously. What is certain is that the relationship between him and McGoohan rapidly disintegrated into constant arguments about the direction of the show. Markstein felt that McGoohan's 'allegory' was unfocused and confusing, continuing to dislike what he perceived as being the gimmickry of the more surreal aspects of The Village.

Dance of The Dead and Chimes Again

'Dance of the Dead' was to be a particularly surreal episode, possibly sealing the series' fate in Markstein's mind. With little briefing, Skene had devised a story rich in symbolism with a female-dominated cast led by Mary Morris as Number 2 and Norma West as Number 240, Number 6's observer. Both actresses, who developed a firm friendship during the production, found the script confusing but noted that McGoohan was not forthcoming with any of the answers about either the episode or the series. According to West, he would rarely talk to anyone but Tomblin or Chaffey in the evenings. I imagine this was largely a result of the production problems the show was suffering and because the 'actor-manager' was keen to plan for the next day's work as efficiently as possible. McGoohan was well-known for being a meticulous planner and, to judge from the finished episode, both West and Morris were quick-witted enough to pick up on the subtexts in the script. Both turned in excellent performances, with Morris' being a particular stand-out. Both actresses also found favour from McGoohan. The actor worked particularly well with Norma West who, like many guest stars in the series, had previously appeared in *Danger Man*.

Also in production at the same time was Vincent Tilsley's episode 'The Chimes of Big Ben' which starred, as Number 2, the noted Australian character actor Leo McKern, later to find fame as 'Rumpole of the Bailey'. McKern recalled his initial impressions of meeting McGoohan in a 'behind the scenes' documentary of 'The Day The Earth Caught Fire':

> 'When he called me, "You're a funny little fucker, aren't you?" and I thought, "Oh, it's going to be that sort of relationship, unfortunately," and that was said in a bar when we were drinking before we even started the series'[37]

McGoohan was typically confrontational but McKern was not to be put off. He became fascinated by the series, feeling that it very much fitted in with his own opinions about the rights of the individual and freedom not only of speech but of thought. According to Norma West the actor was desperate to find out the truth of what the series was all about but McGoohan stayed typically tight-lipped. Production continued on both episodes, with McGoohan now advising in-depth on the directing but at other times being very reserved and quiet. The workload was starting to get to him, with actress Mary Morris observing to the star in the make-up room one morning that he looked 'terribly ill' ; a fact which McGoohan accepted. His behaviour continued to verge towards the eccentric. He refused to have any physical contact with Norma West in the scripted dancing scene from 'Dance of the Dead', with the actress observing in amusement that they delivered their lines standing six feet away from each other.

Chaffey vs McGoohan: More Casualties

With the conclusion of filming on 'Chimes', another casualty around the end of November 1966 seems to be Don Chaffey. Chaffey had been instrumental in shaping the first batch of episodes and, as noted earlier, had been so closely involved with McGoohan's vision that they were able to share directorial duties on two episodes.

Chaffey had contributed enormously to the show, helping to hire key personnel. However, the star and the director had finally come to a point where they could not agree and the former departed after completing production of 'Dance of the Dead' and 'The Chimes of Big Ben'. Sidney Cole, producer of *Danger Man*, recalled hearing that Chaffey had 'finally had a quarrel with Pat' when interviewing Doris Martin for BECTU, with the continuity lady wryly observing that 'most people did'.

As shooting progressed, McGoohan apparently became more and more strained and tense. This now manifested itself in a desire to delegate less and less, in a drive to ensure that it was his own vision that eventually reached the screen. When interviewed for *Six Into One,* Chaffey alluded to some heated moments, but seemed to hold no particular animosity towards McGoohan in later years:

> 'Pat's not an easy person to get on with but at least he knows what he wants and I have clear-cut ideas too ... there were some bitter arguments but that's neither here nor there because out of it came what I think is one of the best television series ever made.'

The first cut of 'Dance of the Dead' was deemed by McGoohan to be a total disaster, so much so that the episode was shelved completely and was only 'rescued' some months later by editor John S Smith who saw great potential in the episode and offered to re-cut the material.

For an entire episode to be so under par must have angered McGoohan deeply. Smith explains how he eventually salvaged the situation:

> 'What had happened is that one of the end scenes hadn't been shot and I managed to overcome that with a few wild tracks and stretched one or two other things out and I got the reputation as the man who saved "Dance of the Dead".'[38]

The stress upon the actor was to increase as he had now taken it upon himself to both write and direct the next episode in production, the semi-autobiographical 'Once Upon a Time'. The production team had been so impressed with Leo McKern's Number 2 that he was asked to stay on for this new episode, a tight two-hander, a psychological confrontation designed from the start by McGoohan to be the first act of a two-part-ending to the series. McKern readily accepted but the shooting was to take a heavy toll on him as well as on the star.

This time McGoohan's script was written under the pen name of 'Archibald Schwarz' since the actor was convinced that he would be ridiculed for its content and it was reportedly distributed late in the day. Props-buyer Sydney Palmer complained on the Steven Ricks' documentary *The Prisoner In Depth* that the lack of scripts made his job extremely difficult. All too often, the buyer was being asked to do things like find an organ on the Friday for shooting on Monday, leaving him in a state of nervous exhaustion by the end of the day. George Markstein was singularly unimpressed by McGoohan's latest piece of writing and remained staunchly hands-off during the production. (He had chosen to remain in his office, despite having little to do, so he was still around at this point.)

> 'Leo McKern ... a very fine actor I think, came in on short notice to do it, and it was mainly a two-hander. The brainwashing thing, he was trying to brainwash me and in the end No 6 turns the tables. And the dialogue was very peculiar because all it consisted of was mainly "Six, Six, Six", and five pages of that at one time.'

Degree Absolute

After McGoohan's typical thirty-six hour writing blitz, 'Degree Absolute' – as the episode was then known – went into production immediately. This was the first almost completely studio-bound episode of the series, which would have pick-ups shot at Portmeirion in the new year. Therefore a great deal more material had to be produced than for the previous episodes and McGoohan proceeded at his usual breakneck pace, driving the crew to the limit.

The bulk of the episode took place on a cost-cutting set, comprised of black drapes and stock props and dressings, and featured only McGoohan, McKern and Muscat in his usual non-speaking role. McKern found that McGoohan was flexible enough to incorporate a particular idea he might have, allowing him to improvise some of his dialogue. This was a sure sign that the director and star trusted McKern's work but the relationship was to sour, like so many before, within a few days. As McKern recalled in several interviews:

'He was almost impossible to work with, a dreadful bully, always shouting and screaming and yelling about the place. Hurrying up, saving money … I used to lie in my dressing room in the short times we had off and worry and be depressed and very silent.'[39]

Bernie Williams recalled that the actor had even suffered from a serious heart problem because of the intensity of making the episode and eventually he was retired from the set for a few days to recuperate. McGoohan remembered in the Warner Troyer interview that:

'I knew he was tired. I went up to his dressing-room to tell him how good I thought he had been in the rushes and he was curled-up in the foetus position on his couch there and he says, "Go away! Go away you bastard! I don't want to see you again!" I said, "What are you talking about?" "I've just ordered two doctors," he says, "and they're comin' over as soon as they can… Go away."

And he had. He'd ordered two doctors and they came over that afternoon and he didn't work for three days. He'd gone! He'd cracked, which was very interesting. He'd truly cracked. And so I had to use a double, the back of a guy's head, for a lot, and eventually Leo did come back and we completed them and also he was in the final episode, so he forgave me for everything, but he did crack, very interesting, I thought...'[40]

McKern may have 'cracked' but McGoohan didn't have that luxury. It's almost as if he had passed the point of being able to react emotionally to McKern's breakdown at all. As soon as work on 'Degree Absolute' was completed, the production team spent the final two working weeks of December moving straight on to the next episode. This was Terence Feeley's 'The Schizoid Man'. It would be directed by a newcomer to the show, Pat Jackson who years before had given McGoohan his first ever screen test.

Jackson was delighted with the script though he cheerfully professed that he hadn't a clue what it was about. After the intensity of the previous episode, McGoohan was able to relax slightly, though as the plot revolved around The Village importing a doppelganger of Number 6 in an attempt to destroy his sense of identity, he had more then usual to do in terms of acting. By this point, ITC were keen to see a finished episode to help facilitate sales in the States and in the evenings after filming wrapped, McGoohan was usually to be found in the post-production suites, where he focused on supervising picture and sound editing.

A Schizoid Man

Terence Feely offers an interesting insight into McGoohan's attitude towards scenes of a sexual or even romantic nature that might involve him. During the writing process Feely had devised a scene where a young and attractive woman, Alison, is able to deduce which of the two identical men was the real Number 6 by kissing them. McGoohan, typically, demanded that the scene be removed and a more cerebral relationship was substituted. Feely recalled in an interview with Steve Ricks that McGoohan had told him:

'I have this tremendous guilt inside me and I would not be able to look
my wife in the eye that night. I just can't do it.'[41]

Could it perhaps be that McGoohan did not want to put himself
into a situation where he might be tempted by another woman? He
was clearly capable of enormous appetites in other areas of his life
and work and it is often the case that such driven and energetic people
have tremendous sexual needs. His apparent sense of guilt with regard
to sexual desire, a consequence of his Catholic upbringing, made him
unsuited to the role of leading man. It must have been a considerable
source of conflict.

The episode starred Anton Rodgers as the new Number 2 and
Jane Merrow as Alison, a village resident unusually allowed her own
name. Both performers were, in later years, generous in their praise
of the overworked and stressed star. Merrow found him particularly
rewarding to work with, though she recalled that the actor demanded
total professionalism:

'I got on very, very well with him, I don't know why, we connected very
well and I think he liked me and I think he respected what I did and I
think he could to some extent relax with me because he could … you
know, we were just two professionals working together.'[42]

Rodgers, on the other hand, reportedly found that McGoohan
could be very difficult to work with but that in his opinion that
wasn't a problem. Merrow's comment about McGoohan being able
to 'relax' with her is telling. This indicates that he felt able to trust
her professionalism and her ability to deliver the goods, taking some
of the burden from his shoulders which no doubt contributed to
their working relationship. She was also impressed by the fact that
the exhausted star took the time to stay on set during her close-ups,
providing his own reactions to her lines rather than using a stand-in,
a common technique but one which often throws the performer.
This is further evidence of McGoohan's commitment to the quality
of the series, as well as his unstinting support of those who he felt
were putting in as much effort as he was.

Production continued up until Christmas Eve with McGoohan directing pick-up shots for 'Checkmate' before the cast and crew were finally allowed some time off over Christmas and the New Year. I've not been able to verify the rumour that Markstein came into work on Christmas day itself, to be dismissed by McGoohan, the only other person present, with the words, 'Everybody gets a day off on my birthday.'

CHAPTER 6
The Prisoner: Obsession

It's Your Funeral

With production of episode seven on the schedule, 'The Schizoid Man', completed in early January 1967 the pressure was back on. The next episode, 'It's Your Funeral' was to prove a trial for both McGoohan and the production team. The star had invited his old friend Robert Asher, who had recently directed the Norman Wisdom film *Press for Time*, to direct the story, which was by Michael Cramoy. No doubt McGoohan felt that the director would be a safe pair of hands, as he had mentioned that there was the possibility of further work on the series. In keeping with an all-too familiar pattern, both the working relationship and the friendship would break down, spectacularly early on in the shooting.

McGoohan was becoming more and more involved in production. He would frequently distribute handwritten script amendments on the day of filming, which the cast were, of course, required to learn immediately. Cast as Number 2 in 'It's Your Funeral' was another old friend of McGoohan's, Derren Nesbitt, who recalled being utterly confused by the script. He received little help from Robert Asher, who was no more enlightened than the actor. Neither man was offered clarification from McGoohan who was now becoming increasingly tetchy with everyone involved. In *Don't Knock Yourself Out*, Nesbitt remembered McGoohan's dissatisfaction with his confused performance:

'McGoohan came up to me and he said, "This is not a comedy! Why are you doing … you look like you don't know what it's about!". I said, "I have got no bloody idea what it's about! You tell me what it's about!". He said, "Well I'm not sure." So I played him *totally* confused."[1]

Perhaps 'It's Your Funeral' was a particularly tricky episode to make. Nesbitt may have been confused but actress Annette Andre, who played the Watchmaker's Daughter in 'It's Your Funeral', was on the receiving end of McGoohan's ire. In *Don't Knock Yourself Out* she explained that:

> 'I hated very single minute of it. And that was down to Patrick, totally. It's no secret that I just loathed Patrick from the minute I started. I tried to be nice and he … doesn't work with actresses at all well. "

Whether or not McGoohan was a misogynist is hard to say from the varying responses of the actresses he worked with. Andre was working with McGoohan at his most stressed, as he frantically rewrote and rewrote this episode, attempting to clarify the narrative. He couldn't tolerate the inevitable compromises of the production process and began drinking heavily, which would have made his behaviour even more erratic.

It wasn't only Annette Andre who was having problems with the 'actor-manager'. After a number of disputes, matters between McGoohan and Robert Asher came to a head. McGoohan fired the mild-mannered director, humiliating him in front of the entire crew. Annette Andre recalled:

> 'He had a crushing row with Bob Asher and tore him apart in front of the entire studio, the crew, everything. And in my set of ethics, you don't do that to an actor and you certainly don't do it to your director. And the next day I went to my agent and said, "I can't stand this." However, I finished the whole thing but I hated that. I hated the whole thing!"[2]

Jekyll and Hyde

By this point, McGoohan's increasingly dictatorial behaviour indicated that he little respect for other people's feelings. The suave and charming Dr Jekyll had metamorphosed fully into Mr Hyde, with an overwhelming drive to make the show succeed at whatever cost. Asher left the production reportedly in tears and McGoohan once again wearily took directorial control. According to fellow actor Mark Eden, who took a significant role in the episode, McGoohan was now on the verge of mental collapse:

> 'I think he was having a bit of a nervous breakdown to be honest, he was terribly uptight … he had a terrible row with the director, on the set, screaming! And he sacked him.'[3]

Watching the episode in hindsight, there does seem to be an edge of barely-restrained fury and hysteria to McGoohan's performance that is absent from other episodes, with Number 6 almost racing through the episode as if determined to get it over and done with. Though the actor was always very truthful and believable in action scenes, to the point of genuine violence at times, Mark Eden recalled that the climactic battle between Number 6 and his own character, Number 100 became a genuine life and death struggle:

> 'There was a bit where he had to get on top of me and strangle me and I had to push him off … and he got on top of me and he was really strangling me! There is a way of doing it you know without actually hurting … and I looked up and I could see these mad eyes looking down at me and I thought "He's gone, he's gone…" and his face was contorted with rage … and he's a big man and I had to push him off. Fortunately in those days I was quite fit … but it took me every ounce of strength that I had to push him off.'[4]

The attitude of the consummate professional seems to have deserted McGoohan by this point, perhaps due to his alcoholic intake. It seems a reasonable conclusion that McGoohan was now suffering from some form of depression, brought on by stress. The episode is not fondly remembered by anyone who worked on it. As an added note to his comments above, Eden mentioned in *The Daily Star* that, 'Later I found out he was having terrible emotional and mental problems.'[5]

Thankfully, the troubled shoot wound down before any major disasters could occur and the next episode, 'A Change of Mind', swung into production. History was, however, about to repeat itself.

A Change of Mind

Roy Rossotti had been brought in to direct this new episode and actress Angela Browne, cast in the pivotal role of Number 86, recalled that the novice director spent his first morning on set taking great care setting-up his shots but also taking up a great deal of time. This annoyed McGoohan, who by now was feeling a new pressure, that of Lew Grade and his financiers. Grade had remained remarkably calm and hands-off during the making of the series so far, but *The Prisoner* was well behind schedule and rapidly going over budget. McGoohan felt extremely indebted and responsible to Grade (who had, after all, taken a terrific gamble with one of his most favoured leading men). He resorted to his usual solution: if you want something done, you have to do it yourself.

Perhaps feeling some guilt over the blazing public altercation with Robert Asher, McGoohan quietly fired Rossotti during the first lunch break. The young and ambitious director was extremely upset by the dismissal and was later found crying in the car park by Bernie Williams. McGoohan suggested to the crew that Rossotti had fallen ill and would not be returning to the production and once again took control.

It is not known whether McGoohan used Rossotti's camera scripts or prepared his own in record time for the shooting of 'A Change Of Mind' in late January and early February 1967. For the uninitiated, a camera script is an annotated breakdown of every shot, every angle that will be used being referred to as a 'set-up'. According to Tomblin, McGoohan averaged twice the usual number of set-ups per day and it is remarkable that there is no perceptible drop in quality because of the breakneck speed.

His intimidating presence on the set of 'A Change of Mind' ensured that every crew member did their very best and, unlike Annette Andre, in her role as Number 86 Angela Browne found the star incredibly supportive. She was required in one scene to deliver a great deal of very complicated medical and scientific dialogue and her concentration had been broken by on-set chatter during the set-up. McGoohan noted that her confidence had been dented and roared at the crew to be quiet under threat of dismissal, pointing out that the actress was doing her best and needed to concentrate. Browne had previously worked with McGoohan on *Danger Man* and had always been treated to the 'Dr Jekyll' side of his personality. From an interview on The Unmutual website, she recalled:

> 'I don't know about the other actors experiences with Patrick, but with me he was always terribly patient, really kind, he gave you all the time in the world. And I really did love him, I thought he was smashing. Some people found him a bit fierce, and he was fierce because I think he was a perfectionist. He knew what he wanted and if you went all the way along with him he was on your side. And that was the thing I liked about him. He was only angry with people he felt weren't doing the job properly.'[6]

Quoted in an earlier chapter, Browne also recounted how on the set of *Danger Man*, she had 'fallen in love' with McGoohan. I am assuming this to be nothing more than a mild crush but she recounts that when she met him again on the set of 'A Change Of Mind': 'I was still quite keen … not as keen as he was…!' Could it be that the man in the ivory tower actually lowered his defences and flirted with the classically beautiful actress or was she just a fantasist? In the oft-repeated words of Number 6, 'You'll never know…'

McGoohan declined to take a director's credit on the finished episode, pointing out that, 'The other fellow had done half a day,' and so the episode went out under the name 'Joseph Serf'. Did McGoohan perhaps feel that he had become a slave to *The Prisoner*, choosing this name as a tongue-in-cheek gesture towards that fact? Certainly, the production was by now consuming all of his time leaving little room for family or socialising with any but the crew.

By the beginning of February, Lew Grade had asked that there be a completed episode to show to a group of executives from CBS who had agreed to buy the series and McGoohan was now extending himself still further by working with the editing teams to ensure that 'Arrival' would be completed in time for their visit. Time was against 'the prisoner' of his own dream.

In recent correspondence I have shared with Eric Mival, who worked as music editor on *The Prisoner*, he recalled that at this point McGoohan was a surprisingly frequent sight in the post production department.

'When you work in the cutting rooms your encounters with the shooting side of the series tend to be infrequent. However, Pat had been responsible for the shooting of the opening sequence to *The Prisoner*, which was down to Geoff to edit, so he did pop by at the end of a shooting day to check how it was going. As Geoff was an excellent and highly experienced feature film editor … he was a bit put out when Pat would urge him to speed-up the cuts he had already made, giving the opening title sequence more pace.'

A, B and C

With money running dangerously low, another writer, Anthony Skene was asked to come up with a cost-cutting script that could be filmed on an especially low budget. Initially, David Tomblin had instructed him to make an episode that would use as many Portmeirion stock shots as possible but Skene felt this to be, and I quote 'crappy'. So he instead walked around the MGM back lot, conceiving of an episode that would use the already standing sets. 'A, B and C', as it would come to be titled, was an episode that found great favour with Tomblin who explained that he feared the series was becoming too claustrophobic, trapped in the confines of The Village. The storyline dealt with the attempts of the new Number 2 to influence Number 6's dreams with drugs and electronic control methods, in an attempt do get his subconscious to divulge his secrets. This plot placed the character outside The Village confines for several dream sequences, giving the viewer a glimpse of Number 6's life before his abduction. Directed by the reliable Pat Jackson (replacing original director Michael Trueman who was forced to leave the episode through illness before shooting began) the episode encountered no major traumas during its production, though the actor's workload was still phenomenally intense.

McGoohan was now so heavily involved with the production and post production of numerous other episodes that he had less time to spend on the set of 'A, B and C' than he might have liked. Unlike the experiences of actress Jane Merrow, who had enjoyed McGoohan's undivided on-set attention filming episode six (see previous chapter), actress Sheila Allen found that all her close-ups were performed to the director, Jackson. She was playing Number 14, the expert brought in to carry out the procedures on Number 6. Alongside her, playing Engadine, was French actress Katherine Kath, who recalled that McGoohan didn't smile very much during this period, though he did manage to crack a grin once, at her teasing. She also remembered, amusingly, that he was even able to catch up on some sleep during the filming of the scenes in the Laboratory, most of which involved Number 6 unconscious on a gurney. Interviewed by Steven Ricks for his aforementioned documentaries on *The Prisoner,* Kath's recollection was that the episode was very pleasant to work on, describing it as being, 'Beautifully produced … by Patrick McGoohan'.[7]

Though it is not known if McGoohan took any active part in rewriting this episode, there is a scene at the conclusion where a mysterious figure in Number 6's dream (of which he has now taken control) is unmasked to reveal the face of Number 2: a major victory for the Prisoner and a crushing defeat for the Village administrator.

One can sense McGoohan's dissatisfaction with what he perceived as the dumbed-down narratives of most spy thrillers, as Number 6 wryly observes that the unmasking must happen to satisfy the curiosity of 'the people who are watching'. He is, of course, referring to Numbers 2 and 14, who are watching the dream on a large screen in the operating theatre, but another interpretation – that the viewers of the episode would also feel cheated – no doubt amused the actor.

The CBS Deal

McGoohan was less amused by the visit from Michael Dann and his team of executives from CBS in February that year. The actor had been working to the limit for the five days prior to the meeting, to ensure that 'Arrival' would be able to be screened. The print was finally being delivered to Grade one hour before his meeting was due to begin. Dann liked what he saw but had reservations about the fact that every episode ended with Number 6 still a prisoner, fearing that the American audiences would not take to a hero who essentially loses every week.

Grade arranged that McGoohan should come to his office to meet the representatives and having listened to Dann's concerns, McGoohan retorted that he thought the executive had outlined a wonderful series. However, it wasn't the one that he was making, nor was it one in which he had any interest. McGoohan then departed the meeting, his standards entirely uncompromised, leaving a bemused Dann to ask Lew Grade if he ever had any problems with the recalcitrant star. Grade replied that he had an excellent working relationship with McGoohan and when Dann questioned how on earth the ATV chief managed that remarkable feat was given the answer: "I always give in to what he wants".[8]

The Prisoner Theme Tune

Around this time, the music which would become the final theme for the series was being composed. There had so far been two attempts at recording a theme, neither of which had met with McGoohan's approval, and the production team had now turned to the experienced TV and film composer Ron Grainer. Grainer was best known for his wildly different themes for *Steptoe and Son* and *Doctor Who* and had recently been working on another ITC series in production concurrent with *The Prisoner* called *Man in a Suitcase*.

However, according to film librarian Tony Sloman, the basic melody for the new theme came from McGoohan himself. Apparently, he had walked into one of the film editor's cutting rooms one day, whistled the tune and asked for the editor's opinion before passing it on to Grainer. Originally, Grainer composed a version of this theme, known as 'The Age of Elegance', a light track based on harpsichords; but McGoohan, while liking the basic melody, wanted the music to have a great deal more power. Eric Mival, music editor for *The Prisoner* recalled to me:

'The incident of his getting Ron Grainer to "beef up the music" happened a few weeks later, after I had been given the music editing job. As with Geoff, the pace of the music appeared to be the problem: i.e. too slow and somewhat gentle, as far as I can recall, which no doubt would have frustrated Pat, who attended the music session. I have this mental image of him remonstrating with Ron with arms flailing to encourage him to "beef it up" and speed up the pace. Fortunately he did, and the music was transformed for all of us.'[9]

Eric went on to question his own recollection:

'In retrospect, I find what I am saying to be somewhat suspect, because if you change pace on something designed to fit picture edits inevitably it will go out of sync.'

But he ultimately supports the story he has told:

'To have the memory and know that there's a huge difference between what Ron released as his theme on a record (slow and gentle), and the final *Prisoner* theme tune, makes me believe something along the above lines did happen that day, as the two versions are as different as chalk and cheese.'

The General

By the time episode 10, 'The General', went into production, Markstein had very little day-to-day involvement in the production of the series. However, he kept his office at the studios and the script for this next episode was one from his friend and colleague, writer Lewis Griefer. In fact, the storyline of 'The General' did not find favour with Markstein, but McGoohan approved of it immensely.

Griefer chose to write about the confines of standard educational practices, the freedom of the individual to learn in their own way.

'Originally, you've got this guy trying to escape ... but that was an easy way. But since I decided that it was slightly more than that ... I went for "The General" because it was an aspect of life at that particular time. Well the idea was ... I had children then that were going through their "O" and "A" levels and both of them were feeling very hostile to the rote learning that they were going through.

They were both very intelligent kids who liked information and would have liked to study things in their own form. What they hated was having to pass exams. I think kids are pretty open to education but at the same time they are pretty opposed to being forced into a sort of sausage grinder.'[10]

With such a theme, it was inevitable that McGoohan should express his appreciation of the episode. As Griefer recalls:

'Pat loved "The General". He thought that it was just what he wanted to do, it was exactly his cup of tea. George less so if you know what I mean, but George and I were great mates anyway and we could talk to each other any time we wanted to … he didn't raise too much rumpus but Pat actually thought that it was exactly what the series should be around and that sort of slightly mysterious area.'

Interestingly, Tony Sloman (the film librarian mentioned earlier) recalled that McGoohan thought the episode was 'stupid'. How this tallies with Griefer's memory is not clear, perhaps this was another case of McGoohan's increasingly split personality manifesting itself. In any case, with a script that was good-to-go, and mindful that the finances were now tighter than ever, McGoohan turned to experienced TV director Peter Graham Scott to helm the episode – observing that he was hired because, 'He's quick. And cheap'.

All Change: Firing Directors

It seems that, yet again, McGoohan had been dissatisfied with the first director assigned to the job. If a director couldn't realise his vision or meet his extremely high standards, they wouldn't last a day. Peter Graham Scott explained how he got the job in *Don't Knock Yourself Out:*'

'My phone rang on a Friday night and a voice said, "Peter, this is Patrick". He didn't say Patrick whom, but I knew who it was. And he said, "I've fired the director, we're going to start all over again on Monday and you are directing.'"[11]

There was no invitation, just a simple command and Scott took the job. It is not known exactly what the previous director, Robert Lynn, did to raise McGoohan's ire, but the implication is that some shooting had already been conducted on 'The General' and that it was not to the star's satisfaction.

Though Peter Graham Scott was at the time a staff director at the BBC, McGoohan took it upon himself to phone Scott's ultimate boss (the legendary Sydney Newman – himself a formidable and abrasive figure) to persuade him to allow McGoohan's team to 'borrow' the director for the duration of the shoot. Colin Gordon, who had just played Number 2 in 'A, B and C', was flattered to be asked to return to play the same character. Veteran character-actor Peter Howell played the role of the ill-fated professor who created the supercomputer of the title. Howell echoed what many fellow actors have said about McGoohan's power as a performer:

'Patrick McGoohan has an extraordinary personality. When you were sitting next to him in the make-up room where this man's electric personality and burning dedication to what he was doing … and the fact that he had more panache, more electricity flowing through him … he wasn't frightening, he was exciting and you could see how it was that he could have the energy to write and direct and star in this extraordinary piece and it's a quality that is very rare indeed and I remember (him) particularly on the stage in Ibsen's *Brand* and the same quality was there. He just took you with him and just took over in a way that very few performers in my lifetime certainly, have done.'[12]

Magnetism and Intuition

Howell clearly liked and respected McGoohan, as both a person and a performer, and his observation that McGoohan's intense energy was exciting rather than frightening is intriguing. Howell was an extremely experienced actor, no doubt completely secure in his own abilities and therefore quite happy to serve McGoohan's vision and let himself be carried along by the burning energy of the star player. Perhaps others, like Roy Rossotti, were less secure and felt greatly intimidated by such a presence hanging over them. It seems a reasonable conclusion that McGoohan could, as it were, 'smell' fear and insecurity in a performer or a crew member, making him feel nervous in turn.

Howell went on to recall that McGoohan was involved in every single aspect of the shoot, though without, as he saw it, getting in the way of Peter Graham Scott's own creativity. He also recalls an incident during filming which illustrates McGoohan's incredible self-belief:

'Patrick McGoohan brings the stick very hard down and cracks this mask. He was very clever ... because he said, 'I don't want to go too close to your face because it might slip and I might hit you.' ... and then when it came to the actual take he did it very, very hard indeed. And I think what he was saying, rather typical of him really, was that he didn't want to frighten me but he had total control, he was absolutely certain that he could do it without catching my hair. And so he put my mind at rest and then did it ... pretty close!'[13]

Always looking for inventive visual devices to add into the series, McGoohan had spotted a black plastic moneybox, the kind popular in the 60s and 70s which, when a coin was placed in a slot, would produce a small plastic hand to grab the coin and whip it into the interior. Delighted and fascinated by the toy, McGoohan presented it to Sidney Palmer the props buyer and it was worked into the episode as an unusual and amusing security mechanism, accepting tiny penny-farthing stamped passes.

Concurrent with the shooting of 'The General' in the studio, David Tomblin took a second unit back to Portmeirion for two weeks of shooting. While stuntman Frank Maher spent most of his time doubling for McGoohan, the star appeared each weekend, travelling from London to perform as many shots as possible before turning around and heading straight back, getting a few hours sleep before starting work again at 4 am on the Monday. Though he frequently claimed to need very little sleep, the physical strain of working seven days a week must have by now been intense and the mental strain was certainly taking its toll.

Hammer Into Anvil and Many Happy Returns Run Parallel

It is perhaps unsurprising that during these difficult months, with the weight of the series, the expectations of Lew Grade and of his crew resting on his shoulders, McGoohan's temper became more prone to fraying and his actions more unpredictable as he turned more and more to drink. He remained focused however, to the point of obsession, determined that his voice be heard through the narrative.

McGoohan had it slightly easier on 'Hammer Into Anvil', a tightly scripted battle of wills by Roger Woddis, directed once more by the talented and, above all, safe pair of hands Pat Jackson. For once, there were no major setbacks during the shoot and Jackson with his usual flair, efficiency and understanding for the material delivered the goods with apparent ease (though he was quoted in *Six Into One* as saying he had no idea what the script for 'The Schizoid Man' was about when he first received it).

Patrick Cargill, who would also play a small role in the later episode 'Many Happy Returns', was cast as a neurotic Number 2. In a dramatic turn, Number 2's arrogant confidence in himself and in the systems of The Village are systematically torn down by Number 6, leaving him at the end weeping and broken. Another victory for the individual.

The constant changing of the nominal head of The Village was a deliberate attempt to make sure that there would always be a strong guest role available, something to break any monotony that could ensue if Number 6 were pitted against the same man week-in, week-out. McGoohan also saw it as a comment on the bureaucratic practice of many companies and governmental organisations who would replace one operative with another from a different department, usually meaning that any applicant going through a system has to repeat the entire process so far. Number 6 may break one Number 2, but there will always be another to take their place.

'Many Happy Returns' had begun filming back-to-back with material for 'Hammer into Anvil' and all of Tomblin's second unit material in Portmeirion. Yet this was to be another episode which ran into problems. Michael Trueman, who had been hired as director, was unwell (possibly a recurrence of the illness which prevented him from directing 'A, B and C'). More crucially, according to second unit cameraman Robert Monks, McGoohan and Trueman did not 'see eye to eye'.[14]

As we have seen several times, this usually meant the end of the line for any director and indeed, Trueman left the production after only a few days filming. This left McGoohan to take command once more.

Series producer, David Tomblin, recalled in *Six Into One*:

'As it progressed and we got further into it, being the man he is and being the man I try to be, we put all our time into it. In fact, we worked seven days a week, sixteen hours a day and we tried to make every episode really 1,000 percent. And eventually it became fairly obvious that we couldn't sustain this… well, pace… the level of quality in the time that was left, because we were running out of time because the showing dates were fast approaching.'[15]

Written by Anthony Skene, from an idea given to him by Tomblin, 'Many Happy Returns' was another episode that opened out the scope of the series. Number 6 wakes one morning to find The Village deserted and dead. Realising that this is his chance, he constructs a raft and sets sail for freedom, eventually managing to return to his London home, where he immediately starts carrying out his threat from 'The Chimes Of Big Ben' to 'escape, come back, wipe this place off the face of the Earth'.

Markstein Departs

The storyline was favoured by George Markstein, whose original intention was to complete the full run of twenty-six episodes that Lew Grade wanted to facilitate sales. His vision was that as the series progressed, Number 6 would find himself back in the real world where he would discover that he was just as much a Prisoner as he had been in the Village. It's an intriguing idea, that would have fitted in well with McGoohan's core intentions, but it was not to be.

With the production now heavily behind schedule, largely due to the lateness of scripts, but compounded by McGoohan's perfectionist drive, Markstein felt that it was finally time to bow out. In 'Many Happy Returns', he made his last contribution to *The Prisoner*, by reprising his role as the-man-behind-the desk from the opening titles. This episode sees Number 6 revisit his old employers to begin his campaign of vengeance. In *Six Into One*, Markstein explained his reasons for his own resignation:

> 'When egomania took over! You know, when McGoohan was everything! When McGoohan was writing, was conceiving, was directing … and didn't know where he was going. My presence was superfluous – and we've seen the result after my departure.'[16]

That Markstein felt his presence was superfluous is hardly surprising. McGoohan was taking on more and more of the responsibilities of production and no doubt felt that his story editor had let him down. Had Markstein taken a more professional approach, then many of the early script problems would not have arisen and the series would not have fallen so far behind. But any writer is an artist with a desire to express their own ideas in their work. Markstein remained critical of the direction the series had taken after he left but McGoohan now had a free hand. Unfortunately, he also had no one else bar Tomblin to source new scripts.

Ice Station Zebra

'Many Happy Returns' saw the conclusion of the first shooting block of *The Prisoner*. The series was far behind in production, with few episodes in a fit shape to be sent to the ITV network. This had begun to damage the relationship between McGoohan and Lew Grade who had to contend not only with the ITV network but his overseas buyers. Grade, quite reasonably, was now unwilling to continue to pour money into the project without seeing much in the way of an end result, but to McGoohan, the inevitable decline in quality that would come with a reduction of finance was of course unacceptable.

McGoohan had been chased by Hollywood for several years but had always declined to be involved in the movies he was offered, either for artistic reasons or because the shoot would take him away from his family. He claimed to dislike the idea of uprooting and relocating to the States and certainly held a deep contempt for the idea of becoming a Hollywood 'puppet star', paraded out at every red carpet ceremony. However, this time he had little choice. *The Prisoner* needed money and the responsibility for earning it fell upon his shoulders. In June that same year, he accepted a part in the John Sturges thriller *Ice Station Zebra* (released 1968). Upon completing his duties on 'Many Happy Returns', filming fight scenes until 4 pm, he showered, changed his clothes and drove straight to the airport, taking his secretary with him so that he could dictate letters on the way.

Adapted from an Alistair McLean novel, *Ice Station Zebra* saw McGoohan playing a British spy once more, though this character was no moralistic John Drake. David Jones, the character he played, was an amoral self-confessed 'bastard' who would do whatever was necessary to achieve his goals. Interviewed, albeit grudgingly, at first for the magazine *Photoplay* on the set of *Ice Station Zebra*, McGoohan explained:

> 'I have admired Sturges' work for a long time. When he rang me up about it I liked the way he talked and I accepted the film even though there wasn't a script at the time. Then I read the book and I had no qualms whatever playing it because it was a completely different type of secret agent from the one I played for years in *Danger Man*. A first class part.'[17]

Though away from the MGM lot, the themes of *The Prisoner* were still very much on McGoohan's mind.

> 'I'm not particularly ambitious to be a film star or to earn millions. Being a film star is probably one of the most confining occupations in the world. The last word I would associate with it is "freedom". And freedom in my work and in my private life is something I have always wanted.'[18]

In an interview for TCM's 'Private Screenings' show, co-star Ernest Borgnine recalled of McGoohan:

> 'He was a good man. A little crazy but by golly he got it right. But when we were shooting *Ice Station Zebra*, he seemed a little high. He kept doing odd little things; but, hey, the filmmakers liked it and they kept it in and that was it.'[19]

The comment about McGoohan being 'a little high' is difficult to interpret. Borgnine could simply be referring to the actor's mood or might perhaps be implying that McGoohan was by this point using cannabis as a form of relaxation. Certainly he had been a heavy cigarette smoker for most of his life. Nothing is known about McGoohan's attitude to recreational drugs although many actors used them at the time. McGoohan managed to spend some rare time with his family during the shooting of Sturges' movie. They had been, as ever, unfailingly supportive and it is rumoured that Catherine even made an appearance as an extra in 'Dance of the Dead'.

Characteristically, McGoohan had moved his entire family with him, during the production of *Ice Station Zebra*. He explained in another *Photoplay* interview that because of her upbringing, he had little concern for his daughter's well-being in the glamorous city:

> 'I wasn't alarmed in the slightest because of the way Cathy was brought up. My wife is a very good wife and mother and out daughter was brought up to be a very self-possessed girl. She went to the Sunset Strip and I didn't worry. If you were to tell me that there was the most depraved nightclub somewhere I wouldn't tell her to stay away. I doubt she would want to go but if she did I'd send her on her own. She has always had complete freedom and she's never abused it.'[20]

The shooting must have seemed like an idyllic holiday compared to the production of *The Prisoner*. McGoohan had no other responsibilities than turning up on set and performing. He relished having the extra time to spend with his family, stating in the interview that he and Joan had put a lot of effort into their new temporary accommodation and making a brief comment which supports the theory that he would have been against the use of drugs:

> 'Whether we're living in a cabin or a tent … I hope it is a place where my daughters will want to bring their friends. If they can find all the excitement they want at home then I don't think there's anything to worry about. When kids have to go outside to find excitement, then there's trouble. All those poor kids running around taking drugs. I feel sorry for them. I also have great sympathy for their parents but the first thing I wonder is "What is their home like?"'[21]

Prisoner Block Two

While McGoohan was in Hollywood, the crew he had left behind made a start on the second production block of *The Prisoner*. The series would contain only four more episodes, bringing the total (including the held back 'Once Upon A Time') to seventeen, a number which Lew Grade felt he could sell to the States. Block Two began shooting on the August 26th 1967, with Pat Jackson returning once again to direct the first episode of the series. This was unique in that it didn't feature Patrick McGoohan in any significant way. Instead, in 'Do Not Forsake' the role of Number 6 was taken by Nigel Stock, who had worked with McGoohan in *Danger Man*. Writer Vincent Tilsley wryly took advantage of the change of lead actor to give Number 6 a romantic sub-plot involving his hitherto unmentioned fiancée, Janet. Amusingly, Zena Walker, playing Janet, recalled that she was looking forward to being the first actress to get to play romantic scenes with McGoohan and it was only when she was attending her wardrobe fittings that she realised that Stock would be standing in.[22]

Aside from Markstein, there had been some changes in the crew. One casualty was props buyer Sidney Palmer who recalled to Steven Ricks that although he would normally see a production through to its conclusion, he had been given another offer and that because of the stresses of the production, he accepted it:

'If an art department can't prepare then it's very difficult and you do get friction … At times, the scripts did not come up quick enough and you were working on information obtained at meetings and we in the art department used to have different ideas to other people … and it did cause some friction.'[23]

McGoohan returned to a show that was still behind schedule, still under-financed and with most of the pressure on his own shoulders. He took a dislike to the material he viewed for 'Do Not Forsake' and immediately set about rewriting, before performing his one day of filming on the episode. Though Nigel Stock was himself an excellent actor, he lacked the great passion that McGoohan brought to his performances. The episode, while successfully filling the gap in production, is lacklustre compared to the rest of the series. The 'mind-swap' plotline veers a little too much towards *Star Trek*-style sci-fi to be credible, even in the advanced world of The Village. It is also unfortunate that the 'Janet' sub- plot is never developed enough for her to be interesting as a character in her own right.

Living in Harmony

The production team moved immediately on to the next episode, the surrealistic western 'Living in Harmony'. This narrative transposed the character of Number 6 into a completely different setting. However, it kept the basic theme – of the coercion of the individual – intact. The character is made the new sheriff of the town and is exhorted by both the townspeople and his supposed 'boss' to pick up his guns, something he refuses to do until finally pushed to breaking point by a sadistic act of murder.

The idea behind 'Living in Harmony' had come from two sources. Initially, it was Frank Maher who suggested the idea of making a western to McGoohan over a drink after their usual late night game of squash. Coincidentally, assistant film editor Ian Rakoff had also been toying with the idea after a stressed-out David Tomblin had put out a general call for script ideas to the crew. Rakoff recalled a meeting with McGoohan, not long before he departed to work on *Ice Station Zebra*, that shows the frame of mind the tortured star was now in. This explains in part the difficulties that the crew must have had working with him:

'I'd gone up very nervously to MGM and Pat wasn't there. And I waited … one o'clock, Pat still hadn't turned up. Anyhow, two minutes after one he turned up in a very, very bad mood. Marched into his office which was huge! It was just disproportionately large. And he made me sit down in this couch which sank to the ground so I was practically sitting on the floor. And Pat was lurching around absolutely incensed with me and he's a big fellow, he's a big presence, but when you're sitting on the floor, obviously, he becomes a lot bigger. And I remember he slammed a briefcase onto his desk, he whacked a bottle of Malvern water onto the table. Then I couldn't get out. He was pacing about like an agitated caged tiger and all I could do, after an hour I was thinking, "Am I gonna get out of here alive?" Because he was just getting more and more angry he was saying he thought my stuff was very good but I'm writing totally the wrong sort of thing, I've got the wrong idea of this and that and the bottle of water was an example of what I should be writing about! It was totally incomprehensible to me. All that I could perceive was that this man was very angry.'[24]

Having ranted thus for a full hour-and-a-half, McGoohan dismissed the by now terrified aspiring writer. However, as Rakoff reached the door McGoohan called out, 'Ian, how would you like to write a western with me?' Maybe this performance had been one of McGoohan's 'tests' to see if Rakoff was up to the stresses of working with him, maybe it was simply drunkenness (the meeting did occur after lunch and McGoohan was still using alcohol to cushion the stress of making the series). In any case, having developed the concept further with Rakoff, McGoohan promptly departed to the States again for further shooting on *Ice Station Zebra*, leaving Rakoff in the hands of David Tomblin. Rakoff's experience, despite McGoohan's assuring him that Tomblin would 'take care of you', was not a happy one. Though Rakoff had worked extensively on the script, Tomblin took over and rewrote it himself, giving himself sole writer credit in the process (though Rakoff was still credited for the initial idea). Tomblin did, however, give the young writer an extra fee to cover his residuals, wryly commenting that it was out of 'The money this series won't be making' and advising Rakoff that he should 'Count yourself lucky that you'll be out of this mess.'[25]

McGoohan as Mentor

Production of 'Living in Harmony' commenced on McGoohan's return. In the key yet mute role of 'The Kid' a young Canadian actor called Alexis Kanner was cast. Kanner, who had gained a reputation as a hellraiser, had recently appeared in the BBC police drama and spin-off from the hugely successful *Z Cars*: *Softly Softly*. Despite some internal resistance to his casting, McGoohan and Tomblin were resolute and Kanner got the part. Kanner was extremely impressed by McGoohan as an actor, describing in an interview reproduced on The Unmutual website how even the way that the actor handled props was remarkable.

> 'Patrick's way of handling objects – props – which is very persuasive, and very articulate and very sharp and precise and very graceful. The way he flips off the transmission switch at the beginning of "Kings and Desperate Men" when he and the judge are leaving – and the way he ties the gun on in "Living in Harmony". The way he flips the coin down to pay for the drink … When he's given an object – when it's put in his hand, he does something with it. He doesn't really adopt it. It becomes something to wrestle with – he takes – a stance with it.'[26]

McGoohan rapidly became attached to Alex Kanner and came to treat him as a protégé. Speaking of her experiences on a film the pair would make many years later, *Kings and Desperate Men,* actress Andrea Marcovicci remembered that:

> 'Alex and Patrick fascinated each other and it was wonderful to see two men who fascinated each other in such a way.'[27]

What was it in Kanner that appealed to McGoohan? I suspect that McGoohan was drawn to Kanner's eccentrically rebellious personality, seeing a great deal of himself in the younger man. Kanner also responded well to McGoohan's forceful nature. Interviewed on *Six Into One*, he recalled one of McGoohan's typically challenging moves in a communiqué issued before production began, while McGoohan was acting on the second shoot for *Ice Station Zebra*:

'The thing about Patrick is that he loves challenge, he loves competition and he loves there to be an edge on the set, he hates complacency, so it's quite within his character to send a telegram which I received two weeks before we started "Living in Harmony" which said, "Am taking lessons from Sammy Davis Junior and Steve McQueen on quick draw, hope you live up to expectations, McGoohan." Which made it incumbent upon me to go out and get myself a 45 Colt peacemaker and practice with the whole deal. The day we finally shot it I'd gotten quite good at it. A lot of bets were being placed around the set by the crew and the stuntmen and everybody as to who would out-draw who and we were both so adept by that time that even though we both drew, only one shot was heard though both guns went off. And it wasn't until the next day when the film came back from the lab that the editor was able to hold it up and count the frames and discovered that I'd got mine out in nine and Patrick had done his in eleven or twelve, about a sixth of a second difference and then everyone had to pay up. It was very typical of Patrick to do that kind of thing.'[28]

That Kanner had gone to so much effort to rise to McGoohan's challenge (and win!) would surely have impressed the star who always reacted well to strength of character.

In Relative Harmony

Initially, McGoohan was watchful of David Tomblin's direction. This was Tomblin's first time as a director and, having been burned so many times before, McGoohan was nervous even of his closest friend and ally on the production. However, once McGoohan had ascertained that Tomblin not only knew what he was doing but was directing with style, he became surprisingly 'hands-off' and gave his friend and business partner the freedom to plan and shoot in whichever way he desired.

During the production of 'Harmony', the press launch for the series was staged in one of the studios, occupied by sidepieces and props from the show. McGoohan appeared first to the press in his bright orange 'Kosho' uniform from 'It's Your Funeral' and wearing a Russian fur hat. He offered no explanation to the press for this bizarre apparel and went on to answer none of the questions that were posed to him, characteristically countering them with his own. McGoohan conversed with the press from inside the cage set used in 'Once Upon a Time' and which would reoccur in 'Fall Out' as the final means of escape from The Village, feeling perhaps that the bars symbolised the theme of the series. Having questioned the bemused reporters about the possible symbolism of Rover, and of the penny-farthing, McGoohan departed the scene. He briefly returned dressed in his 'Harmony' costume before leaving to continue filming, no doubt irked at having to attend the press call at all. Kanner was on hand to demonstrate riding the ancient bicycle and took over the duties of speaking to the press.

Penultimate Episode:
The Girl Who Was Death

Production lurched on with the filming of the penultimate episode of *The Prisoner*, 'The Girl Who Was Death'. This was an idea that Tomblin had idly devised as a *Danger Man* episode, several years before, and now that the production team were desperately scrambling for ideas, the producer gave the concept to Terence Feely to write. It is a largely comedic tale, the lightest that the series ever gets. With no explanation, we find Number 6 outside the confines of The Village once more, a secret agent tracking down the crazed Professor Schnipps and his murderous daughter, Sonia, the 'girl' of the title. Even though it is revealed at the conclusion of the episode that this has simply been yet another attempt by The Village to wrest the information they so desperately want out of their star Prisoner (by allowing him to tell a bedtime story to children!), its connection to the rest of the series is tenuous at best. It served only to reaffirm in the minds of many viewers that Number 6 was John Drake, setting them up for the ending they expected, one that would answer all the questions and finally put their minds at ease.

McGoohan's behaviour on set for this episode was typically unpredictable. He roared that actress Justine Lord, playing Sonia, was a dreadful actress, yet spent time with actor John Drake (a coincidence?), who had a bit part as a cricket bowler, discussing the actor's recent divorce sympathetically. He also spent time with Kenneth Griffith, who had worked with him on the final colour episodes of *Danger Man*, wanting to renew the acquaintance. Griffith would return immediately after production ended to play a major role in the finale.

Grade and McGoohan: The Final Turn

Although neither man ever alluded to it and both remained glowing and warm in their appreciation of the other in interviews later, there had been a severe falling out between Grade and McGoohan. This was, unsurprisingly, over the fact that the series was now only seventeen episodes long, generally chaotic and over-budget. Writer Roger Parkes remembered:

> 'When Patrick McGoohan and George Markstein talked Lew Grade into launching the series, he saw it as a long-term investment and he fell out, quite substantially I believe, with McGoohan when McGoohan effectively killed it off ... Also Grade didn't like the way it was moving away from reality, which was something McGoohan was quite determined to do. He wanted to break the mould of *Danger Man*. There's a little suicidal element in him! That's probably the wrong word but he likes to kill things off.'[29]

McGoohan had drafted a version of the final episode on the plane returning from filming *Ice Station Zebra* but wrote this script off as being unusable. Now the pressure was really on to devise a satisfactory ending for his series. McGoohan claimed in the *TV Times* that he had the idea for the conclusion in his mind from the start. However, in *Six Into One*, Lew Grade remembers differently. He says that after consistently promising that there would be a definite ending with episode seventeen, McGoohan came into his office and simply admitted that he had no idea how to end *The Prisoner*.

> 'He came to me and he said, "Lew, I just cannot find an ending. I've got too confused with the project." And I thought it was very nice of him to come straight out with me and I told the networks, "We have no ending."[30]

This frank admission of defeat – to the man who had bankrolled the series and put his reputation on the line for McGoohan – would have been a courageous move. It's not clear exactly what happened though. David Tomblin's version accords more with McGoohan's take, that he knew what he was doing from the start.

> 'The ending was in the style of the series. I think that in a strange way it went back to conversations right at the beginning of the series, that one needed a conclusion, obviously. We had a lot of conversations and discussed various possibilities and over that period of time all these things went into the mental computer and it came out at the other end, not quite as we discussed but sort of.'[31]

Even if McGoohan did have many of the plot elements for the finale of his Opus in place while he was formulating the initial concept (as the greater number of accounts suggest) there were significant problems. One of the major stumbling blocks, as McGoohan alludes to himself in *Six Into One,* was finding a resolution to the identity of Number 1.

Resolution: The Identity of Number 1

In normal narrative terms, the series consisted in a build-up to this final confrontation between The Prisoner and his Captor. Number 1 is the force behind the Village, controlling all the Number 2s via the big red telephone, the hotline to God, or maybe to Satan. Never seen, never heard, merely referred to, we are given no clues about his identity or his intentions bar that he wants Number 6's information and that he doesn't want Number 6 to be permanently damaged. This strange protective streak serves an obvious narrative function, if the Village could just threaten him with death then it seems likely they would simply strip the information out of his brain by force and leave him in a vegetative state.

There had to be a revelation, there was no way that the audience would accept a finale without Number 1. Looking again at McGoohan's strong, almost consuming identification with Number Six, there was only one way it could go.

'Who was going to be Number 1? Well I'll level with you, nobody knew that. Nobody knew that. The first person to discover that was after I'd dragged myself out of the office and it was complete after its thirty-six-hours-childbirth thing, y'know, a lot of labour, we had the scripts run off very quickly so I got a copy of this thing and before I caught up with a few hours sleep before working on Monday morning I sat with David and we were having tea or something, in some tearoom and I said, "You'd better read this." I gave it to him and I just sat at another table and sipped tea until he'd finished then he gave it back to me and he said, "I thought it might be you in the end," (McGoohan chuckles). There's nowhere else to go! Who could it be? You know? I wasn't gonna ring up Sean or Roger or any of these fellas, who could it be? I don't know who it could be."[32]

That he 'wasn't gonna ring up Sean [Connery] or Roger [Moore]' shows that right up until the end, McGoohan had no intention of producing the ending that might be expected from his show. The revelation of the 'secret villain' at the heart of a technological web, supported by violent lackeys and brilliant scientists had become a cliché long before 1967 (led by the Bond franchise and perpetuated in hit TV series on both sides of the Atlantic from *The Avengers* to *The Man From U.N.C.L.E.*). Naturally, McGoohan wasn't having any of that, the conclusion to his opus was to see the series at its most allegorical and deliberately impenetrable.

Quoted from an interview on The Unmutual website, stuntman Frank Maher's recollection backs up McGoohan's version of the genesis of the final episode.

'I'll tell you the story of the last episode. This is unabridged. It is the truth and I don't care what anybody else says because I was there. My house was right opposite MGM Studios, a five minute walk, straight across the road. It came to episode sixteen and I remember the dialogue so well because it was a real kick in the teeth for all of us. Pat came to me on Wednesday and said, "We've only got one more show." I said, "What are you talking about?" because we were booked for twenty-six. He said "That's it!' He went and told the rest of the crew and there had to be a final episode which hadn't been written. Nothing had been done because it wasn't expected. So we finished on the Friday night. Patrick disappeared into his dressing-room and he wrote until Tuesday morning. I know because I used to take in a bottle of scotch a day to him and sandwiches. I got the first of five scripts and we started shooting. That is how the last episode got written. Make what you will of it but that is the absolute truth. I know 'cause I was the only one there.'[33]

The Final Episode

'Fall Out' was, according to McGoohan, written in a concentrated thirty-six hour burst. It was designed to follow directly on from episode sixteen, 'Once upon a Time', that was originally meant to mark the end of the first season and now forming a two-parter with this new conclusion.

Production began immediately and McGoohan gathered his strength for one last push. Griffith remembered that the finale was under-resourced for what McGoohan was trying to achieve but that the star pushed ahead anyway. Kanner returned once more as the personification of youth culture and formless rebellion, while Leo McKern had been persuaded to reprise his role as Number 2 one last time. After his shattering experiences on 'Once upon a Time', the actor was understandably wary of returning to *The Prisoner* and was reportedly only convinced by Kanner's offer to stay close to him during the filming of every scene he had to appear in, presumably to protect him from 'Big Bad Patrick'. In conversation with Steven Ricks for one of his *Prisoner* documentaries, Kenneth Griffith remembered:

'Rumour had it that Leo, in those interrogation scenes ... Patrick would challenge people, you know, and ... Leo McKern is a pretty tough Australian but I think it had a pretty shattering effect on him. That's before that last episode.

From the start, the production was somewhat chaotic. McGoohan was determined that the finale should represent his creative vision but as always that means he was unselfishly open to ideas that might be better than or which would build upon his own.

I mean he had great big ideas like the rocket taking off ... I know he didn't have the facilities of some directors on a big feature film for that sort of thing but I know it was tremendously important, he worked so hard to get the right effect, I remember, he worked *so* hard, he almost killed himself with hard work. Killed himself. He was doing everything. And yet he wasn't selfish. He was extremely free with people to use their creative energies.'[34]

McGoohan gave Griffith responsibility for writing the President's speech and accepted it in a workmanlike manner by simply not objecting to the content and shooting what Griffith had written. Though this behaviour might seem unforgivably curt to many, Griffith was able to shrug it off. He recognised that from McGoohan, who was the first to complain if something had fallen below his expectations, to simply include the piece without any alterations from himself was high praise and that no doubt the highly pressured star saw little point in wasting time in thanks.

McGoohan seems to have given his naturally collaborative nature free reign in 'Fall Out'. This may have been due to exhaustion or that 'end of an era' feeling that comes at the completion of a long project. Indeed, there is a feeling of incredible exuberance and triumph in 'Fall Out', McGoohan almost seems to be screaming, 'Look, I've done it!' as he tears down the prison he has created for himself. It must have been such an incredible relief to have reached virtual completion. The sense of impending freedom would have been intoxicating.

That McGoohan worked best with those who understood him must have been acknowledged by the *Prisoner* crew by the end of series. That Kanner and Griffiths had a natural affinity with their fellow actor-manager was certainly reflected in their working relationship with him. Griffiths explained to Steve Ricks:

> 'I really do admire him and like him very much. His difficult behaviour or sharpness comes out of … you see a man's talent and his private behaviour is not divisible.'[35]

It appears that Griffith and Alexis Kanner were in fact working on two completely different productions. In *Six Into One* Kanner recalled:

> 'The thing was in a continuous state of evolution, a continuous state of flux, Patrick was writing in aeroplanes and on sets and in the middle of the night and just before the take even, right on the set, but when he had something set he would hone it and it would stay set and remain precise that way for all takes.'[36]

Kanner became close to McGoohan during the filming, particularly on the intense production of the final episode. The elder actor cast the younger as Number 48, an epitome of the late sixties counter-culture with 'flowers in his hair, bells on his toes'. The episode, 'Fall Out', takes the form of one long deranged trial scene with two witness appearing. The first, a former Number 2, is a representation of authority and control, the second, Kanner as Number 48, a dissident who can only be tamed by words from the older man who has broken down The Village.

At one point McGoohan even envisaged a spin off series from *The Prisoner,* starring Kanner. It would follow Kanner's character of Number 48 as he travelled around the world, trying to keep away from the surveillance of The Village which had followed them all into the outside world, the Butler becoming Number 48's protector. This would have allowed McGoohan to take a back seat, no doubt writing, directing and producing the series but without the added burden of starring in it, using Kanner as his new mouthpiece. Nobody, not even someone with as much energy and passion as McGoohan, could sustain the pace he had forced upon himself. As Kenneth Griffith observed, in one of Steven Ricks' interviews:

'He wasn't very well at times, I think under the enormous pressure of doing this and that, I mean he worked and worked and worked … I think he took a slug too much now and again. Particularly in the lunch hour. Just to keep himself going, I would say. And I can see him now, tall and handsome and elegant, directing and then he'd act, he'd move over and act and then back to directing … I can see him after lunch now just swaying slightly, swaying.'[37]

Most actors who drank so heavily while working would be regarded as being unprofessional, let alone actors who were also the director and the lynchpin of the whole shoot. But whatever state he was in, whichever demons he was using the alcohol to mute, McGoohan was not going to allow his dependency to interfere with the all important work. Griffith continued:

'And yet from a professional point of view, not a point was missed, you know, nothing. My God, you had to be on your toes with him because if anything wasn't up to scratch, you'd hear about it.'[38]

'Fall Out' itself is worthy of analysis, being a script that must have been exceptionally close to the actor. It begins with The Prisoner being handed back his old suit, the clothes that he was captured in before being forced to wear the uniform of The Village, symbolic of the return of his individuality. From this moment on, Number 6 has won. He is taken to a huge cavern presided over by Griffiths' judge character (called 'The President' in the script) who almost obsequiously informs him that the authorities have conceded, that Number 6's revolt has been 'good and honest' and that, incredibly enough given their treatment of their star Prisoner, they now want Number 6 to lead them. Or leave.

He decides to leave.

Final Shot

But the central character would not be allowed to depart taking the stand to make a final speech to his captors. As in 'Free For All', Number 6 is about to shout and scream his defiance, but this time, his voice is drowned out by the crowd. In the previous episode his words fell on deaf ears, this time his voice isn't heard at all. Did McGoohan feel that it had all been pointless by now?

For such a joyful episode, 'Fall Out' is tinged with moments that make the viewer feel that McGoohan might have finally given up on humanity and written it off as a bad job with no hope of salvation. There is a mile-wide streak of cynicism running through McGoohan's own performance, he conveys the feeling that Number 6 has seen it all by this point and is not going to take this latest trick of The Village seriously. There is also a feeling, I think, that McGoohan senses that upon his imminent release from the series, he will be imprisoned by it all over again.

Public opinion on *The Prisoner* had veered between those who were strongly supportive, appreciative and impressed that such a series had been presented to them and the baffled, infuriated and downright angry, who had felt that although the premise had been promising, the series was becoming more and more incomprehensible by the week. Some viewers liked to be challenged and relished the intellectualism of the series, some wanted only to know when John Drake was going to start winning. With his air of calm detachment during his 'trial' in 'Fall Out' it's almost as if the final act of the confessional starts with him holding up his hands and saying to the press and the public: 'Right then, here you go. Get stuck in!'

Having been shouted down, his final words to The Village drowned in an orgy of repetition from the assembled delegates – all in monochrome masks, one side white, one black, their bodies hidden behind identical white cloaks – Number 6 is informed that the time has now come for him to meet Number 1. Shaken by his experience on the stand, for the first time in the episode Number 6 displays confusion and uncertainty.

Who is Number 1?

McGoohan now elegantly riffs off the aforementioned cliché of the big reveal. The journey from the cavern to Number 1 is down the same underground corridor set that had been used in several previous episodes, silver and arched, something one would quite happily expect to be owned by anyone from Blofeld to the Daleks. I use the word 'happily' here with reason, after presenting the bemused audience with the surrealistic polemic of the 'Trial' McGoohan reverts to exactly what they would be hoping for, a build-up of tension to the moment where everything will become clear. It's a simply-directed scene, by the book. As Number 6 slowly ascends the spiral staircase to the chamber where Number 1 is waiting for him, he is treading in the footsteps of countless John Steeds and James Bonds, eventually gaining admission to a chamber packed with technology, flashing lights, beeping and hissing. Finally, the viewers were back in their comfort zone, finally being given exactly what they expected.

But we don't even get the reveal straight away, Number 1 is standing hunched at a set of controls on the other side of the room, as much hidden by his cloak as McGoohan once hid in his mackintosh outside Sheffield Youth Club. Number 1 turns, masked like the delegates in the 'trial', offering a crystal ball, implying a vision of the future. All Number 6 sees within the ball is the repeated image that has sealed his fate in every episode thus far. This is the image of his face being imprisoned behind a set of animated sliding bars, his title sequence battle cry 'I am not a number, I am a free man!' ringing around the chamber, the soundtrack suddenly condensing to just the word 'I' repeated with increasing speed and distortion. But Number 6 has won. He smashes the crystal ball in defiance of that future. The audience cheers their hero on as he reaches out and whips away the mask. At which point McGoohan decides to pull the rug away with equal speed and anger.

The face revealed isn't even human but that of a gibbering ape, gabbling in time to the repeated vowel 'I'. We are wrong-footed and then treated to a brief shot of Number 6, face twisted in a smile saying to Number 1 'Oh, come off it!' before he tears the second mask away to finally reveal a human being.

The Reveal of a Demented Madman

When I first watched 'Fall Out', the reveal of a demented madman and subsequent action scene was good enough for me. Seeing Number 1 laughing hysterically in the face of Number 6, before the sequence devolves into a frantic twisted chase around the room, with the eventual apparent escape of Number 1 up a ladder into a chamber which Number 6 then locks, was a quite sufficient finale. The series was so clearly about the triumph of the individual. That the being at the pinnacle of an empire dedicated to controlling and subverting that spirit was depicted as a bestial, fractured and ultimately impotent character made perfect sense, a minimisation of the oppression.

It wasn't until a second viewing that I grasped the true identity of Number 1. I'm not alone, a great many people watching originally, and since, have initially missed the fact that Number 1 is in fact Number 6 himself. No doubt that was part of McGoohan's intention.

There are probably a thousand theories as to the meaning of the polar opposites being the same man. McGoohan's explanation was simple: Number 1 represents all that is evil and base about one's character. So for McGoohan the act of sending his 'bestial side' into space in a rocket is a cleansing process. He is wiping the stain of The Village and his time there from his soul, using the opportunity to become a more pure person, unfettered by base desire or by the motivation to do harm to others, to restrict them. His intention is apparently to purge the devil.

It's all terribly Catholic and herein lies one of the great contradictions of *The Prisoner*, that a series so much about the personal freedom of the individual should exclude sexual freedom altogether. It is all the more remarkable that in the era of sexual liberation, a TV series should counteract the social mores of the day.

Beyond Breakpoint

The final drama of this sequence is also an insight into the workings of McGoohan's mind. By this point, he had given everything he had to *The Prisoner* working himself to breaking point and then beyond. His behaviour had become erratic and unpredictable. Editor Noreen Ackland recalled an incident during the post-production of 'Fall Out', where the actor made her repeatedly view one single piece of film, backwards and forwards again and again so many times that the editor was reduced to tears. When she asked what he was trying to say with the scene, she received the reply that he didn't know and that she was to continue running the sequence back and forth. This was an utterly irrational action and one that had a complete disregard for Ackland's feelings. It also shows the state of creative exhaustion that McGoohan was now in. He had acted appallingly to co-workers throughout the making of his series, had lost friends and had jeopardised his reputation.

The episode plays to its conclusion as Number 6 launches the rocket containing his alter ego into space and escapes in the company of Number 2, Number 48 and The Butler. One-by-one they return to their old lives, the actors' credits flashing up over the characters, subtly implying that the fiction and fact have become indivisible. Number 2 heads towards Parliament, apparently ready to raise hell, continuing the rebellion inspired by his former Prisoner. Number 48 takes to the road, his rebellion apparently directionless once more.

At The Last Count: McGoohan is Number 6

Number 6 returns to Number 1, Buckingham Place; the name of his home now loaded with so much more significance. He slips back into his Lotus, while the Butler dutifully takes up residence in the abode of his new master, the door opening and closing with the same automatic buzz that characterised that of his Village residence. Far from having escaped, Number 6 has willingly taken a tiny piece of the Village with him into his future. As he drives once more through the streets of London in stock footage filmed for the opening titles, instead of the credit granted other performers, the single word 'Prisoner' flashes up to represent the lead actor and creator. The inference is hardly subtle but it is interesting.

While McGoohan's primary intention was to suggest that we are all still prisoners of ourselves, a secondary interpretation is that he already realised that this series would come to define him for the near future and maybe longer. The caption is also a final act of identification of Patrick McGoohan with Number 6.

There was a general sense of elation during the final days of shooting 'Fall Out', many of the crew have referred to an 'end of term feeling'. Summed up by Kanner during his Unmutual interview, he says

'The location footage for "Fall Out" was shot right at the end. Boy – we were really happy to be in that van, with the cigar and the tea-tray, just dancing around away from the set, out in the fresh air. We were really happy. I mean, Leo and I were dancing ... The out-takes of "Fall Out" would make a full-length motion picture. Amazing footage. There were enormous numbers of takes, but there were so many new angles and so many new ideas, chunks of script.[39]

McGoohan himself seems to have been as much a part of the frivolity as anyone, no doubt feeling that an enormous burden was about to be lifted from his shoulders. He had made his statement and, more than anything, had not compromised himself for a moment. The price, however, had been that McGoohan and Number 6 had become indivisible. Oddly, it is George Markstein – who in McGoohan's eyes perhaps least understood the actor's vision for his series – who best describes the influence of the series on its creator, in *Six Into One*:

'I think that in many ways *The Prisoner* is a tragedy ... because McGoohan became a prisoner of the series and it's never nice to see that happen to a human being, the combination of ambition, frustration, wanting to be writer, director, actor – you name it. It was sad, it was very sad I think. It did something to him that wasn't very good and it was reflected in the series and that's why the series ended like that and that's why people have said, "I don't understand the end". Of course, they don't understand the end, because there is no end ... I don't think even McGoohan understood the end, or if he does, well, perhaps he does, but that is the biggest tragedy of *The Prisoner*, that Patrick McGoohan became a prisoner himself.'[40]

The strain had undoubtedly been intense, the pressure from every quarter was extraordinary and his perfectionist drive had brought him to the point of complete collapse. It is a testament to his strength that he was able to continue and finish the series, keeping his commitment to Lew Grade and to his dedicated crew who worked almost as tirelessly as he had to deliver his vision. But a great deal of damage had been done. Word of McGoohan's ferocity on set had spread throughout the industry and stories had even leaked in the press. In interviews McGoohan had shown typical honesty in admitting that he could be difficult to work with.

In later years, McGoohan stated several times his belief that only seven episodes of *The Prisoner* really count and that the rest are just fillers. His original vision was to create a perfect series of seven episodes though he never revealed which those seven were. The general consensus is that they would have certainly had to include the first and last two episodes and I suspect that the McGoohan-authored 'Free For All' would have been in place. He had been impressed by the themes of 'The General' and 'Change of Mind' and may well have been inclined to include 'Living in Harmony'.

Typically, however, McGoohan never revealed which of the episodes formed the core of the series so it is impossible to surmise much from them. An erroneous list was compiled for a hugely inaccurate book, White and Ali's *The Official Prisoner Companion* (1988), which McGoohan derided:

> 'We were talking about the seven episodes which form the true basis of *The Prisoner*. Well, they picked their seven, but they're not my seven. They claim they're mine, but they're not. Everything they claimed that I said, apart from two things, is inaccurate.'[41]

The interpretations that have been put on *The Prisoner* are appropriately, numberless. To me, at least in its distilled form, it's almost entirely about Patrick McGoohan and his major concerns. To create, shape, write, direct and embody *The Prisoner* was for McGoohan the ultimate catharsis. I said earlier that McGoohan found a shield in the craft of acting. Now, he had shifted to a full-blown confessional.

Perhaps the last word on the series should come from McGoohan himself.

> 'Somebody needs to yell a warning. I hope I'm giving some kind of warning. My village is not 1984 but 1968. More than anything else I believe passionately in the freedom of the individual. I want to yell back: "That's our right. The loss of one's own individuality is a nightmare."

And if I haven't made my yell back clear in *The Prisoner*, the individual viewer has the right to shout: "Nuts to you, Paddy boy!"[42]

And they did.

CHAPTER 7
Fall-out: The USA

Courting Controversy

The immediate and most obvious effect that the making of *The Prisoner* had on Patrick McGoohan personally, was that it amplified his dominant personality traits to extreme proportions. It's as if the man psyched himself up to number eleven on the dial to make the show, trampling over a lot of people in the process and becoming downright unbearable. Using alcohol to manage the stress can't have helped either. On the other hand, it was McGoohan's single-minded drive that ensured that *The Prisoner* was of such a high quality, sufficiently well-executed to ensure its longevity. Divisive from the start, Don Chaffey, director of several early episodes, recalls his personal experience of the public reaction:

> 'The pub would be empty, the landlord would be in there and I could hear the final bits of *The Prisoner* going on and I'd say, "It's me!" and he used to say, "Pour yourself a beer, I'm just watching this bloody rubbish you've been making". And he'd be sitting there and then gradually the village would come creaking back to life and would come into the pub and twenty minutes later there would be the most almighty row going on in the public bar with people yelling at me saying what a load of rubbish it was and I would reply, "Well, why do you watch the stuff then?"'[1]

McGoohan had achieved one of his aims for sure, that of courting controversy and provoking debate with his new series, though perhaps not quite in the way that he would have wished. A great many of the complaints seemed to be directed at the fact that *Danger Man* had suddenly become extremely weird and what had once been a straightforward, entertaining spy series had now become an incomprehensible piece of televisual surrealism.

The response was by no means uniformly negative, though, with one critic hailing the show as being, 'Television's first work of art'.[2] Slowly, more and more positive reactions emerged in print from critics and letters from viewers in the *TV Times* and newspapers. In that he managed to raise such a public furore over a television show, McGoohan's struggle could be seen as an unqualified success. In fact, in those terms, the initial reaction to the final episode was magnificent. Reportedly, the switchboards at ATV were jammed with complaining callers, all feeling cheated by 'Fall Out' and demanding to know just who Patrick McGoohan thought he was to do this to them? Chuckling with apparently genuine delight, McGoohan later recalled the reaction:

> 'Of course, I wasn't angry, not in the least! I just had to go and hide myself that's all in case I got killed. But I wasn't in the least angered, I was delighted! It's marvellous when people feel enough to be angry, righteous indignation is terrific and they're entitled to it. I'd have been very, very angry and disappointed if they hadn't watched, if they hadn't jammed the switchboards at ATV, I would have been outraged and would have slunk around for years with my tail between my legs, instead of which it was just terrific! Loved it. And if I can do that again I'll do it again, god love 'em, millions of them. Watch it and be outraged. As long as people feel something, that's the great thing, it's when they're walking around not thinking and not feeling, that's tough. That's where all the dangerous stuff is because when you get a mob like that you can turn them into the sort of gang that Hitler had. We don't want that, we want people to say, "Hey, wait a minute, you daren't do that to me, I'm gonna call Lord Grade about that."'[3]

His aims may have been grandiose, but it cannot be denied that McGoohan created a series which still divides opinion to this day. His sacrifice of time, effort and occasionally his own sanity may have seemed in vain at the time, but over the years, *The Prisoner* has come to be one of the most highly regarded, inspirational and influential TV programmes ever made. It has dedicated admirers to this day and continues to win new fans, many of whom are now influential in television and film. It has entered the canon of popular culture, considered sufficiently popular and iconic for two mainstream television advertising campaigns to use the imagery, music and themes from the series in the early 1990s.[4] More words have been written about the seventeen episodes than are contained within the episodes themselves and it has been subjected to a great deal of academic and critical analysis, belying its status. Amusingly, considering McGoohan's stated aim of provoking dissent and discussion, there is a significant proportion of the TV-watching population who still regard the series as a jumbled nonsensical mess in which 'that bloke is chased around by a big white balloon'. The ongoing quest for answers from *The Prisoner* is pointless. Its purpose was never to provide answers but to provoke questions.

No doubt the ITC publicity machine and the media, hungry for copy, exaggerated the public reaction to the broadcast of 'Fall Out'. However, there was undeniably a level of persecution that forced McGoohan into his decision to leave England at this point. Already the actor had been on the defensive when conducting the final round of promotional interviews and articles that accompanied the end of the series, a typical example coming from this exchange between McGoohan and his interviewer Anthony Davis:

'I told him the thing that bothered me most about *The Prisoner* was the absence of any continuity between the episodes; that there was no logical progression in his captors' extraordinary attempts to break him, no logical pattern to his escape bids – or, indeed, to anything else.

He snapped back. "Let me ask you two questions. You're living in this world? You must answer 'yes' to that," he went on helpfully, without a pause. "Do you find it always logical? No? That's your answer to that."

I said some people had found the obsession with medical experiments on Number 6 verged on the sick or sadistic.

He was back fast again. "A man died after a heart operation. You read about that? How about that operation? Do you find that sick or sadistic?"

And so the conversation went on, mainly question for question.'[4]

Always moving immediately on to the next idea (or often set of ideas) upon the completion of any project, McGoohan rapidly tired of being asked to explain or defend the series. Most of this harassment would probably have taken the form of incensed letters or perhaps shouted altercations in the street. While I'm sure McGoohan could have coped with the letters, he would have had great difficulty with being approached in the street and remonstrated with, especially if his family were with him. In an interview with Jeannie Sakol for *Cosmopolitan*, he explained some of the problems he was having with life in London:

> 'The conversation turns to family life. The McGoohans, he tells me, divide their time between a house in Switzerland and one in Mill Hill, ten miles from London. Last June, Patrick created a bit of a kerfuffle with the town council by erecting a six-foot-fence to keep Sunday day-trippers from peering in at him and his family in their backyard. Because he had not requested permission to build the fence, the local powers wanted him to tear it down. "While I readily accept this sort of exposure for myself," he told reporters at the time, "I think my wife and children are entitled to privacy. My wife was particularly affected, as she was cooking in the kitchen."
>
> The privacy of Joan and the girls (there are now three – Catherine, seventeen: Frances, nine; and Anne, eight) is sacrosanct. No interviews. No photographs. Those who know them say that Joan at thirty-six is a radiant beauty in full flower who worships Pat and couldn't care a fig about having given up her acting career. "She's loving, demonstrative, vivacious – must be that Viennese blood! Absolutely devoted to Pat and perfect for him," a friend said.'[5]

As the decade turned, like many who relocated as the 60s subsided, McGoohan took his family away, choosing a retreat in Vervey in Switzerland. I imagine that this must have been as much for his benefit as for theirs. The production of the series had left him exhausted and he needed time to recharge his creative batteries. In *Six Into One*, he explained:

'I think I was fortunate to get out of England alive because I imagine a lot of people watched the last episode expecting a conventional end in which the evil person personified as Number 1 that we had never seen, this mystery character who brooded over everything ... What was he going to be like, was he a Jekyll and Hyde? ... No, not a Jekyll and Hyde, I think they expected more a sort of James Bond villain at the end and I think they felt that they had been robbed with what they got. A lot did, though I would argue against that, I don't think they were robbed because going back to the allegory which was what it was, it had nothing to do ... it was very difficult for people to understand that I was not John Drake, it's not a James Bond, right? ... You can't expect it to end like James Bond, you've got to have an allegorical ending.'[6]

That McGoohan might allude to Robert Louis Stephenson's famous schizophrenic before correcting himself is telling, he was very clearly aware of his own failings. Interestingly, in the fascinating book *Inside The Prisoner* (1998) by Ian Rakoff, assistant film editor and co-writer of 'Living In Harmony', there is reproduced a snippet of a questionnaire which McGoohan filled in. Amongst a litany of one word responses are the intriguing exchanges:

'Q.   What is your greatest thrill?
A.   Living
Q.   What is your greatest disappointment?
A.   Living with myself.'[7]

I return to the idea of McGoohan having a depressive side, one which he kept at bay with constant work, the mental activity simply not allowing him time to dwell too on other things. Unfortunately, in the coming decade, he was to find that he had a great deal more time on his hands than he had had for the previous twenty years and he was once more to find solace at the bottom of a bottle.

New Era

McGoohan's career as it had been was over. He would never again be offered the level of control he wielded on *The Prisoner* and the public's reaction to the series was to remove forever the stamp of John Drake and replace it with an image of a slightly unhinged, intense, angry and somewhat paranoid individual. Here was someone who had the arrogance to challenge the audience in their own homes. Or, from another viewpoint, here was someone who had the audacity to put out such 'drivel' in the name of entertainment. McGoohan discussed this in an interview on the set of *Ice Station Zebra* with Mike Tompkies, published in *Photoplay* in 1969. Presumably motivated by the stress of production on his series back in London, he stated that:

> 'I think I've had enough of TV series for a good while, but one must have a perspective about TV. It's entering a new era today. Two hour TV premieres are the new thing – they will be top shows with top stars in them and with budgets of around £350,000. These shows will be networked on TV first then released in the regular movie theatres like films here now. TV almost killed Hollywood, people said, but now the biggest boom of all time in film-making is coming up. In a few years you won't be able to get on a film stage in Hollywood because it's just not possible to keep the TV screens filled with enough original material. Look how many repeat shows there are on TV today.
>
> I intend to go into producing some of these shows myself. With a million dollars spent on them, actors will no longer have to do the hop, skip and a jump type of TV exposure And big stars who now shy away from TV will be drawn in too. I own several properties myself and I intend to go into this sort of deal in a big way.'

Though McGoohan intended to take time away from television as indeed he did, it is clear that he was already making plans for the future. His prediction about the future of TV was correct. During the next decade 'made for TV' movies would become increasingly dominant, used either as series pilots or one-off crowd-pleasers and ratings-pullers, sometimes even 'prestige' events particularly on the large American networks. McGoohan had a very clear intention to remain active in the production of these films. McGoohan's mind, it seems, was always crammed with ideas, potential projects, scripts and stories.

Editor John S Smith, interviewed by Ian Rakoff for *Inside The Prisoner* spoke of McGoohan's mindset at this transitional time, offering an insight into the actor's ideal working scenario after his experiences of making his own show. Once again, the actor-manager theme is at the forefront of his plans:

'He was saying how he loathed the studio system and how he would much rather gather a nucleus of people around him and get an old stately home or a castle way up the country. No factory regulations and tea breaks, no artificial sets but real rooms. He was never particularly happy with the end result of *The Prisoner*. He was frustrated and I was very sympathetic.'[8]

In the Absence of Heroes

McGoohan's apparent dissatisfaction with the final result of *The Prisoner* may in part be down to the backlash. Contemporary accounts from several co-workers indicate that he was, to an extent, personally hurt by the negative comments flung at his creation. McGoohan had been extremely lucky in that his talent was recognised and seized upon by the critics, he had rarely received anything other than glowing praise for his performances. Now, he had put his other talents on the line, was being judged as a writer, director and producer and had been found wanting. Even his once seemingly impregnable self-confidence must have been dented and England was fast becoming an unwelcoming place, eager to tear down the home-grown yet adopted small screen star of the decade. In the Sakol interview for *Cosmopolitan*, conducted while the furore from *The Prisoner* was still raw, McGoohan mused:

'Why must we kill our heroes? We need them now as we needed them in the past. Julius Caesar, Henry the Fifth at Agincourt … Every real hero since Jesus Christ has been moral. We need moral heroes because they represent the generous, questing spirit of man. Without that we cannot survive.'[9]

Not a Number

Referring to the deaths of the Kennedys and Martin Luther King, McGoohan goes on to ask:

> 'Why must our heroes die? Don't we want them? These men were heroes – they're dead – and there are no replacements.'

It's tempting to theorise that McGoohan spoke these words at a time of great self-reflection. Maybe he was now starting to regret tarnishing his *Danger Man* image, with what was largely seen as a spin-off series that had gone horribly wrong. He had destroyed his own hero, despite believing heroes to be of great importance in society, whether fictional or not. Perhaps he felt that he had abused his position of power.

As the family relocated to Switzerland, McGoohan was thinking to the future. America had been very welcoming to the actor during the production of the Sturges movie *Ice Station Zebra* and he had begun to think that a move to the States would be the next logical step, while considering his post-*Prisoner* options. He already had strong opinions about the country, as he expressed in an interview to Joan Barthel to promote the screenings of *The Prisoner* in *TV Guide*, May 1968:

> 'I've always been obsessed with the idea of prisons in a liberal democratic society. I believe in democracy, but the inherent danger is that with an excess of freedom in all directions we will eventually destroy ourselves.
>
> You take a great nation like the United States of America and you find its run on opinion polls. It's an incredible situation! The poll investigator goes through a general cross section of the public – butchers, bakers, candlestick makers – and asks them how they think the war in Vietnam should be conducted … Well, these people may be very good butchers and bakers and candlestick makers, but I can't believe they know enough about the political and psychological situation to say how the war should be conducted.
>
> The reason we're so concerned with these polls is that we're so desperately concerned with saying, "We're free!". And I want to know, how free are we? I think we're being imprisoned and engulfed by a scientific and materialistic world. We're at the mercy of gadgetry and gimmicks; I'm making my living out of a piece of gadgetry, which is a television set,

and anyone who says there aren't any pressures in it has never watched a commercial!'[10]

Technology: Advance or Threat?

McGoohan was to return to this theme in interviews throughout the following decade, clearly concerned that technology, in this case that of the media, was advancing more quickly than our ability to control or perhaps to regulate it. In the previous chapter I briefly wondered what he would have made of the internet, a largely unregulated system where a variety of content can be obtained at the click of a mouse. I imagine that he was horrified by the internet's potential for corruption and the unregulated dissemination of pornographic and violent material.

It is unlikely that the wider implications of globalisation and the potential threat to cultural and individual diversity that the internet has helped to advance would have escaped him either. There is a scene from 'The Chimes of Big Ben' in which Leo McKern's Number 2 expresses his desire to see 'The whole earth, as The Village' which takes on a particular resonance in the face of globalisation. McGoohan remained convinced of the power of television and the wider media to persuade and influence public opinion, and he wanted to be part of that, to loudly rail against this power from the inside. He was now a sort of 'accepted rebel', an extremely rare position for anyone working in Hollywood, let alone an actor who had transformed his reputation and image in such a stark and profound way. McGoohan was no longer flavour of the month.

Despite this, he was still held in extremely high regard as an actor and with good reason. Whatever personal problems he may have been suffering, his professionalism in front of the camera never once deserted him and though reactions to *The Prisoner* had been mixed, he had at least been rewarded with positive reviews for his performance as Number 6. There was no questioning his authenticity and commitment to the role.

However, it was as the actor-manager figure that McGoohan still wished to style himself. Looking at the projects on his production company's slate from 1968-1969, this is immediately clear. Though

McGoohan was partially absent from the UK during his self-imposed exile, Everyman Films had been continually developing a number of projects. Unfortunately, with McGoohan and Grade falling out, many of these planned projects had lost focus and were eventually abandoned.

Back to Brand

McGoohan was very keen to return once more to *Brand*. Having produced the definitive stage and television versions to date, he wanted to make Ibsen's play dance for him on film now. Another motivation to achieve this project was the desire to appear in the film with Joan playing Brand's wife, Agnes. McGoohan probably felt a certain amount of guilt and regret that Joan's stage and film career had ended while his had flourished. He now wanted to give her something back for the time she had devoted to the family, a move he had been planning since at least 1965. He contacted Michael Meyer at some point in 1968, the man who had translated from Ibsen's original for the 1959 stage version, and arranged a meeting at MGM. Meyer recalled that the actor was 'shooting something, maybe *Danger Man*'. This shoot was most likely to have been for the concluding chapters of *The Prisoner* and Meyer's recollection is that McGoohan went into great detail about various scenes he planned to shoot for the film. He also remembers being slightly taken aback when McGoohan announced that he would also be directing the movie.[11]

Dylis Hamlett, a fellow cast member from the 1959 production of *Brand,* had been privy to industry gossip about McGoohan's new celluloid version. She recalled that Ingmar Bergman's cameraman, Sven Nykvist, was attached to the project, which was obviously intended to be a high profile and high quality piece of filmmaking. It was an intelligent choice for McGoohan at that stage, re-linking his name and currently damaged reputation with a highbrow classic in which he had already achieved great critical success a decade earlier.

Lew Grade – not yet ready to give up on McGoohan in spite of their differences – had given Everyman Films £900,000 to develop and produce two feature films, *Brand* being the first. Ibsen's joyless play was, however, going to be a hard sell, so as a sweetener, Grade asked for a standard action/adventure, starring McGoohan. The proposed idea was that McGoohan would portray a mercenary who becomes sickened by his trade and decides to opt-out by taking refuge in rural Ireland. However, there he becomes embroiled in the troubles between the IRA and the British forces. Conceived with a huge fight scene towards the end, it does seem like Everyman Films was doing its best to offer Grade an easily saleable product. The basic theme of this film bears a remarkable similarity to the 1979 movie *The Hard Way*, concerning the attempts of an IRA hitman to lay down his guns, in which McGoohan would later take the leading role. The similarities are so marked that this seems more than coincidental. Perhaps when the project didn't work out for Everyman Films, someone else took up the idea.

Production went as far as location scouting in Ireland for the action movie and in Norway for *Brand*. It was during this trip that McGoohan gave the interview (mentioned previously) to Jeannie Sakol from *Cosmopolitan*. The interview is entertaining, not just because it offers an insight into McGoohan just post-*Prisoner* but because of the fact that Sakol is so seduced by him. She falls head over heels in a matter of days, casting him as a 'good guy' who 'projects the kind of tender strength that could pull a tree out by its roots or fix the hair-ribbon of a weeping child'.[12]

McGoohan starts the interview in fearsome mode, barking 'Mind your own business' to the innocent opening gambit, 'How's everything going?'. Having thus tested his new opponent, McGoohan allows himself to relax. He seems, on the whole, to have been honest with the journalist, especially when focusing on his past work and his upcoming projects. Now the weight of the production of *The Prisoner* had been lifted, McGoohan was actively looking for the next project in which to wholeheartedly immerse himself. The offers of work weren't as numerous as his pre-*Prisoner* days, but McGoohan seemed unconcerned by this, preferring to pursue his own projects under the aegis of Everyman. He explained his motivations to Sakol:

'I have a virile hope for the future. That's why I did *The Prisoner* ... an allegory ... a fable ... a protest against regimentation and the loss of individuality. We must not become puppets. That's why I'm doing *Brand*, a passionate rebuttal of our own times. Ultimately, each of us must live within themselves and I'm just an idiot like the rest of the crowd.'

Everyman vs The Individual

Everyman Films had been developing several potential ideas during the final months of production on *The Prisoner*, some original pieces, others adaptations of books or plays. *Blackjack* was a proposed feature-film adaptation of a Leon Garfield novel, concerning a criminal who manages to escape hanging by inserting a silver tube into his throat to avoid his windpipe being constricted. Blackjack himself was conceived as an innocent character, a case of arrested development, who finds himself being used and manipulated by those around him until he finally finds his own way. Garfield was delighted and flattered that McGoohan and Terence Feely had taken an interest in his novel but was unaware that a full script had been prepared by the duo. When, many years later, he was able to read the pilot episode, he was impressed at how closely the adaptation had kept to his story and how the writers had kept in all the material that he considered vital to the narrative.

Having been impressed by *The Prisoner* and the attention to detail that had been put into it, Garfield also felt that McGoohan and Tomblin would have done his work justice on screen, expecting that they would favour impressionism over realism, exactly as he would have envisaged it.

The Outsider was an idea for a series centring around the adventures of a traveller, a man of the road: Johnny Quill, remarkably well-kept despite his slightly worn clothes and with a slight Irish accent, was obviously developed with McGoohan in mind. With proper development, this concept from Lewis Griefer could have become a remarkably entertaining series and it is interesting to speculate what McGoohan might have intended for the project, which topics he would cover this time. Once again, we have the individual, the outcast, the loner. Whilst obviously a less 'way out' concept than McGoohan's previous series, no doubt it would have sailed as close to the wind. McGoohan was not yet one for compromise. *When Trumpets Call* was a script that originated from an external source to Everyman, and was adapted from material by Rudyard Kipling. This appeared to have been earmarked as a potential TV Movie for CBS in the States and again featured as the lead character a man out of step with his surroundings. However, ultimately all of these interesting plans were to come to nothing. There had, by this time been a fatal falling out between Everyman Films and Lew Grade and this, it appears, was as a direct result of McGoohan's increasingly eccentric behaviour. The previously over-tolerant Grade simply withdrew the backing for Everyman's projects. Terence Feely, the scriptwriter who by this point was part of the company, explains that he felt little animosity towards Lew Grade on his departure:

> 'Because of … some difference of opinion between Lew and ourselves he withdrew the finance. For which I don't blame him because… erm… I think he was entitled to. I think we were probably being unreasonable in our last push for something that we didn't really need.'[13]

Magic Numbers and Tantrums

With Tomblin as the experienced producer and McGoohan as star name, Feeley had come aboard the company as a writer and ideas man. However, McGoohan had become utterly unpredictable and while wilfully inventive, he was again proving difficult to work with. Feeley elaborated in a later interview for Ricks which revealed the reason for the financial collapse of Everyman and ultimately, of McGoohan's grandiose plans:

> 'One day Pat came in with that look in his eye. You often read in melodramatic novels about the red light in the madman's eye. It's not entirely untrue because Pat came in with this look … and I thought "Uh oh…" And I said "What's up Pat?" And he said, "We haven't got the magic figure," and I said "Sorry?". He said, "The magic figure is a million pounds," I said "Yeah, I know, but we've got nine hundred thousand." I mean, we all know, David was there as well, we all know it's more than enough to make a cheap action adventure and Ibsen's *Brand*.'[14]

McGoohan's comment about 'the magic number' echoes a story from Ian Rakoff in *Inside the Prisoner*. Not long after Rakoff had joined the post-production team as assistant editor, assisting John S. Smith in assembling 'The General', Rakoff recalled Smith asking McGoohan during one of the actor's frequent cutting room visits, his opinion of the fact that their edit suite was located in room number 6:

> '"Number Six, the perfect number," Pat muttered. "But it's not a magic number though, it's perfect according to numerology. It doesn't do any good to read more depth than there is. If you get too intellectual, you could end up with something Satanic like 666." Pat looked straight at me. Whether he was serious or joking I couldn't tell.'[15]

It's hard to say which numbers were 'magic' for McGoohan, and indeed why. Perhaps this apparent belief in mysticism was tied to his religious beliefs or perhaps it was his interest in mathematics which caused his tendency to favour certain 'magic' numbers. Whatever his reasoning, with typical ferocity McGoohan was not to be persuaded from his ideas on this front. It hadn't previously been a problem that he frequently claimed to have little commercial sense and no such thing as a career plan but things were different now. Feely recounts how McGoohan's behaviour impacted badly on the company:

> 'What we'll do I said is announce to the trade papers that we've got a million. We know we only have 900,000 but that doesn't matter." And he grabbed hold of my lapels and said, "Don't you know you can't cheat magic?" So I said, "Well what's the answer?" and he said, "Well, this afternoon I am going to go and see Lew Grade, who loves me like a son. I'll get the other hundred grand."
>
> Now I afterwards heard what had happened. Lew, being an entirely practical man, knew we didn't need the other hundred grand. And despite loving Pat like a son, which he did, said 'No'. Whereupon Pat, like Douglas Fairbanks Senior, with one leap, landed on the middle of Lew's desk … and kicked everything on it to the four corners of the room. With the result that when he came in in the morning, he didn't have the million and we didn't have the 900,000 either.'[16]

Exit Lew Grade

McGoohan had refused to listen to reason and had now thoroughly bitten-off the hand that had so diligently fed him throughout most of the decade. This eventual breakdown was the result of months of tension between the two men over production costs, abandoned scheduling and McGoohan's refusal to compromise on quality by producing the promised twenty-six *Prisoner* episodes. Production manager Ronald Liles remembered the final conflict as follows:

> 'He'd had so many ups and downs with Lew Grade, over not doing any more than the thirteen, then finally deciding he would do another four but that would be the lot, that I think he got discontented with ITC. And I know he went to Vervey in Switzerland where he had a house and from there on he went to the States.'[17]

For McGoohan to have had the naked arrogance to be 'discontented' with ITC is astonishing. Lew Grade had, after all, given him the TV break that eventually gave him the power to make his own series and had been unfailingly supportive of that series while money was poured into its chaotic production. He had done his best to accommodate McGoohan's demands and had every right to be furious at how his trust in McGoohan had been abused. He now had a hugely expensive series to sell which, while of excellent quality, was not going to bring anything like the expected financial return in overseas sales. *The Prisoner* was to become a cult but it would never be a mainstream hit worldwide like Gerry Anderson's technically inventive puppet series *Thunderbirds*, *Captain Scarlet* and *Stingray* etc or Roger Moore's suave, sexy and straightforward *The Saint*. Having complete control over *The Prisoner* had clearly gone to McGoohan's head. (If the above story of his tantrum on Grade's desk is indeed true, this was a classic case of kicking the toys out of the pram.)

As Terence Feely recounted, McGoohan's desire to achieve the 'magic' million was ridiculous and the pragmatic Grade, fond as he was of McGoohan, was a businessman first and foremost. He certainly had a flair for spotting promising talent and supporting often wild ideas.

However, to Grade it now seemed like working with McGoohan was a gamble he was no longer prepared to take.

McGoohan later reflected on his state of mind at the time in an interview for the *Sunday Telegraph Magazine*:

> 'The hardest thing to hold on to was perspective,' he reflects. 'I got spoiled because I had complete control, down to every last nut and bolt.'[18]

With the finance suddenly pulled out from under them, there was little else that Everyman Films could do as a creative team or as a company. In 1974 it would be dissolved, with debts of over £60,000 and more than half owed in taxes to the Inland Revenue. It was at this point that McGoohan decided it was time to leave England and apart from the occasional visit to the UK he was never to return.

Departing Britain

Though there are persistent rumours that McGoohan left the country as a tax exile at this point, this decampment may also have been the shrewdest career move of his life. Lew Grade was an exceptionally powerful, well-connected and, importantly, well-liked figure; a dominant presence in the British media. By all accounts an extremely honourable businessman, Grade would be unlikely to divulge details of McGoohan's behaviour to those outside his trusted circle. But the close knit, sometimes cliquey, nature of the industry would mean that tales of McGoohan's temper would spread fast. It's not as if McGoohan had left *The Prisoner* set without making a few enemies on route; even if there were many who remained loyal to him. Ultimately, he would be viewed as less employable.

McGoohan was contracted to make three pictures for MGM, the first having been *Ice Station Zebra* which had proved to be a critical and commercial success. He was therefore required to spend more time in the United States. For now, however, Switzerland would give the family a neutral territory in which McGoohan's face was not as well known as in the UK and where the ghosts of his recent past could fade.

The fact that Joan's parents now lived in Switzerland would have contributed to their decision to move, as McGoohan had as strong a familial bond with them as with his own parents. Having made his big statement, there is the sense of a wounded animal returning to the safety of the pack to lick its wounds. Whilst McGoohan must have felt some dismay at the direction his career had now taken, he was already planning new projects, scripts and film ideas. He would have appreciated the chance to repay his family for their patience during the making of his series, as he was finally able to devote some time to them. He could relax and play his favourite role: that of the dedicated family man. The family took up residence in Vevey on the banks of Lake Geneva, in peaceful and calm surroundings, far removed from the intense scrutiny and constant activity of London. McGoohan had become disenchanted with the city, identifying it with one of his current concerns, as he revealed to Joan Barthel in *TV Guide*:

'Only occasionally, "out of great pressure", does he come into the mechanised, computerised city. "Computers have everything worked out for us. And we're constantly being numeralised. The other day I went through the number of units that an ordinary citizen over here is subject to, including license plate numbers and all the rest, and it added up to some 340 separate digits."'[19]

McGoohan was probably aware that he had lost his way as a person during the production of *The Prisoner* and was ever fearful of losing the down-to-earth attitude that had previously characterised his approach to work and colleagues. It was time for a rest, time to recuperate and plan for the future, to take stock of his situation. Fully aware of his nature McGoohan explained that:

'I like working under pressure. I, unluckily, only have two gears. Very low and very high. I wish I could cultivate the middle gear but I can't. At MGM, Elstree, where my offices are, I allow my desk to get cluttered up for three days. I look at my "In" tray till it won't hold any more, descend upon it and clean it right up. It's a bad way to work but it's the way I'm made.'[20]

The Moonshine War: New Projects

McGoohan was now able to switch into low gear, financially secure for the time being due to his large pay cheque and profit percentage deal from *The Prisoner*, happy to take things a little more slowly for while. His next career move, in 1970, saw him returning to his previous life as purely an actor. Any wider-reaching ambitions were temporarily on hold after the falling out with Lew Grade, though Tomblin and Feeley would continue to develop ideas for the ultimately crippled Everyman Films.

The actor who had for so long resisted the lure of Hollywood, now relocated temporarily to its environs, not far from his birthplace, and took a role in a film called *The Moonshine War* (1970). He played Frank Long, a greedy and somewhat stupid villain, a role as far removed from the intellectual fire of Number 6 as possible. This was a shrewd move. Whilst his appearance in *Danger Man* had never impacted upon his career, the public had typecast him in the role of the upright spy/hero, with the character of Number 6 further reinforcing this image.

The Moonshine War, adapted by Elmore Leonard from his own novel, is set towards the end of prohibition. It follows the attempts of McGoohan's character, a revenue man by trade but infinitely corruptible, to track down one remaining stash of alcohol. Frank Long finds himself increasingly out of his depth as he becomes more deeply involved in the lives and machinations of real criminals. Directed by Richard Quine, the film itself is somewhat disjointed, losing its way halfway through. It's never quite sure enough of itself to run with the initial rather light-hearted tone set at the start. McGoohan, however, is once more excellent, throwing himself into the part with familiar gusto. At the time it may have been said that he had failed as a producer and director, but there was no denying that he retained his power as a performer. Unfortunately *The Moonshine War* was too cynical for McGoohan's taste, though it apparently influenced Quentin Tarantino (who McGoohan later vilified for his penchant for the artistic glorification of on screen violence).

There is a fascinating, short, behind-the-scenes documentary, made as a promotional piece for the film, which shows McGoohan apparently at his ease during the set-up of a car stunt involving him. Though the fierce concentration is still present in the eyes, the actor is full of smiles and co-operation. Not one to play the media game, he nevertheless knew that he had to rebuild his reputation in the eyes of both the public and potential employers, especially if he were to be once more given the power to pursue his plans.

While undoubtedly enjoying the free time he could now spend with his family, McGoohan was still on the look-out for projects. He was easing himself back into the working world with appearances in films, which were likely to be more highly paid and more creatively satisfying than most television work.

Consequently, in 1971 McGoohan accepted a part in the Universal film *Mary Queen of Scots* (1971). Costume dramas were becoming increasingly popular and McGoohan took the role of the treacherous James Stewart in this film. Vanessa Redgrave was cast as Mary and Glenda Jackson played Elizabeth I – a role she was often identified with after the success of her highly-acclaimed BBC TV series of the same name. The film was shot at Alnwick Castle in Northumberland before the crew returned to the familiar environs of Shepperton Studios, for the interior work. Surrounded by such an excellent cast, McGoohan was outstanding in what was, for him, a relatively undemanding role. Moreover, he was given an opportunity to show that he was working once more back in his home country, to repair some of the damage caused by *The Prisoner*. This was a period of rehabilitation for McGoohan, certainly as far as popular opinion was concerned and he did all that was required of him. He produced a controlled performance, perhaps lacking in some of the fire of his earlier work, but pitched perfectly for the production – a watchable but worthy tale which took great liberties with historical accuracy. My feeling is that, oddly enough, the script would have translated better to the small screen as a series of multi-camera TV plays, the medium in which McGoohan had once found such success.

Catch My Soul

After their time recuperating at Vervey, McGoohan and his family left in 1974 for Santa Fe, New Mexico. Here, McGoohan was able to take the directorial helm again, making the film *Catch My Soul* (1974) a rock version of *Othello*, for Metromedia productions. The ambitious premise of this project must have appealed to McGoohan; it was certainly an unusual idea and not without risks. He would also have relished the chance to prove himself as a director once more. Unfortunately, the production did not go as planned and McGoohan was not at all happy with the results. He spoke briefly about this frustratingly elusive piece in an interview given in 1995 to French movie magazine *Premiere*:

> *'Catch My Soul*, yes, with Ritchie Havens, Tony Joe White … I lived in New Mexico at that time and the producer did too. He'd heard I was available and that's how, after the hiatus that followed *The Prisoner*, I came back to the profession. Unhappily, in the process of making the film, he got religion … Catholicism. He became a convert; he took the film and re-cut it. The editor warned me, I asked that my name be taken off it, and, unhappily, that was not done. The result is a disaster. What's more, he added eighteen minutes of religious stuff. Ridiculous. But the music was good. Ritchie wrote one or two marvellous songs. Again, it's one of those typical show business stories… Very sad…'[21]

The reviews were scathing, spotlighting McGoohan's handling of the movie as one of its weakest points, amongst a plethora of others. It had clearly been clearly another disappointing creative experience. McGoohan had no doubt expected, perfectly reasonably, for the director to have a degree of control that he was not afforded. The fact that he refers to the period after *The Prisoner* as 'a hiatus' confirms that while he did work during that time, he was no longer the powerhouse of activity that he had been. McGoohan's reputation had made him too hot to handle for many producers and directors and it must have been a crushing blow for him to realise that he was unlikely to be able to fulfil the actor-manager role in any particularly meaningful way, maybe for a very long time.

CHAPTER 8
Kings and Desperate Men

Working with Lt. Columbo

In 1974, McGoohan accepted a part in the popular detective series *Columbo*, featuring Peter Falk as a shabby, down-at-heel detective, apparently with a mind as shambolic as his clothes but hiding a burning intelligence behind the façade. As with McGoohan in *Danger Man*, Falk wielded a considerable amount of control over the direction the character and indeed the series would take. In keeping with the casting of most big-name guest stars, McGoohan was to play the villain of the piece. His character was a military man, Colonel Lyle Rumford, now retired from active service and working at a military academy. A man of extreme convictions, he kills the grandson of the academy's founder, in order to prevent the academy from being converted into a co-ed school. Though a ferocious authoritarian, McGoohan elegantly brings out the more caring motivations of the man, who acts only in the best interests of the school. It is one of McGoohan's greatest on screen performances and the rewards of his effort were twofold.

Firstly, and most significantly in the short term, the role won him a prestigious Emmy award for 'Outstanding Single Performance by a Supporting Actor in a Comedy or Drama Series'. When an actor wins such an award, it is said that their fee triples overnight. McGoohan, with this one TV appearance, had restored much of his reputation as an actor of depth and power and he would be invited back to the *Columbo* set the following year.

Secondly, and probably of equal importance to McGoohan himself, he was to develop a long-lasting friendship with Peter Falk. This had the added benefit that he was asked to appear in the series again and again.

McGoohan had thoroughly enjoyed his experience on the set
of *Columbo*, finding Falk to be on a similar wavelength, as well as
passionately committed to the quality of the show. He was delighted to
be asked not only to appear in but to direct the episode 'Identity Crisis'
in 1975. In a later interview for a 1977 edition of *TV Guide* in the US,
he spoke about his experiences:

> 'One of his greatest friends in Hollywood is actor Peter Falk – Lt.
> Columbo. "He's a rebel like me … *Columbo*," he says, "it's the one TV
> show he's worked on where 'they give you time and money to spend
> on quality.'" Not that he's ever around to watch the finished results.
> "Unless I'm directing – and have to cut – I never watch myself on film
> or television," he states. "I've never seen a movie I've made. I'd be sick
> if I saw myself on screen. If I'm directing, I can look at the rushes
> and at myself dispassionately saying, 'He's done a lousy job' or 'that's
> not bad' as if I were some other actor."'[1]

Speaking in an interview with Howard Foy in *The Box* in 1991,
McGoohan describes the particular appeal of working on the series, as
Foy perceptively asks: 'And Peter Falk will be happy then for you to do
anything or everything on that episode?'

> 'Oh yes, and that's the best way to work because it short circuits the
> complications of having a lot of writers and a lot of people making
> decisions. Just the two of us get together and what we decide – that's it.
> It's a very simple way of working and the best one I know and it's very
> rare one has the opportunity to do that, being episodic TV, because you
> know the old sausage machine is in-and-out, in-and-out, but at least with
> Peter you get the chance to prepare properly and debate before you get
> to actually shooting. So by the time you come to shoot it, you've decided
> what you're going to do and you just get on with it.'[2]

McGoohan's preferred working method was warmly embraced by
Falk, laying the bedrock for their close friendship, to the extent that
McGoohan would many years later remark that Falk was the only
person to whom he would never say 'no'. McGoohan would rarely

take a project that he felt was beneath him, yet in Falk he found the same desire to achieve the highest possible quality with the resources available; even if this meant alienating friends in the process.

Unfortunately, both were known for their drinking and there are various rumours about their outings as drinking buddies, over-indulging to a worrying degree, each encouraging the other.

A Genius, Two Friends and an Idiot

Saying 'no' is something that might perhaps have been a good idea on his next venture, the Italian-funded movie *A Genius, Two Friends and an Idiot* (1975). Shot in the US, this was intended as a comedy spaghetti western and the chance to play in such a piece would have intrigued the actor. He felt that he had never really explored his comedic gifts since the stage play *Ring for Catty,* although the *Prisoner* episode 'The Girl Who Was Death' is played mostly for laughs.

Though McGoohan may have had a great comedic flair, his decisions in this movie are questionable at the least. No doubt lured by the fact that director Sergio Leone was associated with the movie, McGoohan accepted the part of Major Cabot. Though his comedy timing is excellent, and his gift for physical humour apparent, the performance is a little too strange for the material. McGoohan seemed slightly out of step with what is ultimately an amusing but pedestrian film. Fortunately, soon after, he made another appearance in *Columbo*. His friendship with Falk and shared desire for quality no doubt helped to banish any disappointment at the unimpressive western. It received lukewarm reviews and vanished without trace, much, no doubt, to McGoohan's relief, as he passed it off with little positive comment (though some humour) in *Premiere*:

'I've never seen it. For all I know, it was never released in England. And, thank god, never in the United States. It was a spaghetti western and the first time I'd worked in Italy. Very funny, in fact. In Italy, most films are dubbed in post production, and one of my friends who saw the film in Spain told me I spoke with a voice like Mickey Mouse.'[3]

Silver Streak and Rafferty: Heroes and Rebels

1977 was a comparatively good year for McGoohan. Catherine was now married and gave birth to a daughter, Sarah. The hellraiser became a grandfather. He had also recently appeared in Arthur Hiller's comedy thriller movie *Silver Streak* (1976). McGoohan played Roger Devereaux, an art dealer and murderer, alongside unlikely co-stars Gene Wilder and Richard Pryor. He had been cast as another villain, no doubt reinforced by his appearances in *Columbo* in which he excelled at playing the bad guy. Predictably, McGoohan was beginning to tire of this typecasting, claiming in a *TV Times* interview:

> 'I've played similar parts before but the suits were better and the ties were more expensive in this film … I'm a heavy, a one-dimensional heavy. It's the last heavy I want to play – I'm looking for heroes now.'"[4]

McGoohan had often mentioned that to him, doctors, nurses and especially plumbers were heroic figures; important people without whom modern life would become impossible. It must have been a welcome change for him to play such a pillar of society, a doctor, in his next project, the TV series *Rafferty. Rafferty* is considered a precursor to the Hugh Laurie-centred medical hit *House,* as both feature unconventional, irritable and brilliant doctors working against the clock to solve that week's medical problem. However, though *House* has long since reached the point of parody, *Rafferty* was to run for a mere thirteen episodes. In *The Daily News* of July 13th 1977, executive producer Jerry Thorpe revealed that it was the casting of McGoohan that had clinched the deal with CBS.

> 'The concept was taken to the network which was interested enough to order a script and then a tentative casting. "When we were lucky enough to get Mr McGoohan," Thorpe says, "The show was on the air".'[5]

Rafferty was a character that McGoohan took to his heart, producing a performance that evoked melancholic emotions through little activity other than unpredictable flashes of anger. The character, a widower, had several pictures of his deceased wife on the walls of his study. Touchingly, these were all of Joan, who was paid a fee for the use of her likeness. Another rebel, McGoohan delighted in the fact that Rafferty was an anti-establishment figure and was quite prepared to draw comparisons between actor and character:

> "Rafferty has traits close to my own personality," McGoohan says. "Crusty. He's a crusty man." Patrick McGoohan, star of a television series. Earns thousands of dollars a week. Owns a piece of the show. Yet drives a Honda. Wouldn't drive even that if he could get about Los Angeles on foot. Says he doesn't know why he's doing a doctor show.
>
> "Doctors are important," he concedes. "But plumbers are even more important. And garbage collectors. If plumbers and garbage collectors go on strike, that's when we need doctors!"
>
> "Enigmatic," a producer says about him after the interview. "A strange man."[6]

Jerry Thorpe, the show's executive producer, who, along with Warner Bros., owns the rest of *Rafferty*, thinks McGoohan is shy.

> "If there's anything that people find abrasive, it probably grows out of his shyness. He doesn't like people poking into his private life. I like him personally, but we have not socialized. I don't think we will."[7]

As might be expected, McGoohan was concerned with every aspect of *Rafferty*. Thorpe noted that the actor could be difficult with scripts but always constructively so, with 'inordinately high' standards. Amusingly, in the *TV Guide* interview, Thorpe echoed several other publicity pieces about the series by highlighting McGoohan's 'low-key sex appeal' (with co-star Millie Slavin crooning, 'He's so sexy!' in the *Boca Raton* news). In this piece it was intriguingly revealed that McGoohan had been asked by Peter Falk to take charge of *Columbo*, Falk feeling that McGoohan had 'the goods'. However, studio bosses had apparently scuppered this plan. Maybe one of them had thought fit to ask Lew Grade's advice? McGoohan was instead involved in the rewriting of scripts and managed to direct one episode.

'In the new series, McGoohan not only acts but writes and directs occasional episodes. He didn't go out of his way to land the role. "I don't like to read pilot scripts. Too many pilots never sell. But my agent sent me this script, I liked this doctor guy.

Rafferty is scheduled Mondays opposite NFL football and a network movie, "If OJ is on. I'll be watchin' him." McGoohan says. Then quickly: "I'm not denigratin' my show. I never watch my show, except when I have directed it."

He isn't denigrating the industry, either, but he's not very thrilled by it. The first four years in this country the McGoohans did not own a TV set. "When we finally got one. I made a verbal contract with the kids. I told them: 'Go through the TV listings and pick out the seven things you want to watch this week. Remember, if you see two things one day, there'll be another day you can't watch anything.'"[8]

Poet and Romantic

The Hano interview for *TV Guide* states that McGoohan was living in what Hano described as a 'Cape Cod cottage' with McGoohan revealing that, 'The view is of trees and flowers. It's absolutely enclosed. Very private.' It went into a little detail about McGoohan's poetry. Always an avid writer, McGoohan spent a great deal of his time writing teleplays and poems, some of which he would collect together and bind into private volumes to be distributed amongst friends. It would be fascinating to read such a collection but these tomes, like his home-made movies, seem destined to remain as secret as their creator intended them to be, despite the fact that according to the interview he had at the time had five editions published with a print run of a hundred each. In a 1995 interview for *Premiere*, McGoohan commented that: 'I don't want to talk about them, they are very personal things for my family, my wife. When I am dead, my children can publish them.'[8] No such collection has so far been forthcoming. The *TV Guide* interview also revealed that McGoohan's romantic side had survived the traumas of the late 1960s intact, as he was planning to give Joan the white wedding he had once promised:

'My wife, Joan, and I are getting remarried next Saturday. A re-affirmation. When we got married twenty-six years ago over in England, we were too busy for a church ceremony. I was rehearsing for Petruchio in *Taming of the Shrew* and Joan was playing Ophelia. I said to Joan, "I promise you a white weddin' some time, but not now."[9]

According to Arnold Hano, who was conducting the interview, McGoohan showed off a ring that he planned to give to Joan, somewhat shyly, with the words: 'A white ring for a white weddin'. My wife is dark, a dark angel.' The shyness is entirely in character and is always a humanising touch in a man who could often be remote at best or wilfully incomprehensible at worst. It is genuinely moving that he took such pride in the fact that their marriage had survived untouched by the potential ravages that showbiz could inflict upon a couple. His family life was an unqualified success, he and Joan were as close and loving as they had ever been, while in other ways, his daily routine for years remained unchanged:

'He keeps in shape playing racquet ball, shoots occasional pool, and plays high-calibre chess. His wife's game though is gin rummy. "She's very good at it. I t'ink we're runnin' neck and neck. We'll play ten games: if she wins, we go away for a weekend."[10]

McGoohan revealed that he still kept somewhat unusual hours. He had never required a great deal of sleep, averaging just two hours a night towards the end of *The Prisoner*.

"I'm an insomniac," he says. "I sleep four hours maximum. I get up at 2.30 am, I read or write, and then I'm out of the house to walk on the beach. It's lonely then, just people with their dogs and some surfers. I walk, and I talk to the dogs."

Another interview appearing around the same time revealed that McGoohan had now bought a plot of land in Montana, where he was building a secluded retreat, intended to be powered and heated by solar panels and a waterwheel. The actor liked the idea of being independent and self-sufficient, commenting that: 'We'll go up there to suffer a little cold and realise that life can hurt sometimes.'[11]

McGoohan alluded to his occasionally mentioned tax problems, saying that he had paid his debts and affirming that neither he nor Joan had any immediate plans to return to England.

That he should have been afforded such a stable and loving home life must have been of great comfort to McGoohan as *Rafferty* failed to make much of an impression in the ratings – no doubt most of the audience 'watching *OJ*' along with McGoohan himself. Reviews were mixed, though uniformly positive towards the actor who seems later to have been disappointed with the direction the series took.

Disappointment seems to have been a common response for the actor who, with the exception of his work on *Columbo*, had been largely unimpressed with the productions he had appeared in during the decade. The critics seemed to agree that the storylines were predictable and the format largely uninspired, saved only from mediocrity by the lead performance. *Rafferty* ran for just thirteen episodes before time was called.

With the cancellation of what must have been a promising long-term commitment for McGoohan, he appeared in *The Man In The Iron Mask* (1977). This was to be a lavishly-budgeted TV movie costume epic starring Richard Chamberlain, previously a heartthrob in TV series *Dr Kildare*. McGoohan was magnificently arch as Fouquet, the minister of finance to Louis XIV, a character driven by the kind of ambition and ferocious self-belief that McGoohan himself had demonstrated so often in the past. Significantly, this was the first time McGoohan had worked for ITC, Lew Grade's company, since *The Prisoner*. Time had passed and McGoohan must have felt encouraged by the fact that he had not been blacklisted by the powerful mogul.

Perhaps mischievously flying in the face of all the critics who had called him 'prissy Pat' back in the days of his conservative approach to *Danger Man*, McGoohan made a short but memorable appearance in low key WWII thriller *Brass Target* (1978). He played Macaulay, a colonel who is living in a captured German castle. His appearance lasts for only half-an-hour and sets up the plot of the film. However, it is memorable for two reasons. Firstly, he again affects a bizarre style of delivery, seemingly aiming for comedy. Secondly, he is seen in a bedroom in this film, lasciviously observing Sophia Loren as she strips for his pleasure. Knowing McGoohan's forthright views about such matters, that he took this role seems to have been a minor act of rebellion in itself, against his own self-cultivated image. Presumably, he also no longer felt the restrictions of being the responsible father of young children, as all of his family were quite old enough to distinguish fact from fantasy by now.

Kings and Desperate Men

McGoohan spent much of the later 1970s relaxing on his farm at Montana or at home in Pacific Palisades, always with his family. But a figure from the past was about to re-enter his life. Alexis Kanner had decided he wanted McGoohan involved in his new film *Kings and Desperate Men* (1981).

Coming in late to *The Prisoner*, Kanner had found McGoohan at his most controlling: writing, directing and producing one of the episodes in which he had starred. He had been enormously impressed by the star's drive and determination to make the series his own. Kanner had collaborated on the screenplay of *Kings and Desperate Men* with Edmund Ward, a British TV writer who had recently created episodes of the ITV action series *The Professionals* and would direct the movie, as well as taking a leading role.

Andrea Marcovicci took the role of 'girl' in the film *Kings and Desperate Men*. Recounting in detail her experiences on set to the Confluence Film blog online,[12] she reveals a production that was crippled by the drunken antics of its two prime movers from the outset. Her initial meeting with Alexis Kanner saw the actor/director falling asleep in his soup, with Marcovicci initially passing this off as jet lag. Her first impressions of Patrick McGoohan weren't much better. She had been really looking forward to working with him, having long been impressed with his work, but his and Kanner's drinking habits were playing havoc with the production schedule.

'I thought the experience was going to be unforgettable because everyone in my family were all fans of *The Prisoner*. I mean, how could you not be?

The show was just one of the things you had to watch. It did wind up being unforgettable, but in a very different way than what was expected … you had two English drunks who really didn't mean any harm, but they thought they were creating something new, creating an art that was theirs and theirs alone, this profoundly original work. In attempting to mount this, what they were doing so frustrated the crew. Now, it's one thing if you try to do that and you're sober. However, trying to do that when you're not sober didn't make for a positive experience for anyone but themselves. So everyone starting calling the production *"Kings and Desperate Crew"*.[13]

By all accounts, the production seems to have mirrored the chaotic shooting of 'Fall Out', which had so inspired Kanner, with a freeform improvisational nature that gave the actors free rein to expand upon their roles but which frustrated the crew who were expected to follow the script. However, 'Fall Out' was underpinned by the great organisational capabilities of McGoohan and made by a crew who had worked together closely for months, supported by a large budget. Kanner had none of these skills or resources, nor perhaps the force of personality of McGoohan which, at full Wellesian strength could have held together such a 'desperate crew'. Unfortunately for Kanner, in this instance, McGoohan was to be of little help.

As Marcovicci explains:

'Patrick … was shockingly mean-spirited, which was a disappointment. Alex and Patrick fascinated each other and it was wonderful to see two men who fascinated each other in such a way. But once we saw how chaotic the shooting was, none of us could really imagine how Alex was going to cut it all together. That was our biggest concern. So little of it was being matched, the script girl was shooed off the set when she complained about it. The sound person was not allowed to do his work accurately. The two of them were really in the world of their own imagination, which was fascinating.'[14]

McGoohan had once more succumbed to drink and Mr Hyde was back in full force, but with ten years of self-loathing added. In this condition, he was liable to snarl at anyone within reach, with the exception of the golden-boy Kanner. The two of them, according to Miss Marcovicci's memories, vanished into a world of their own during the shoot.

'Above all, it is important to remember that Alex and Patrick meant well and they really did fascinate each other. Theirs was a wonderful, fierce madness.'[15]

Co-star Margaret Trudeau, who played Elizabeth Kingsley, McGoohan's character's wife in the film, became extremely irritated that McGoohan would wilfully change the script. Kanner recalled that he would trim many of her lines (though also his own, this was no exercise in egotism) and to an actress used to collaborating, rather than taking orders and being pushed around, this was intolerable.

Alexis Kanner gave a fascinating interview to Rosemary Camillari, in *In The Village* Issue Four, in which he described a particular moment of inspiration from McGoohan. Kanner recalls how he slightly altered the words of a song that his character John Kingsley sang to himself in a reflective moment:

'He thought of that himself. 'Cause he got it. Today his life has little merit for him. I distorted the old line of the song "I hear the gentle voices calling" and then with his sardonic wit [McGoohan] says, "Poor old John. He's talking to himself."'[16]

In the same interview, Kanner explained the reasons behind his casting of McGoohan, citing the often-noted air of 'danger' in his performances as being one factor. Ultimately, Kanner concludes that: 'The danger is, in fact, finally, to himself,' and though it's unclear whether Kanner is discussing actor or character , both share a strongly self-destructive streak.

Andrea Marcovicci took great pleasure in retaliating once her commitment to the film had been wrapped:

'I actually chucked a glass ashtray at Patrick the moment we wrapped, and that's not like me at all … Patrick had been so unpleasant to most everyone during the shooting that I just took it upon myself to strike back and, even though I prided myself in being lady-like, felt he deserved it. The crew applauded. He was almost still in character when he asked me, "Miss Marcovicci, whhhy? Why, Miss Marcovicci? Whhhy?"'[17]

The Hard Way

The film would linger in limbo for several years as Kanner struggled to find the resources for the necessary post-production work. McGoohan's unruly and unpleasant behaviour apparently carried on into his next role in the 1979 movie *The Hard Way*. This contemporary piece concerned the troubles in Ireland and, significantly, was a TV movie made by ITC. (As mentioned in Chapter 7, Lew Grade's production company who had withdrawn the funding for a very similar Everyman Films project at the end of the 1960s.) McGoohan plays a hitman, John Connor, a killer who now wishes only to retire. He is confronted by a gangster, Lee Van Cleef, who demands that Connor work for him. McGoohan makes a potentially unlikeable character extremely human, giving a very complex performance which is absolutely right for the material. Perhaps he went the extra mile to impress Grade, knowing that he would undoubtedly see the results. Maybe that ghost too could now be laid to rest. However, as Paul Duane – co-creator of *The Secret Diary of a Call Girl*, who is in touch with McGoohan's contemporaries – informed me recently, McGoohan was on his worst behaviour on set.

'I met the original director of that film, Richard Tombleson, around the same time – '97 or '98 … Tombleson had been responsible for suggesting McGoohan, but told me it was the worst decision he had ever made – the quote I remember is: "If I asked him to stand and look out the window, he would lie down under the bed." He was fired and the film was finished, very poorly, with one of the producers directing, and Tombleson disappeared to Australia.'[18]

The Hard Way certainly rambles and is badly paced at times, but it cannot be denied that McGoohan gives a quietly forceful performance, one of his finest on celluloid, yet again playing the individual, fighting against coercion. Despite this impressive performance, his on set antics would no doubt have been reported to Grade and McGoohan never again worked for ITC. Both men remained loyal and openly admiring of each other but the working relationship was critically severed.

Around this time, McGoohan granted an interview with Bob Kjellin for a 1980 edition of *Tidbits* magazine which offers another glimpse into the private life of the man and his state of mind at that time. He spoke briefly about *The Hard Way*:

> 'I play a hired killer … and that is sort of contradictory to my way of thinking. I have talked about immorality, amorality, dishonesty and violence, yet I'm playing a character who is full of that. But there's less violence in *The Hard Way* than in any Western.'[19]

McGoohan goes on to point out that the irony of the situation is that the character is trying his best to give up that life and put down his guns, in the face of extreme coercion to the contrary, a situation analogous with that of Number 6 during the episode 'Living In Harmony'.

Meanwhile Back on the Farm

The remainder of the interview paints a picture of a rural idyll, McGoohan having retreated to raise chickens on a farm in Montana, cut off from the pressures of the outside world. The farm lay in the middle of a forest, a perfect island for the increasingly reclusive actor to find peace of mind with his family, uninterrupted. He took great joy in reliving his teenage life as a chicken farmer, presumably untroubled by his asthma, and spoke of relaxing by catching trout for breakfast in the morning. I feel that McGoohan was finding it increasingly difficult to fit in with the world of modern media and most likely felt less and less inclined to try. Indeed, he was already branching out into other areas, buying, renovating and selling houses, working with his hands. All his early interests that had been subsumed beneath his desire to act were now finding free expression. Based on his autobiographical account of his time working for the Browns on their farm outside Sheffield, I imagine these precious times in Montana to have been amongst the most relaxed he had during the 1970s.

> 'I suspect I'll retreat more and more into a quiet way of life. And you can't beat this way of life up here. I got this log cabin and a few acres of land a few years ago and it is here where my family and I can really relax totally cut off from the outside world.'[20]

Escape from Alcatraz

A vastly better-known film than *The Hard Way*, *Escape from Alcatraz* gave McGoohan his other major role in 1979. In this classic prison break-out movie, he played the quietly sadistic prison governor in a performance that is controlled and highly unpleasant to watch. He succeeds in creating a genuinely unlikable character, using body language that is completely different from his usual identifiable movements and tics, and he makes the very most of what is a comparatively small yet hugely important role in the movie. It is a remarkable feat that, once again, whenever he is on screen McGoohan commands the viewer's attention, even when up against such an intense screen presence as Clint Eastwood, the star.

When compared to Eastwood during his interview for *Premiere* magazine, McGoohan somewhat coyly commented:

> 'He is very astute, an immense star, a great producer, all the things that I'm not. That's why I don't see how anyone can compare us. Very very skilful. A magnificent career. I very much appreciated the one time I worked with him. Very well organized; never any wasted time. I like that. I dread wasting other people's money. In every film there is so much waste. I think he finished *The Bridges of Madison County* with two weeks to spare, and under budget. Studios really like that.'[21]

In 1981, McGoohan once more appeared on the silver screen, in a low budget horror film *Scanners*. Directed by David Cronenberg, who would make his name with the movie and go on to become a successful director in the genre, it boasted an inventive script and an interesting role for McGoohan. As Dr Paul Ruth, he played a scientist working to destroy a network of 'Scanners', people who have developed horrific telekinetic powers, demonstrated gruesomely at the beginning of the film when a human head graphically explodes on screen. With McGoohan's great dislike of on screen violence it seems surprising that he should allow this scene to make the cut, but at the time he was once more drinking heavily. He simply may not have cared or perhaps he wasn't aware of the full content of the movie (though it would have been hard to miss this scene when reading the script). Shooting *Scanners* was not a happy experience for either McGoohan nor novice director Cronenberg, who noted in *Cronenberg on Cronenberg* (1996):

'...he was so angry. His self-hatred came out as anger against everybody and everything. He said to me, "If I didn't drink I'd be afraid I'd kill someone." He looks at you that way and you just say, "Keep drinking." It's all self-destructive, because it's all self-hating. That's my theory.

He was also terrified. The second before we went to shoot he said, "I'm scared." I wasn't shocked; Olivier said that he was terrified each time he had to go on stage. With Patrick, though, it was just so raw and so scary – full of anger and potent. But he was sensing the disorganization; the script wasn't there, so he was right to worry about it. He didn't know me. He didn't know whether I could bring it off or not. We parted from the film not on very good terms ultimately."[22]

McGoohan's concerns were typical of a man who strove in his own career for perfection, he was always dismayed by what he regarded as shoddy or ill-prepared filmmaking and after the chaos of *Kings and Desperate Men* may have been worried that the low budget *Scanners* would result in a similar mess. In the event, after a low key release, *Scanners* went on to make Cronenberg's name, becoming a cult classic and, in some quarters, a very highly-regarded movie. However, McGoohan was on a downward slide once more. Whenever he was not working, he had taken to finding solace in the bottle. Irish writer and TV producer Paul Duane mentioned on his blog (Some Came Running) that:

'I once met an LA-based actor/bartender who told me that McGoohan came to his bar each morning and drank through till lunchtime, silently. He also told me that McGoohan had, some years back, been told that one of his kids had an incurable illness. Refusing to accept it, he threw himself into amateur medical research and managed, after some years of labour, to find a cure for what ailed his kid. Then he started drinking again.'[23]

This is not the only such story to be found on the internet, usually from eyewitnesses. McGoohan was now drinking all day, every day. Aside from his impressive feat of finding a cure for his daughter, he was effectively an alcoholic. Frustration at the lack of good roles being offered to him and perhaps a sense of failure at not having reached his full potential may have contributed. Perhaps the fact that he had never since found the same creative freedom as he had achieved with *The Prisoner* – and the possibility that he never would again – haunted him.

Enigma

I stated earlier in this book that McGoohan was often referred to in the press as an 'enigma' and during these years he certainly lived up to that epithet. The two most important factors in McGoohan's life had always been family and work. Whilst he still had the close-knit and loving support of his family, work was often more scarce. This would be especially difficult to take for a man who was so used to being able to immerse himself in a variety of projects, a man who thrived on the pressure and challenges of his job.

On July 1st 1982, McGoohan was stopped by the police and charged for drunken driving. Upon being tested, he was found to have three times the legal limit of alcohol in his bloodstream. In addition, it was found that he had been driving with a license that was suspended until 1985 because of an earlier accident. (Nothing further is known about this bar the comment from Assistant Criminal Attorney Schuyler Sprowles that the accident had not been as a result of any criminal activity.) It was clear that McGoohan's alcoholic intake was now making him a threat not just to himself but to others. His battle with drink was to continue and although reports are conflicting, it seemed that

McGoohan managed to abstain from alcohol for long periods at a time, before once again being drawn to the lure of the bottle.

Jamaica Inn and Trespasses

In 1983 McGoohan returned to England once more, making the film *Jamaica Inn*, another high budget TV movie made by HTV, part of the ITV network. Though extremely dismissive of television at the time, he was prepared to accept roles in halfway-house productions like this when it suited him. While TV movies have comparatively parsimonious budgets when compared to their cinema counterparts, their finances and production values are usually much higher than the average TV programme. McGoohan co-starred with Jane Seymour and played the uncle of her character, Mary. This uncle, Joss, was a wild and untamed figure with a Heathcliff-ish air, bent on making her life a misery. Unfailing in his levels of performance, no matter what demons his personal life might contain, McGoohan is at his best. Watching the film now, it is clear that he enjoyed the role and gave it his full care and attention.

Perhaps this was down to the location. Upon his return to the States, he gave an interview to chat show host Mike Bygrave in which he talked about the fact that he rarely returned to the country that had been his home for so many years:

'He denies having been a tax exile these past years.

"I never had a penny in a Swiss bank," he says. "I just felt like a change and that I had done all I could in England. I'm trying to break away from the one-dimensional characters like the warden in *Escape from Alcatraz* and others I've done."

He talks enthusiastically about *Jamaica Inn*. "We had a terrific crew – including some people who'd worked with me on *Danger Man* – as well as Jane Seymour, who's also done well in America and came back for this. It's a melodrama. I went all out for it. Did a bit of roaring. I think we all took our parts by the throat."'[24]

Seymour, though she later recalled being 'tested' by the actor before he would accept her, was equally enthusiastic in her praise for her now-veteran co-star. A strong-willed personality in herself, she would no doubt have found favour with the challenging McGoohan, paving the way for a comparatively easy-going relationship. She stated that:

> 'He's electric, one of the best. To me, in *Jamaica Inn* he was always Joss, not Patrick McGoohan. He's totally professional, very underrated.'[25]

Surprisingly, for someone battling an addiction, the hellraiser had lost none of his power.

Trespasses was a character piece, a movie made entirely in New Zealand. Joan may have decamped with her husband once more for the duration of the shoot, though the career she had built in recent years working as a realtor may have interfered with this. McGoohan plays a lonely widower who is shocked and furious when his daughter runs away to join a commune with sexual morals that do not match his own rather puritanical views. This was ideal casting for McGoohan who, unusually, was full of praise for the project. For the first time in a long while, he enjoyed a satisfactory creative experience. In the US film magazine *Sequence,* he was quoted as saying:

> 'Making a film in New Zealand turned out to be one of the happiest and most rewarding experiences of my professional life. The quality of craftsmanship was a pleasure to be associated with. *Trespasses* is a film in which I have the highest possible expectations. When I first read the script, I was attracted to the idea of conflict between generations. Her (the daughter's) need to break away from a puritanical upbringing – his (the father's) need to keep her love and respect. The challenge of playing the father, the kind of complex character I'd never had the opportunity to show on screen before, was too much to resist."[26]

Also, around this time. Alexis Kanner's troubled post–production work on *Kings and Desperate Men* finally came to an end and the film went on a limited release. McGoohan was yet again being praised to a great extent by critics and noted as giving a standout performance.

Appropriately, as his 'Fall Out' co-conspirator released his own movie, McGoohan's opus was about to make its presence felt in the actor's life once again. In England, Channel 4 was preparing to re- screen the entire series of *The Prisoner*.

The Prisoner Resurfaces: Six Into One

In an effort to keep operation costs within achievable parameters, the channel had been showing a wealth of material which was by this point considered archive programming. The vaults of ITC were being mined particularly deeply as their output mostly existed in colour and in an easily transmittable format. To celebrate the show, now considered a highly-regarded if cultish classic, Channel 4 had commissioned a documentary about the series. Called *Six Into One: The Prisoner File,* Illuminations were hired for the project – one of the small production companies that flourished in the early 1980s with the advent of the publisher/broadcaster. Made from 1983-84, the documentary featured interviews with many of the cast and crew, including David Tomblin and George Markstein. Though he had become increasingly reluctant to discuss the programme during the 70s, a recalcitrant McGoohan was even persuaded to talk about *The Prisoner* for this one-off production.

The agreement was a major coup for the documentary makers and negotiations took some time. McGoohan was happy to play a game of cat and mouse with Chris Rodley and Laurens C. Posthma who would be travelling to the States to conduct and shoot the interview. On the Illuminations website, producer John Wyver reminisced:

'Eventually, Laurens and Chris got on a plane with the promise of a meeting but nothing more. McGoohan directed them to his neighbourhood bar for an early morning get together and they spent a day, with an expensive local crew in tow, driving around the city before, towards twilight, McGoohan relented and sat down in front of the camera with a view of Los Angeles behind.

By the end, it was getting so dark that Laurens had to bring up the camera car and switch on the headlights to illuminate McGoohan's face. Job done – and the interview was thoughtful and comparatively expansive.'[27]

McGoohan gave his most revealing on screen interview about *The Prisoner* during this session. He was just being his usual wary self when meeting strangers he would work with. Before he would sit down and commit his thoughts to tape, McGoohan would (like any high profile actor) have wanted to test these two new interlopers, making sure their motivations were honest and that he was not going to be misrepresented. Through previous experience with journalists, as well as his own understanding of the post-production process, he would have been familiar with the way in which judicious editing can alter the meaning of a person's utterances. Rodley and Posthma had evidently met with approval, however, and with the interview successfully concluded, they must have breathed a sigh of relief. This was perhaps premature; McGoohan was never going to let them off so easily. John Wyver recounts:

> '…true to his reputation, McGoohan wanted nothing to do with a release form to allow us to use the interview. (He had supposedly never signed his contract with Lew Grade for *The Prisoner*, which it's said is one of the reasons why no movie version has appeared to date and why it's taken so long for the television re-make, now shot but not yet screened, to appear.) Chris and Laurens flew home and negotiations continued about the release form. I think McGoohan flew to Paris just before Christmas, and the faxes followed him there. We, however, had to own up to Channel 4 that we had a great interview, a pretty good programme, but no release form. Eventually, I was summoned to a meeting with Channel Controller Paul Bonner. He growled at me, and right through Christmas I worried about whether Illuminations would get paid and whether the documentary would be shown. McGoohan never did sign a release, but Channel 4 went ahead anyway.'[28]

Upon seeing the completed documentary, before it was broadcast on Channel 4, McGoohan was incensed; mainly at the commentary from George Markstein. He had expressed displeasure earlier about the inclusion of Markstein, growling that 'If he's on it, then I'm off,' but had nonetheless consented to the interview. As mentioned earlier, Markstein was not impressed with either McGoohan or *The Prisoner* and used the documentary to make his feelings quite clear about both. In his interview, Markstein claimed once again that the original genesis of the series was his and, whatever the truth, McGoohan did not come out of the documentary untainted.

Though sufficient time had elapsed for McGoohan to be openly reflective and regretful of his behaviour at the time, to have Markstein twisting the knife on screen was more than he could bear. He was motivated to take a stance once again and with the help of his daughter Catherine, made a short 'right of reply' video which he sent to the production team. Generally known as 'The LA Tape', this consists of an interview with McGoohan in which he states his own feelings about the series. Designed to be re-cut into the documentary, replacing the original footage shot by the production team, the tape arrived too late to the office for inclusion, though it is obliquely referred to at the very end.

During the course of the new interview McGoohan takes particular issue with Markstein's assertion that Number 6 was John Drake, pointing out that John Drake would most likely have escaped from The Village whereas, in one of the most definitive statements he ever made about the series, Number 6 'Never did. He thought he did'. He is careful to appear generous enough to give Markstein due credit for finding the series writers and helping to craft the script of 'Arrival' and runs through several of his usual themes – the meaning of the penny-farthing, the genesis of Rover – obviously answering the same general set of questions, sometimes giving the answers almost verbatim. McGoohan chooses to expand, however, and includes an interesting response to the question of whether he found it difficult to direct himself as an actor:

'In some respects it's easy, because you certainly can't blame anybody else if you get it wrong and it does save a lot of discussion between the director and the person playing the leading part, I think it saves time. The danger of it is that one has to always be extra self-critical and it is essential to always have someone behind you … you think you can see yourself as well as doing it but I don't know anyone who can do that, you have to have someone behind the camera that you can rely on.'[29]

McGoohan goes on to comment that the writing of the partially autobiographical 'Once Upon a Time' had allowed him to 'get that stuff' out of his system, then reiterates his point that the ending of 'Fall Out' depicts a man who has failed to escape. He leans into the camera at this point and directly address the audience, softly asking, 'We never escape … do we?', his voice rising with a quizzical tone at the end. (No doubt the question was addressed not only to the audience, but to the filmmakers also.)

When fed his own question asking whether he has any further plans involving *The Prisoner*, McGoohan answers, while casually playing with a pair of tiny child's shoes, that he has re-cut the entire series into four hours' worth of film. This has been done, he notes, off-handedly demonstrating his fascination with production technology, on 'one inch videotape.' This had rapidly become the predominant broadcast production format at the time and indicated that there must have been some budget attached. The re-cut would be fascinating to watch. However, like many of McGoohan's semi-amateur productions alluded to over the years, it remains tucked away in the family archives, maybe never to see the light of day.

In any case, when discussing this piece McGoohan wryly suggests that he is 'open to offers' on this piece before he responds to another question: 'Do you believe in fantasy and fairytales?'. Still fiddling with the shoes, he answers: 'I don't know how anyone can live without fantasy and fairytales.' He then speaks of a 'distant cousin' of *The Prisoner* that he has been developing which is set in the year 3000. The human race has lost the power of speech, long since having abandoned such crude means of communication for telepathy and other types of computerised thought-transfer, all of which suddenly goes wrong at a point of national conflict. In order to save their civilisation, these advanced humans have to visit a tribe who have been exiled from society for keeping alive the gift of speech. McGoohan explains with relish how the advanced species have to abandon their progressive ways and revert to what they consider as primitivism. The tribe was expelled because they were rebels who refused to conform. It's an intriguing, if heavy-handed, concept that expressed the actor's familiar concerns: the speed of progress, the importance of the individual. The title of this piece was '*Stop*'.

McGoohan is asked finally what his current projects are and he speaks with surprising enthusiasm about his latest role in a Walt Disney movie *Baby: Secret of the Lost Legend* (1985).

> 'This is, I think, a lovely delightful story and it's called *"Baby"* and it's about things that go on in Africa where a little baby dinosaur is discovered and a mama and a papa dinosaur and I think that's nice. And the same fellow that made *ET* has made the dinosaurs so they've got to be very lovable and I'm looking forward to that very much indeed, I have great hopes for it.'[30]

Where McGoohan's original interview ended with him declaring that 'the sky is the limit', he makes a direct reversal in this version, ending with the words:

> 'One can think that, after all, the sky is not the limit. We've found that out haven't we, since we've been exploring a bit. Be seeing you. I hope.'

The LA Tape then segues into a peculiar, presumably improvised sequence. McGoohan is seen wandering his favourite beaches, where he once took early morning runs, occasionally drawing coat hangers in the sand, to the soundtrack of 'An English Country Garden'.

It could be argued that McGoohan plays these scenes in character as Number 6 and the use of coat hangers is certainly open to interpretation (perhaps he was taking advantage of the fact that at the top of every coat hanger is a question mark). The audiovisual montage continues with snatches of interview inter-cut with beach footage. Then it ends with an amusing sequence in which a conversation between McGoohan and the off-camera personnel is slowly drowned out by Ron Grainer's music, echoing Number 6's attempted speechmaking in 'Fall Out'. He reiterates that the sky is not the limit and confesses that he finds this 'frightening'. Then he simply walks off into the sea – like the lead character from the classic UK sitcom *The Fall and Rise of Reginald Perrin* (though without the nudity) – as the music ends and Leo McKern's mocking laugh echoes over the final frames.

Baby In Reality

Despite his hopes for the project, *Baby* would turn out to be an extraordinarily bad film, let down hugely by the astonishingly unconvincing dinosaurs. 'The man who made *ET*' must have found his genius deserting him when he crafted these creatures and their lack of authenticity undermines any scene in which they feature. Delighted to have the chance to once again make a family film for Disney, McGoohan had taken the role of the villain, Dr Eric Kivat, in opposition to sappy palaeontologist couple William Katt and Sean Young.

Though intrigued by its premise, McGoohan was later to regret his involvement in the film, which had no doubt been instigated by casting director Rose Tobias Shaw (who worked also on *The Prisoner*). While the film depicted a surprisingly realistic South Africa, full of warfare and bloodshed, the awkward nature of the dinosaur effects gave the finished movie an uneven texture. Though the production was besieged by technical hitches, mostly concerning these animatronic dinosaurs, McGoohan explained what to his mind had been the greatest problem in his *Premiere* interview:

> 'That all took place in the Ivory Coast. A remarkable script! When I read it, I thought that it would be a new *ET*. I play a kind of mad palaeontologist who believes that there are still dinosaurs in out-of-the-way places…
>
> Unhappily, once we were on location, the producers called in another scriptwriter, who rewrote the story and destroyed it … That was just the intervention of imbeciles. The Disney company was doing very badly at the time. Very disorganized.'[31]

Once again, McGoohan had been disappointed, his continual quest for excellence, not just in his own performance but in the material in which he was appearing, thwarted. Fingers badly burnt, he would not take on another film role until a little-known actor named Mel Gibson got in touch in the middle of the next decade.

Disenchantment and Broadway

McGoohan's career follows a pattern of disenchantment. Virtually repeating his activities of the late 1950s, after his disillusionment with Rank, now heartily fed up with films after the *Baby* debacle, McGoohan returned to television, to appear in the American Playhouse presentation *Three Sovereigns for Sarah*. This was a TV movie starring Vanessa Redgrave, set during the Salem witch trials. At short notice, McGoohan took the small but prominent role of chief magistrate, replacing James Mason who had died not long before production began. His faculty for memorising lines would have come in useful, his Rep training allowing him once more to go on with little preparation time. But then working at speed was always McGoohan's natural preference. He took on little other work around this time, presumably throwing himself into unrelated projects and for his next acting role, decided once more to eschew Hollywood.

In December 1984, *The New York Times* announced that McGoohan was to return to his original home, the stage, in a Broadway production of Hugh Whitmore's *Pack of Lies*.

There had been hints that McGoohan was considering such a move before. Around the time of filming *Jamaica Inn*, he remarked in an interview for *The Mail on Sunday* that he was considering appearing in a new production of *Moby Dick*. This would be staged in Manchester, set up by Michael Elliot, one of the founding members of the Theatre 59 company that had produced McGoohan's groundbreaking *Brand*.[32] However, a later report had a source close to the project commenting that McGoohan had pulled out, saying that he no longer had the confidence to act on stage. Just like his shy sixteen-year-old self, it seemed McGoohan was once more unable to summon up the courage to get through the doors. Perhaps his long absence from the stage had taken its toll on his confidence.

Thankfully, he evidently managed to conquer his anxieties enough to return to the theatre in 1984 for the 120-night run of *Pack of Lies*. In this spy thriller, based on a true story, McGoohan played a British Intelligence operative called Stewart: a cold-hearted agent, dedicated to his work. He admitted in several interviews to going into the performance in a state of total fear, perhaps exacerbated by the fact that although he had played on many high profile stages in his time, this was the actor's first appearance on Broadway.

In a rare interview from this time, McGoohan confided that whilst the play was in good shape, the rehearsals were at 'that awkward stage when you've just learned the lines and therefore haven't been able to do anything with them.'[33] He also appeared on *The Today Show* in the states to promote the piece and gave an interview with freelance journalist Gay Search. McGoohan seemed to be enjoying himself, giving a precise if somewhat extensive account of the plot of the play, and offering the opinion that his character was a good man. The interview features a brief clip of the play which shows McGoohan giving a clipped and largely emotionless performance. Though it is impossible to ascertain his range in the part from less than a minute of footage, it seems to be of his usual high standard.

The play was a character piece about two families who were neighbours. When McGoohan's character arrives at the house of one couple, he informs them that their neighbours are spies, then commandeers their domicile as the base for his own activities. The reviews, thankfully were almost uniformly positive, with only one critic noting that he had found McGoohan's 'automaton like condescension unreal'[34] but this criticism was swamped by glowing praise from other sources such as:

'a performance of glinting power'[35]

'Mr. Martin, as Miss Harris's congenitally weak-kneed husband, and Mr. McGoohan, an icily silverfox of an intelligence technician, are ideally cast.'[36]

'McGoohan was charming and bitterly cool in a smart, powerful, superbly-placed performance, in a role perfectly suited to the grey-haired actor.'[37]

The play became a Broadway hit, and McGoohan felt vindicated. He had taken something of a personal gamble by returning to the stage, exposed and as he noted 'without retakes' for the first time in years.

That he was once again able to demonstrate his mastery of the craft to himself as well as to an audience would have bolstered his confidence. Perhaps McGoohan merely wanted to prove to himself that he could still excel on stage, for he never again trod the boards after this final long run on Broadway.

'The basic function of our business is standing up on a little raised platform and saying words with people watching and listening. I think I've been negligent in not going back oftener in all these years. You have one take, and if you make a mistake they're all watching you make it and that's a good challenge. It gets the adrenalin going'.[38]

CHAPTER 9
An Enigmatic Legacy

McGoohan entered 1986 with a lead role in the TV movie *In Pure Blood,* an involving character drama about the Nazi's eugenics program. Lee Remick played Alicia, an American beauty who finds that her DNA hides a sinister secret. Her uncle, McGoohan, idolised her father, an SS officer, who was expected to produce a certain number of offspring as part of the program, which he still upholds. By the conclusion, the uncle is forced to confront his beliefs, finding that his love for his niece overrides them. McGoohan gave a complex performance to suit the character, allowing the viewer an insight into the mind as it slowly changes, again apparently without doing very much. For a performer who could so easily portray explosive emotions, McGoohan was still a master of minimalism, able to convey meaning with the tiniest of facial tics or gestures.

Lee Remick, as the niece, gave a performance worthy of her co-star who seemed to have found a natural home in the TV movie. The film also featured, in a small but prominent role, McGoohan's daughter Catherine, now a successful actress in her own right and the only one of his children to follow him into the profession.

In 1987, McGoohan took a role in the hugely popular detective series *Murder She Wrote* staring Angela Lansbury. As much of a US TV legend as *Columbo*, this was another high profile appearance in what was generally considered to be a high quality series. McGoohan played Oliver Quayle, a Defence Attorney, and approached the part with an overblown relish that was perfectly judged for the material. His performance is by no means naturalistic and is all the better for it, making him intensely commanding on screen. It seems he spent the remainder of the decade away from work, presumably relaxing with his family, spending time in Montana and endlessly writing. Ideas had begun to ferment in his mind, loosely based around the same themes that still vexed McGoohan, themes he had explored in *The Prisoner* and now felt able to return to.

When interviewed for Issue 31 of *Number Six* magazine, published in the spring of 1991, Bernie Williams, who was the production manager of *The Prisoner* and long-time friend of McGoohan, tells an intriguing story.

> 'I was approached by Samuel Goldwyn Jr about two or three years ago and asked if there was any way I could get Patrick interested in doing a movie about *The Prisoner*. So I said "Yeah, I think so. It's possible, I don't know. I haven't spoken to Pat for so long." So I got together with Patrick and he showed a sort of interest but he felt that *The Prisoner* had been done and finished and completed and there was no more *Prisoner* for him other than to move on with it.
>
> So we went to meet Samuel Goldwyn Jr who is a typical Hollywood mogul who wants you to go out and write the script at your own expense in your own time – however long it takes – then you come back, show him the material and he can say whether he likes it or not ... that's not a good deal, that's a stupid deal ... Patrick took that position: "Hey, if you want to make it come to me with an intelligent offer and I'll get on with it, otherwise, forget it."'[1]

This anecdote demonstrates that McGoohan's series was not only held in high regard by discerning TV critics and viewers, as well as a growing legion of fans, but had also attracted the interest of one of the major names in Hollywood. It also shows his reluctance to be treated in the same way as many writers and actors involved in the Hollywood machine.

Acceptance and Respite

Despite the abuse of his body with alcohol, tobacco and perhaps other substances on occasion, McGoohan had aged well. He continued to be defined by *The Prisoner*, most of the interviews from the last decades of his life still concern the series. His perspective on the series fluctuates between irritation and acceptance, and sometimes even pride. By now, the series had grown to be a highly respected cult show. It was widely regarded as a gem of 1960s television, a remarkably prescient work which would continue to find new fans (newcomers finding its themes are as relevant today as they were at the time of its conception). He must have been touched to know his work was held in such high esteem, not just by its fans but by fellow professionals, his peers.

In 1977 he had graciously accepted the honorary presidency of Six Of One, the appreciation society set up around the show, professing to be 'profoundly grateful' for their continued interest. By the late 80s he appears to have come to terms with the fact that although he had been profoundly disappointed by the series, it had survived intact and with its release on VHS was undergoing a resurgence of interest. He became prone to giving more in-depth interviews about the show, perhaps no longer feeling the need to distance himself from what had once been viewed as a glorious failure, a mere folly. Consequently, he was happy to talk about it in some detail in 1990 with Howard Foy, editor of the television magazine *The Box*.

McGoohan was making a brief visit to England appearing at the NEC in Birmingham where the annual motor show was being held. There, he was presented with his own Caterham 7, the first of a limited edition range of the kit car painted in its *Prisoner* livery of green and yellow and with McGoohan's signature embossed into the dashboard of each one. No doubt McGoohan was in a good mood, having been presented with his own sports car for a programme he had made over two decades previously. He certainly gave Foy an expansive interview, revealing that he had advanced plans and scripts for a mini-series that could loosely be seen as a continuation of *The Prisoner* and that he was currently looking for a natural home for the project:

'It's finding someone who is sympathetic to it who is going to give it the freedom really, and that could be in the states or here or who knows, it might be in Australia! It's got a lot of deserts in it! It's also got igloos in it!'[2]

McGoohan revealed nothing particularly new about the production of the series or his feelings about it but did use the platform to express his fury at two advertising campaigns which had used the themes and iconography of his series. One particularly invoked his ire, for the extremely middle of the road vehicle the Renault 21:

'My first reaction was fury. First of all, not knowing about it – I was told about it by people that wrote to me and called me from England – but also the fact that they're using the series to promote a family car. I think it was a con job.'[3]

McGoohan is presumably railing against the homogeneity of the car rather than its ability to carry a family. However, it must have been galling to see his defining statement against the establishment co-opted into a sales pitch – particularly given his views on the subtle and pervasive influence of advertising. He also expressed a certain discomfort about how much of a cult his series had become referring to the fan club Six of One in provocative tones:

'I don't want to knock Six of One. There are a lot of innocent people there who genuinely believe that that is something very important and with Six of One one has to be careful about it. But when one is talking in general about fan clubs that become cults no matter whether it is that or whether it is the followers of rock bands or whatever it is, there comes a point which is a crossover point when the appreciation which is what it originally was intended to be turns into something else and I can't think of the word … it's a step into cultism. In the end it's got nothing to do with the subject it's become a sort of entity in itself.'[4]

Of course, his comments could apply to any of the *Prisoner* fan clubs that have since emerged. McGoohan had always disliked the idea of being put on a platform simply because of the job he did for a living and no doubt felt a sense of responsibility in part for those 'innocent' members of Six of One and other groups, who had succumbed to his 'cult'.

He continued his discussion with Howard Foy by mentioning that he was currently writing two novels, completely unconnected, one of which was called *'Escape'*. He also expressed his distaste for the idea of walking into a bookshop and finding an unauthorised biography of his life, though he enthuses about his love for biographies of others.

The interview reveals that McGoohan remained engaged by the possibilities now emerging in television, the digital revolution was underway and new channels were being created and disintegrating with great speed on both sides of the Atlantic. The stranglehold of the biggest media providers had been shaken apart and through the cracks flourished new companies and ideologies. McGoohan explained that he felt the time was right to make a return to his original intention of the actor-manager, taking on complete control of another TV programme, exercising the auteurship he had wielded over *The Prisoner* once more. The wounds from that series had clearly healed, but then a free sports car will always help with that:

'I think at this time it is probably very good. The market has become so diverse and the networks are being challenged left right and centre by these sort of maverick companies like Fox who are doing extremely well right now with these far out shows … you know *The Simpsons* is on against *Cosby* on Thursday nights over in the States and doing well and there are three or four others that knock the old formats. I think it's a good time now and these guys in the networks are looking for something different. Well, by golly, I've got it if they want it! But I don't want to go in half-assed as they say until I've got it in a form that I can say, "This is it. This is the way it will be and if you don't like it…"[5]

What became of this new idea is unknown, but McGoohan would return in interviews several times to a series or film which expressed the same basic concerns as *The Prisoner* and sometimes even had direct connections. As with every creative, the public reaction to his work mattered and McGoohan could now, if he wished, hold his head high and accept that he had created something remarkable. He had just been given a fantastic car and was about to receive the second affirmation of his talents in as many days. A short time before *The Box* interview was conducted, McGoohan received the news in his Birmingham hotel room, that he had just won another Emmy for an episode of *Columbo*, 'Agenda for Murder', in which he had played Oscar Finch, a brilliant attorney who murders a man to cover up his own past. The visible interplay between McGoohan and Falk was sparkling in this episode and it is usually rated as being one of the best. McGoohan must have been doubly pleased at the honour as he had also directed the instalment. In *The Box* interview McGoohan explained in typically down-to-earth terms how the assignment had come about:

> 'Peter (Falk) gave me a call and I got one together for him and I directed it and he talked me into acting in it so I acted in it and it turned out all right ... As a job? Well if it means writing it and directing it and acting in it and winning an Emmy I think that's a good formula.'[6]

Back to Britain: Best of Friends

No doubt the confidence instilled by these events, and by McGoohan's eventual realisation that *The Prisoner* was indeed of some worth, would have triggered a flurry of activity in the early 1990s. Unfortunately, in 1991 McGoohan fell ill. He had planned that in May that year he would take Joan back to Sheffield for their wedding anniversary. They would hire a tandem on which they could ride around the city and the peak district, visiting their old haunts and reliving their earliest days together. To his annoyance, McGoohan had to abandon this romantic plan. He just wasn't well enough to take on anything physically taxing.

He did, however, manage to make the trip back to England to appear in a videotaped drama of the play *The Best of Friends*. This was shot in a multi-camera studio, much as his early teleplays had been, though with the benefit of an edit suite that relied on sophisticated electronics rather than a razor blade and Sellotape.

The Best Of Friends was directed by Alvin Rakoff, a veteran of Armchair Theatre, which was known for the groundbreaking series of original plays produced by Sydney Newman for ABC television between 1956 and 1974. Rakoff had never worked with McGoohan during that time. He had, however, come close to casting the actor for various productions and had submitted a script to *Danger Man* at one point. Later in the decade, he had also been fascinated by *The Prisoner*. Rakoff had a great deal of respect for McGoohan as an actor, ranking him as one of the best he had ever seen, and offered him the part of George Bernard Shaw.

Rakoff was kind enough to explain to me the circumstances of how McGoohan had come to be cast. He was brought in to replace Ray McNally, who had played Shaw in the stage version, alongside Sir John Gielgud, but who had since died:

> 'We … the writer Hugh Whitmore and I … we thought of this crazy idea of seeing whether Patrick would be interested. He was. The initial approach was very simple, I sent him the script, told him that it had Sir John and Wendy Hiller in it, and he came back almost immediately saying he would do it.'

Rakoff was prepared for fireworks. Hugh Whitmore had written *Pack Of Lies* which McGoohan had performed in Broadway and had been exposed to the star's fiery persona. He had no doubt warned Rakoff off, though by this time it was hardly industry news that McGoohan could at times be very hard to handle. He was certainly strongly opinionated and liable to ride roughshod over any director he did not think was pulling his weight or lacked the capability to create a quality production. However, quite unexpectedly, Rakoff was immediately put at his ease as McGoohan made a generous gesture to his fellow actors:

> 'On the first day of rehearsal, the first thing he did was to go up to Sir John and Wendy Hiller and say, "I'm sorry Ray isn't here to do it for you." This was a wonderful thing to say and such the antithesis of what I had expected because Hugh had worked with him before, Hugh knew him and I didn't, but within the first few minutes of meeting him he did this gesture which I thought was so wonderful. So any fears of irascibility disappeared and I realised that he was a very genuine man who took his work seriously.'[7]

McGoohan and Rakoff developed an instant rapport and enjoyed a fruitful working relationship. Both men held the other in great esteem, McGoohan being quite aware of Rakoff's remarkable record as a director and his passion for quality that matched the actor's own. Though he was prone to 'testing' his colleagues, Rakoff recalled no such occurrence, enthusing at how ready McGoohan was to collaborate and give the director what he wanted:

'I've always found that actors who have directed themselves are very directable. They always know where you're coming from. He was a very directable actor, for me, at that stage. He was an older man so maybe a lot of the fire had gone out of him but I don't think so, if you watch the performance it's in there.'

In 1984, Jane Merrow, McGoohan's co-star from *Danger Man* and 'The Schizoid Man' met up him while working in the States. She later described in an interview printed in Issue One of *In The Village* that:

'I went down and had lunch with him and he was a very mellow man. He was not the powerhouse that I remember which was probably happier for him but I thought it was rather sad in a way because he was such a dynamic man'.[8]

Though McGoohan had become disillusioned during the filming of 'The Schizoid Man', which may explain his subdued air at the time, there are several stories throughout the 80s and 90s that have him as somehow a shadow of his former self, drained by illness and perhaps by alcohol abuse. There was, however, nothing of this kind on show during the making of *The Best Of Friends*. McGoohan was energised and inspired by his co-stars and director. As Rakoff recalls:

'He enjoyed the rehearsal period, he admired Sir John, he admired Wendy, they were a happy trio, they arrived together, they worked together very hard. We experimented with a few things. He was a perfectionist and so am I and the other two were not slouches at that. Patrick was a very fine actor. A great help, a great support.'

Rock Solid Marriage

As on many other occasions, McGoohan had brought Joan and one of his daughters with him for the short production period. Joan often accompanied him to the rehearsal rooms, no doubt providing the same quietly whispered support and relevant notes as she always had. Rakoff's impression of Joan was that she was as devoted to her husband as he was to her.

> 'He and I were both well married men. We both knew that marriage is not easy and that a good marriage … you hold on to! He was very considerate of his wife … You could see it was a good relationship. Some marriages pretend to be good relationships, some really are.'

This first hand account echoes everything that has been said or written about Patrick and Joan. Though Alvin Rakoff also recalled an event that took place in a private rehearsal room, where one of McGoohan's old bugbears raised its head during the rehearsal period, perhaps due to his wife's close proximity:

> 'I only saw his anger or annoyance once, I had a very good dance instructor, Geraldine Stephenson and she was trying to teach him how to do the tango, and to do the tango, she was saying "Imagine you have a woman there…"
>
> And Geraldine was older than any of us, she was well past Patrick's age but a dancer, with all the lithe movement, you know. She said, "Come on, grab a hold of me!" … they were back to back, her back was in his body, and she said, "Come on Patrick, grab me like you want to fuck me!". That brought a certain coldness to the dance lesson that day. There was something innate in the Catholicism that got to him in the early days and he felt that was wrong.'

The production was shot over four days, a very leisurely time to produce one hour of material, giving Rakoff and his actors the space to explore and refine. They took full advantage of this, producing some tremendous performances. From four such experienced collaborators, nothing less would be expected, but Rakoff remembers that there was a particular determination in the air, a definite sense that they all believed very much in the project. It was something they all wanted to do and do to the very best of their ability. McGoohan was in his element, working with people he liked and respected and who respected him. However, after many years spent acting in the single camera world of most American TV shows, or lavishly budgeted TV movies, he was less sure than he had once been in the multi-camera studio environment:

'When we got to the studio I rehearsed it on the floor standing amongst the cameras then went to do his long speech, when he talks about his return from Jerusalem, when he's brought the stones for the abbess, and I went to the control room to record it and we started to record it and he suddenly stopped.

We finished recording and I came down and asked, "What's the problem?" and he said, "The problem was I expected you to be standing there." We did it again and this time I stood downstairs and told them to record every camera. So he wasn't as used to multi-camera. I thought it was very flattering that an actor as great as Patrick McGoohan wanted me standing there!'

Despite this minor slip, Rakoff found that there were no insecurities on display. Many actors make a point of saying how down they are on their performance without necessarily meaning it, presumably fishing for compliments. This was entirely possible, of course, but McGoohan had a very deep honesty about him and if he criticised his own performance there was likely a better reason, at least in his mind, than merely looking for approbation. He was always inclined to be less confident in his own abilities when his confidence in the production had been shaken, usually by the director, but in Rakoff he had a hugely experienced and talented guiding hand. He was enjoying himself.

Plot and Reviews

Best of Friends features a parable of 'The Black Girl' shot in a completely different style to the rest of the play, in which the eponymous character is seen nude on screen several times. One might have expected

McGoohan to have been worried by this material but Rakoff recalled no objections being raised. The relevant scenes were shot on a closed set and on a separate day, so the actor would not have been in studio at the same time as the actress appearing naked. More significantly perhaps, the inclusion of nudity was perfectly justifiable in terms of the story. It was, after all, gratuitous nudity and sex which the principled actor objected to. Alvin recalled wryly that the scenes caused far less offence to McGoohan than they did to the American networks when the programme was sold aboard.

The play received excellent reviews in both the UK and America, with all three actors being singled out for much-deserved praise. McGoohan in particular was on stand-out form as Shaw, inhabiting the man completely, so much so that he received the approval of co-star Wendy Hiller who, as a young actress, had been a favourite of Shaw's. It is a performance of which he was rightly proud. The *New York Times* took a particular delight in seeing three such experienced heavyweights taking the TV stage:

> 'Three old pros take over Masterpiece Theatre this Sunday night to illuminate ways of life and methods of acting that have regrettably become endangered species. The three actors are John Gielgud, 88, Wendy Hiller, 80, and Patrick McGoohan, a mere 65. The latter impersonates the playwright George Bernard Shaw. Performing on a fluid set of connecting rooms that can serve as anything from a drawing room to an abbey cell, the actors wander about easily but never touching. Mr McGoohan manages to make Shaw ingratiatingly testy whilst the luminous Miss Hiller's very presence brings an added dimension to the production.'[9]

There is a knowing chuckle to be had at one moment in the play as Hiller's devout Nun describes Shaw thus: 'He has such a pretty knack of turning on one with a whimsical smile, just when you think you've caught him.' A delightful description of Shaw yet an even more apposite one for McGoohan whose attitude had frequently been known to change from approbation to condemnation in a heartbeat.

His association with Alvin Rakoff might have gone further at this point as the director related to me:

'Post *Best of Friends*, he went to see my accountant ... not my agent, but my accountant! I had a call from my accountant saying, "Well, if what I've just heard is true, you're about to become one of the richest men in Britain." And Patrick wanted to start, which we had discussed, a film production company with he and I as co-partners. And we vowed to stay in touch, we did all those things we said we would form this company and erm ... do pigs fly? But we stayed in touch for about a year. But that euphoria of an actor having had a successful collaboration with a director is not something I'm used to. We got carried away, it was a happy relationship that we wanted to go on longer but it couldn't because we were thousands of miles apart. Had the web been in existence then, McGoohan/Rakoff productions might have been a serious contender in the film world!'

I would have liked to have seen that ongoing collaboration, almost as much as Alvin's accountant.

Confidence Tricks and New Ideas

In December 1991, *The Observer* magazine published an interview with McGoohan by Andrew Billen. It wasn't much of an interview to judge from what was printed, with half of the article being taken up with a commentary *about* McGoohan from Peter Sallis, his friend from Sheffield Rep. Sallis explains that McGoohan had kept in touch through the years, taking a particular interest in Sallis' son, Crispian. He had not lost his sensitive side in later years. Apparently he even wrote the boy a poem during a bout of insomnia.

Sallis made a few other telling revelations, about events throughout McGoohan's life, pointing out that McGoohan had very little confidence in his abilities. It seems he swung from supreme confidence to a crippling lack of it, rather than remaining constant either way.

No matter what job he was working on, however, he was always thoroughly prepared and focused. It was this dedication that had ensured such a remarkably positive run of reviews over such a long career. Yet the reviews would have meant nothing to McGoohan if his own personal standards had not been met. He would have considered himself a failure. Sallis recounted why McGoohan had decided to pull out of the new version of *Moby Dick* on the Manchester stage in 1983:

> 'It's the only thing we disagree about. He thinks he can't act and I think he can … he saw the finished product of the *Jamaica Inn* series. Well I thought it was just fine but Patrick wrote to me saying, "It's no good, I can't act!" and pulled out.'[10]

And on recalling *Brand*:

> 'Patrick's wife Joan turned to him and said, very quietly, "You didn't do it, not tonight," and Patrick said, 'I know. I didn't.' Now if I tell you that the only people in the audience not on their feet applauding Patrick were those actually standing on their seats, you will realise that was not how anyone else saw it.'

Joan was more focused than anyone on her husband's performance, knowing intimately his weaknesses as well as his strengths, and was as crushingly honest with him as he was with others. She knew that to improve, he had to be told what he had done badly and McGoohan trusted her opinion implicitly.

The Observer interview 'proper' revealed one major fact. McGoohan stated that he was working on two novels, a *Columbo* script and a major film project. He revealed that the film was going to be a sequel to *The Prisoner*, set on a ruined Earth in 2101 and featuring himself as the great grandson of Number 6. Though he reveals little of the story other than the fact that it is set in a great glass-domed area, all that is left habitable on the planet, he mentioned that the title was '*The Prisoners*' and that he was moving forward in negotiations with a major studio to make the movie a reality. Sadly, like many of McGoohan's tirelessly inventive ideas, it was never to see the light of day. I imagine that somewhere along the line he refused to compromise over an element of the plot or production values, with the usual consequences.

However, plans were now being put in place for a large scale theatrical remake of *The Prisoner*, rumours of which would persist throughout the 90s. David Tomblin recalled in the Winter 1992 issue of *Number Six* that although their partnership had long since dissolved, their friendship had endured. While Tomblin was working recently in the States he had met with McGoohan who mentioned that he had been writing a script which would explore what had happened to Number 6 post *The Prisoner*. It seems that McGoohan had many ideas about a new take on the series, none of which would ever come to fruition but which he must have spent a great deal of time working on in 1993.

The Mid 90s

Back in England in early 1994, an episode of *Danger Man* was shown as part of Channel 4's 'TV Heaven' season. This was followed the week after by 'The Girl Who Was Death', prompting a renewed flurry of interest in McGoohan and in *The Prisoner*. However, by this stage, the actor was a prisoner of his health. He had been unwell for some time but had refused, dogmatically, to seek medical attention. On February 15th 1994, he was suddenly admitted to hospital. US paper *The National Enquirer*, bastion of reliable and unembroidered reportage, ran a piece on McGoohan's illness, inventing a cancer scare that was picked up by several other news outlets. I summarise the piece here:

> '…the once dashing star, now a thin and trembling man of 64, was rushed to St John's hospital in Santa Monica with gut-wrenching stomach pains and an irregular heartbeat on February 15th. "My father had very bad abdominal pain and the first thing any man of that age thinks of is cancer," revealed his daughter, Ann. Ann confided to a friend: "We were all very frightened and concerned because we didn't know what was going on inside him."

Hardly a cancer scare, later in the article McGoohan himself admitted that it was the first thought to come to him but no more than that. McGoohan's condition deteriorated and by the 20th he had developed pneumonia, which made it impossible for the medical staff to perform the tests to ascertain exactly what was wrong with him. Doctors stabilised his condition with massive doses of antibiotics and it was discovered finally that he was suffering from diverticulitis, an inflammation of the large intestine, usually caused by a blockage. Though potentially life-threatening, the condition was routinely operable and on February 29th McGoohan underwent surgery to remove the blocked section of intestine. *The National Enquirer* continues the story:

> 'His daughter Ann and other family members were constant visitors to the hospital. And following the surgery, his wife Joan took up a vigil in the room. "Joan sat by Patrick's bedside, holding his hand and wiping his forehead with a damp washcloth every day and night," said an insider. "She said, 'Please Patrick, tell me you are going to get better. Be strong. I love you very much." Joan stayed overnight, sleeping in a recliner by her husband.'[11]

Though this story may well suffer from the degree of exaggeration one might expect from such a source, there is nothing out of character in Joan spending every hour with her ailing husband. McGoohan was to make a full recovery, though the experience had drained him somewhat and he was apparently inactive for several months (somehow I doubt that he stopped working, even when bedridden). He occupied himself with property affairs, according to the *Premiere* interview at this time, and had been writing a great deal. His name was consistently linked with some form of remake or re-imagining of *The Prisoner* and perhaps prompted by his meeting in the late 1980s with Samuel Goldwyn Jr he had begun to take the possibilities seriously.

In August 1994, during a *Prisoner* convention being staged in Portmeirion by Six Of One, ITC International publicity consultant Frank Ratcliffe announced to the surprised crowd that the cameras would roll on a new *Prisoner* film the following year. A surprisingly bold statement, the proposed film once more failed to materialise. McGoohan's stance on the production at this time is unknown, nor even his level of involvement, if any. However, during my earliest research for this book, I exchanged several emails with Pat Gadsby, previously a props supplier for film and TV, who was looking into props for this new *Prisoner* film:

'It was about sixteen years ago, maybe more, that I was supplying computers, expertise and whatever as props for film and TV productions. I was asked to quote for a room full of computers and to supply a laptop that was to fall out of the overhead baggage storage on an aircraft – it was to land on some poor sod's head. The designer wanted it to be a Toshiba as he thought that was the best model to use (I think he had one). They got a bit concerned when I pointed out that the lightest Tosh available weighed about 15 lbs and would probably brain the actor (assuming that was possible). The production just disappeared without any information as to why it stopped.'

Gadsby also recalled hearing that McGoohan had lost the rights to *The Prisoner* in a game of poker. There were all sorts of stories that would continue and mutate, sometimes McGoohan was involved, sometimes not. There is an entirely separate book to be written about the machinations to bring *The Prisoner* back to the screen. In fact, this feat was not achieved until the ITV remake of 2009, which was received with intensely varied reviews and starred Jim Caviezel, best known for playing Jesus in Mel Gibson's controversial *The Passion of the Christ* (2004).

Braveheart

Coincidentally, it was also Mel Gibson who would give McGoohan his last big film role, that of Edward Longshanks, the villainous king of England, in Gibson's sword-waving semi-historical epic *Braveheart* (1995). Gibson, like Alvin Rakoff, had long been an admirer of McGoohan and particularly of *The Prisoner*. In an unattributed interview that can be found on a variety of internet sites, Gibson explained how he had cast McGoohan:

'I was looking for someone to play King Edward, and no one was right. One day the casting lady said, "Well, there's always Pat McGoohan." I thought he was dead! (laughs). She said, "No, he lives over in Los Angeles." I was like, "Then f**kin' call him!" So I came back here and met him in a restaurant and offered it to him because I remember him in the old days in TV shows like *Secret Agent* and *The Prisoner*, which was very cutting edge for its time, still is actually. Those conversations he gets into with [his captors], it's like Beckett sometimes, you know? Beckett meets Kafka. They actually had approached Pat to play Bond, before Connery, and he turned them down. He was a really handsome guy as a young man. Big guy, very imposing. It's funny, nobody recognized him in *Braveheart* because we put a prosthetic nose on Pat so he'd look more English. Pat has a very Irish nose [laughs]. He has a really startling presence and can just stare at you and make you wilt!'

McGoohan accepted the part but not without some small deliberation. A delightful version of this story is available on the website Catholicism. org,[12] part of which I quote below. McGoohan was approached by a new filmmaker called Dan Guenzel who was preparing a short film project and had contacted the Screen Actors Guild in the hope of making contact. Surprisingly, he was given the actor's home address and he posted a script, eventually receiving a telephoned acknowledgement of receipt from Joan. As Guenzel tells the story:

'About a fortnight later, the phone rings and one of my daughters answers it. We heard a gasp … then she said to me, "Dad, it's Patrick McGoohan." With quivering legs I took the phone and spent the next hour-and-a-half having the most pleasant chat with this wonderful man. Yes, he was interested in doing the project. Yes, he would like to talk more about it, etc. We spoke of many, many things. After that conversation, you could have knocked me over with a feather. He promised to get back to me in several weeks time to see what his schedule would permit. Wow.

Then the next call came, several weeks later. "Dan," he said, "I've got a dilemma. I've been asked to do two projects at the same time: yours and a $50 million Mel Gibson epic, *Braveheart*. Which should I accept?" He was so charming about it, teasing me in this way, and I said, "Of course, obviously mine." We had a good laugh over that. In all seriousness, he thanked me for the interesting offer but thought he'd better do the Gibson film. It broke my heart, because we were *that close* to getting him'

With David Tomblin acting as First AD, the man on set closest to the director, filming proceeded on McGoohan's scenes with a smooth professionalism. McGoohan was extremely impressed by Mel Gibson, clearly recognising something of the younger actor in himself:

'He directs, interprets this enormous role, busies himself with everything. And he treated everybody, down to the smallest role, equally. He slept two or three hours a night and he was never grouchy. If you want to talk about Mel, I'm one of his biggest fans. Great breadth of spirit! Much more than the image that people have who've only seen *Lethal Weapon*. He's all the same a guy who chose to make *Hamlet* when he could have filmed another *Lethal Weapon* for 20 million dollars. Besides, he went on into directing with that nice little film, *The Man Without a Face*. Now, he does this colossal thing. All that is very courageous on his part. I have the greatest respect for that man, although some people don't hesitate to waste their time on other "movie stars".[13]

As well as having the greatest respect for Mel Gibson, McGoohan was also delighting in being allowed to slip a little black humour into his part and turned in what most critics saw as a scene-stealing performance. Indeed, he appears to be relishing the role, never descending into parody, though sailing close to the wind, but with the necessary gravitas to lend the sudden moments of anger or acts of barbarism an arresting power. The film went on general release and became a critically-acclaimed box office hit, reinforcing Gibson's reputation and carrying McGoohan along in its wake. The huge publicity machine for *Braveheart* made sure that McGoohan was once again a name on the public's lips and there was a surge of interest in the possibility of a *Prisoner* revival. McGoohan now had an extremely powerful ally as suddenly Mel Gibson's name was linked with a new *Prisoner* movie, though there were never any official announcements. Once more, a great deal of fanfare came to nothing and the movie resumed its usual position 'on the back burner'. *Braveheart,* however, had done a great deal to popularise McGoohan and he was offered a role in *The Phantom* (1996) another Hollywood action epic based on a 1930s comic hero.

A Final Hollywood Run

The film starred Billy Zane as the eponymous Phantom, Catherine Zeta Jones took the female lead and McGoohan was to play a small part as the Phantom's father. An old-fashioned hero who fights for what he believes is right with no interest in personal gain, the Phantom's character would have appealed to McGoohan who brought a great warmth to his role and made an impression in his short time on screen.

He was afforded a similar sized role in *A Time To Kill* (1996), a high profile movie starring Samuel L Jackson, Sandra Bullock and Kevin Spacey. This was a courtroom thriller about the trial of a black man who killed the two men who raped his daughter, causing interracial tensions to flare up. McGoohan played the presiding judge, worryingly named 'Omar Noose', and he managed to more than hold his own against such A-list stars. During the shooting of these films, McGoohan made several revelations concerning the ongoing saga of the film of *The Prisoner*, which indicate his commitment to project:

> '…that is going ahead, I have signed the contract, Polygram have invested a lot of money in the project, they start filming next year and expect to see it released in 1997. In the project, the television series will serve as the starting point and the memory of the series will be respected … It will not only be for the people who have seen the series, we will return to Portmeirion for the beginning and the end, there will also be the balloon … It will be a film that follows on from the series.[14]

When asked if he would be producing the film, McGoohan replied unequivocally:

> 'No, I have never handled that size of budget, they expect to spend about 65 million dollars. I am sure they would not let me loose with that amount of money, besides that is not what I want, the director will know my ideas and I will be executive producer.'

The interview, which was with *Premiere* magazine, also cast once more a little light on his life outside work:

Premiere:	Do you have an achievement that is of sentimental value?
McGoohan:	No, I have nothing special, I would just like to be remembered as a true professional.
Premiere:	Does that bore you?
McGoohan:	Boredom, that is not a fair term, I also do other things, I write poems, I make sculptures and lots of other things interest me.
Premiere:	What is your official profession?
McGoohan:	My official profession … official profession … living from day to day, that is perhaps my official profession.
Premiere	Is it also a way out?
McGoohan:	No, it is simply the first time I have ever been asked that question, it's the first time I have had to think about it. You get up in the morning and … it's very true … you ask yourself, "And now what?". I do not like every day to be the same.'

By this point, McGoohan seemed to be in semi-retirement and *The Prisoner* film sank without trace yet again. He appeared next in the 1998 movie *Hysteria* for Danish director Rene Daalder. The film was a surreal psychodrama with McGoohan playing Dr. Harvey Langston, something of a mad scientist and certainly amoral as he uses the patients in the asylum he runs for experiments into group consciousness. McGoohan turns in a high quality performance and it is a thought-provoking film, certainly intriguing enough for the actor to want to take part. Yet more intriguing was the offer from Peter Falk to not only direct and star in but also co-write a new episode of *Columbo*, and McGoohan happily accepted:

'It is a series with a slow rhythm, previously Peter Falk was making eight episodes a year, now on the whole it's one per year. When he asks me to write a new episode I have to dine with him for two weeks.'[15]

The episode was entitled 'Ashes to Ashes' and featured McGoohan once more playing the killer, this time named Eric Prince. In what was to become his last major role on film, McGoohan gave what seems a very personal performance as a 'never was' actor from England. He and Falk spar well, sharing a great deal of screen time together, but such is their presence and the admirable tautness of McGoohan's direction, that never once does this seem forced. Catherine McGoohan even gets a part, as Prince's mortuary assistant Rita, and McGoohan goes out on a high note, his on screen presence undimmed by age. McGoohan made a final return to *Columbo* in 2000, directing the episode 'Murder With Too Many Notes', starring Scottish comedian and actor Billy Connolly. Though the premise might have been interesting – it was about the jealousy an older musician feels towards a younger and more talented writer – even McGoohan's adept direction was not able to raise a weak script above the mundane. From that point on he ceased to direct aside from his own personal projects.

No 6 Personified

It seemed that McGoohan had finally made peace with the fact that he would forever be associated with his character in *The Prisoner:* Number 6. In 2000, he appeared in a spoof of his own show, as part of the long-running and highly-acclaimed animation *The Simpsons*. Show creator Matt Groening was a big fan of *The Prisoner* and had already included references to the series in his show. Upon approaching McGoohan he was pleased to discover that the actor was equally admiring of *The Simpsons*, finding it to be an extremely clever series and deserving of its huge global fanbase.

McGoohan was delighted to take part in an episode entitled 'The Computer Wore Menace Shoes', in which Homer Simpson is taken away to an isolated island, analogous to The Village, where he meets Number 6 who has been trying to escape for years and promptly steals his raft. The episode was a warm and closely observed mickey-take of McGoohan's show, ending with Homer Simpson escaping from Rover by judicious use of a picnic fork. Number 6 sounds more like McGoohan '*au naturale*', with his curious twist on an Irish lilt and habit of striking the 'th's from certain words. It is curiously satisfying that

McGoohan's last portrayal of his most famous character was an out-and-out comedy, considering the actor's unfulfilled comedic ambitions.

In 2002, he provided a voice for the animated film *Billy Bones*, which hit cinemas in 2004. This was to be his last released work; ironic considering the problems he had always had with recording voice only.

Variant Profession

By 2004, McGoohan had retired from the industry. He had struck up a business partnership with Larry Green, a dealer in high quality personally-autographed merchandise such as film stills and promotional posters, which soon became a close friendship. Larry was kind enough to speak to me about his years as McGoohan's friend and has enabled me to gain a clearer picture of the last decade of the actor's life:

> 'He had retired, I think he was kind of tired of the whole Hollywood business, as far as future projects and everything, I don't think he had a whole lot of plans, at least not that he discussed with me. Even though I considered him a close friend and we could talk about anything there were still a lot of things that I'm sure I didn't know about him. But unless we lived together we probably wouldn't know all those things!'

It seems that McGoohan had at last found an inner peace which, it could be argued, had long eluded him. As Larry explained when I asked if his friend had been happy in himself:

> 'He was. I think he truly was and I think that's why he lived the life that he did, so he could be proud of himself, so he could be proud to live in his own skin. I don't think he was ashamed of himself in any way, I don't think that he felt that he had sold out in any way. He had a code of ethics that he lived by, just like the old cowboy thing.
>
> We were at his breakfast table one morning and he was talking about how he had been offered the part of Dumbledore and they had offered to come and set up a green screen in his house. My wife, Elaine, was sitting there looking at him and thinking – as Patrick would look over the top of his spectacles with his bright blue eyes and wink at her off

and on during our conversations – "My God, he *would* be the perfect Dumbledore!". He was a very charming guy. But he said, "I'm done, I just want to enjoy life, I've made enough money to retire and I want to enjoy life and my grandchildren a little bit and being here talking to friends like you is my idea of enjoying life."

Larry was also able to give me examples of McGoohan's sense of humour, often completely ignored by the media, describing his obvious talent for entertaining an audience: whether reciting a filthy poem from the 18th century or responding to Larry about his seeing the spaghetti western he had made with Terrence Hill, 'You've seen too much!'. His stories could reduce Larry and his wife, Elaine, to tears of hysterical laughter. This portrait is a far cry from the usual portrayal of 'prissy Pat', the largely mirthless hellraiser, and paints a quite different picture that was echoed time-after-time by those who were lucky enough to get to know McGoohan well. As Larry explained:

'Once you became familiar with Patrick's unique, very dry sense of humour, you could see it in a lot of his character portrayals and writing; even in *The Prisoner*.'

McGoohan was never the anti-social creature others might have expected, though he may have appeared that way, through his tendency to be guarded. He could be great company. Or perhaps he simply loved the company of Larry and his wife in particular:

'When he got to know you, he was so animated! He was just phenomenal. God, what a host! Instead of the British tea like you would expect, it was one cup of coffee after another. He made some damned good coffee! He was always jumping up and fixing us another cup of coffee. Of course, we were up for days afterwards!'

Larry emphasised that he looked upon McGoohan as more of a friend than a client, telling me that whenever he had a problem, he could turn to his friend who would help him through it, drawing on his own vast life experience. Their conversations were wide-ranging and fascinating, with Green gaining an insight into McGoohan's approach to acting, that it was by no means high art. To him it was simply a job and one that required a talent that could not be learned from acting schools. 'You can either do it, or you can't!' he told his friend.

'He was talking about these big name actors who still go to acting school and he said, "I just don't understand that." Well he was *very good* at it! That's why he didn't understand *that*, he was a natural. He was a good observer. I mentioned it to him once, "Patrick, I've got a feeling that no matter which direction you had chosen as a career you would have been a success." He did *not* like to hear that, he didn't like to hear praise of any sort … he was not that kind of man. He didn't need reassurance or self-affirmation!'

Larry openly admitted that McGoohan had meant a very great deal to him, regarding the actor as the closest friend he had apart from his wife. He recalled how McGoohan would give private performances, reciting Shakespeare to warm up before his last ever interview (this was the interview conducted by Larry for the Disney DVD special release of *Dr Syn Alias The Scarecrow*) and giving the Greens what he termed 'an incredible one man show'.

Despite his retirement, in McGoohan's last years his name was continually linked with the remake of *The Prisoner* which finally went before the cameras in 2008. Interviewed at the time of its screening, the new Number 6, Jim Caviezel, said of his illustrious predecessor:

'We wanted to get him for this version, but it didn't work out. But I'm looking forward to going through all of his work. They showed me some of it from *The Prisoner*, especially the framing of the shots. So our version has a lot of homage to the original series. But at the same time, it does stand alone. But yet, it doesn't separate itself at all.'[16]

A few weeks before he died, Elaine, Larry's wife, had a final encounter with McGoohan. She had been caught in traffic on the way to pick up some signed photographs from him and made him late for a doctor's appointment he had booked that day. Larry Green told me that McGoohan had immediately written to Elaine to apologise for possibly making her feel rushed:

'He was so nice about it, he even wrote her a letter saying, "If I was rushed with you, I am so sorry as I was late for a doctor's appointment. I understand with you coming from Orange County how you could be held up by traffic. I hope I didn't make you feel that you had done something wrong." He wrote the most humbling letter and it made Elaine cry. She called him and said, "Patrick, you don't have to apologise! You didn't make me feel rushed. It was my fault. I had just forgotten how bad Los Angeles traffic can be." But she got to see him that one last time and even if I didn't, I'm glad she got to.'

McGoohan died on January 13th 2009. He was eighty years old. Releasing the news to the press, Catherine's husband, film producer Clive Landsberg, mentioned only that it had been 'after a short illness'. Sharif Ali, McGoohan's agent, followed up the announcement with:

'He was fine and we hadn't talked about his health. He was excited about the future. We had an offer for the lead in an independent feature. He was going over the script, and he was offered a supporting part in a larger film. We are a boutique agency and we're young, but he chose to come here. A lot of the larger actors are with the big agencies, all the same places. It is typical of him that he wasn't. It's just how he lived his life. He didn't take the same path as everybody else took and he was better for it.'[17]

Initially, the expected obituaries, all summarising his life in much the same homogenous paragraphs appeared in the major UK and US newspapers, migrating quickly to the internet.

As is often the case with obituaries, the text reduced the man to a series of clichés, which were, in McGoohan's case, accompanied by a picture from either *Danger Man* or *The Prisoner*. *Brand* frequently merited a mention along with sketchy details of his childhood and long association with Peter Falk, but it was his 1960s work for which he was being remembered. However, the reaction in other media was muted with only the sombre current affairs show *Newsnight* carrying the story on UK television.

Joan did not make any public statement, keeping their personal life just that, until the very end. She continues to live in the area where McGoohan spent his final days and, in a rare interview with Michael Aushenker in *Pacific Pallisades,* remarked that she had begun to follow McGoohan's daily schedule. Aside from this, she has rarely broken her silence.

The Legacy Lives On

One could be forgiven for thinking that McGoohan had been forgotten, but in the wake of his death, tributes began to spring up across the internet, individuals who had met or been inspired by him posting their appreciation and their personal stories. His defining traits of power as an actor, individuality as a man and inventiveness in making *The Prisoner* were repeated and strengthened, building on the self-shielding myth that he had casually built around himself. Yet, as I hope this book has demonstrated, there was a great deal more to McGoohan. He had an endless stream of ideas and – the curse of the overly-creative – a thousand unfinished projects which, according to his agent, were still occupying his mind until the end of his life. He had a wide-ranging artistic talent, his experiments in poetry and sculpture often hinted at and never yet revealed. He undertook an extremely diverse range of film and television appearances, as well as his sadly unrecorded theatrical work, which I am sure will continue to be discovered by new fans who will champion his absolute commitment, skill and talent .

Above all else, in making *The Prisoner,* a work into which he had poured every scintilla of energy and creativity he could muster, he had created something that was truly individual and truly his own. Though no one can deny the immense talent of his many collaborators on the series, it is McGoohan's voice that dominates. He had, in his own words as written for the episode 'Fall Out': 'Gloriously vindicated the right of the individual to be individual'. He had created a piece of television art which would identify him as being that individual. *The Prisoner* was a very personal statement from a very shy man.

Not a Number

The publicity surrounding McGoohan's passing drove viewers to assess the new re-imagining of *The Prisoner*, which – perhaps unsurprisingly as it was a remake – proved to have little of the spirit and individuality of the original. As a friend of mine had muttered when news of the series broke, 'What's the point of doing *The Prisoner* without McGoohan?' Though entertaining in its own right, and despite the stellar cast, the new series simply had none of the bite of the original. How could it?

McGoohan's original vision remains the definitive interpretation of that particular everyman. His work has been influential on many creative minds, from Stephen Fry to Iron Maiden, and it continues to inspire, always finding receptive minds who respond to his message. For almost sixty years McGoohan had excelled as an actor, his earliest real ambition. He had managed to make his point, loudly and forcefully, and had been blessed with finding his soulmate early and being with her for the remainder of his days. I leave the last word to Larry Green:

> 'He was a very honest, humble, non-egotistical, hard working, very straightforward and intelligent man. He was a free man. That's why he lived like he did, that's why he was so private. Our lives are a lot poorer now that he has gone.'

Did Patrick McGoohan change the world? No, probably not.

But he did inspire us to stand up and be counted – the individual versus the system.

LIST OF IMAGES

REFERENCES

INTRODUCTION

1. See http://www.theunmutual.co.uk Rick Davy's great *Prisoner* website for in-depth Patrick McGoohan and *Prisoner* news, interviews, events, merchandise and articles.
2. http://www.theunmutual.co.uk/webchat.htm
3. McGoohan developed a lifelong distaste of the media publicity machine during his time under contract with the Rank organisation.
4. Unknown interview.
5. Reproduced on a variety of film websites.
6. 'Buygones', a series of shorts that Victor Lewis Smith made for Channel 4.

CHAPTER 1
An Actor is Formed

1. *TV Guide*, September 1977
2. *Cosmopolitan,* December 1969
3. US publicity brochure, from internet articles by Moor Larkin.
4. *Woman* magazine, October 1965
5. *Photoplay*, November 1957
6. Private email communication with the author.
7. *Woman* magazine, October 1965
8. *Sunday Telegraph* magazine no. 493, March 1985
9. *Six into One, The Prisoner file*, Channel 4 1984
10. *Photoplay*, June 1969
11. *Woman* magazine, October 1965
12. As above.
13. *Woman* magazine, October 1965
14. *TV Times*, November 1965
15. *Woman* magazine, October 1965
16. As above.
17. As above.
18. As above.
19. As above.
20. As above.
21. *TV and Radio Mirror* (date unknown)
22. As above.
23. As above.
24. As above.
25. *Woman* magazine, October 1965
26. As above.
27. As above.
28. As above.

CHAPTER 2
Rising Star, New Romance

1. Arnold Hano interview, *TV Guide*, September 1977
2. Private email communication with the author.
3. Warner Troyer TV Ontario interview 1977
4. http://www.bl.uk/projects/theatrearchive/ewing3.html
5. As above.
6. *Woman* magazine, October 1965
7. *Sunday Telegraph* magazine, August 1984
8. *Woman* magazine, October 1965
9. As above.
10. As above.
11. http://www.palisadespost.com/content/index.cfm?Story_ID=4587
12. *Woman* magazine, October 1965
13. As above.
14. As above.
15. As above.
16. As above.
17. As above.
18. As above.
19. As above.
20. As above.
21. As above.
22. As above.
23. *Photoplay*, September 1968

CHAPTER 3
Not a Brand

1. *Woman* magazine, October 1965
2. As above.
3. As above.
4. As above.
5. As above.
6. As above.
7. As above.
8. Private email communication with the author.
9. *Photoplay*, September 1968
10. *Woman* magazine, October 1965
11. As above.
12. *Plays and Players*, March 1955
13. *TV Guide*, September 1977
14. http://www.bl.uk/projects/theatrearchive/plowright2.html
15. As above.
16. *Woman* magazine, October 1965
17. As above.
18. http://www.wellesnet.com/?p=699

19. As above.
20. From a review in *The Observer.*
21. 'The Schizoid Man' DVD Commentary, Network 2007
22. *Picturegoer,* 1956
23. *Woman m*agazine, October 1965
24. As above.
25. P*hotoplay*, November 1957
26. *Woman* magazine, October 1965
27. As above.
28. As above.
29. *Picturegoer*, August 1958
30. *Woman* magazine, October 1965
31. As above.
32. As above.
33. As above.
34. As above.
35. *Brand* DVD extra, Network 2003
36. *The Prisoner In Depth*, Steven Ricks, TR7 Productions
37. http://www.bl.uk/projects/theatrearchive/knight2.html
38. *Brand* DVD extra, Network 2003
39. As above.
40. http://www.bl.uk/projects/theatrearchive/knight2.html
41. http://www.bl.uk/projects/theatrearchive/murray.html
42. *Woman* magazine, October 1965

CHAPTER 4
Danger Man, Risk Taker

1. *DWB* no. 86, February 1991
2. *Woman* magazine, October 1965
3. *Cosmopolitan*, December 1969
4. *Don't Knock Yourself Out*, Network 2007
5. *Cosmopolitan*, December 1969
6. *TV and Radio Mirror* (date unknown)
7. *Woman* magazine, October 1965
8. As above.
9. *Photoplay*, May 1965
10. W*oman* magazine, October 1965
11. http://www.screenonline.org.uk/audio/id/838166/index.html
12. *Woman* magazine, October 1965
13. http://www.theunmutual.co.uk/interviewsbrowne.htm
14. *TV Times*, October 1965
15. *Sheffield Star*, 1965
16. The *Photoplay* interview of May 1965 can be found at
http://www.the-prisoner-6.freeserve.co.uk/markstein.htm

CHAPTER 5
The Prisoner Arrives

1. *Six into One, The Prisoner File*, Channel 4 1984

2. As above.

3. *TV Times*, October 1965

4. *Sunday Telegraph Magazine*, March 1985

5. *Six into One, The Prisoner File*, Channel 4 1984

6. 'The Schizoid Man' DVD Commentary, Network 2007

7. *Six into One, The Prisoner File*, Channel 4 1984

8. As above.

9. As above.

10. *The Persuader*, BBC 2 August 1994

11. *Six into One, The Prisoner File*, Channel 4 1984

12. Warner Troyer TV Ontario interview 1977

13. *TV Week*, February 1966

14. http://www.theunmutual.co.uk/interviewsmaher.htm

15. As above.

16. As above.

17. Source unknown.

18. Source unknown.

19. *Six into One, The Prisoner File*, Channel 4 1984

20. As above.

21. Warner Troyer TV Ontario interview 1977

22. http://www.theunmutual.co.uk/interviewsmaher.htm

23. *Six into One, The Prisoner File*, Channel 4 1984

24. *Don't Knock Yourself Out*, Network 2007

25. *The Prisoner In Depth*, Steven Ricks, TR7 Productions

26. *Don't Knock Yourself Out*, Network 2007

27. http://www.theunmutual.co.uk/interviewsextras.htm

28. As above.

29. http://www.screenonline.org.uk/audio/id/946020

30. *Six into One, The Prisoner File*, Channel 4 1984

31. As above.

32. *Six into One, The Prisoner File*, Channel 4 1984

33. *The Prisoner In Depth*, Steven Ricks, TR7 Productions

34. *Six Into One, The Prisoner File*, Channel 4 1984

35. *Don't Knock Yourself Out*, Network 2007

36. *Six into One, The Prisoner File*, Channel 4 1984

37. *Don't Knock Yourself Out*, Network 2007

38. As above.

39. As above.

40. Warner Troyer TV Ontario interview 1977

41. *The Prisoner In Depth*, Steven Ricks, TR7 Productions

42. *Don't Knock Yourself Out*, Network 2007

CHAPTER 6
The Prisoner: Obsession

1. *Don't Knock Yourself Out*, Network 2007

2. As above.

3. As above.

4. As above.

5. *The Daily Star*, date unknown.

6. http://www.theunmutual.co.uk/interviewsbrowne.htm

7. *Six into One, The Prisoner File*, Channel 4 1984

8. *The Persuader*, BBC 2 August 1994

9. Private email communication with the author.

10. *The Prisoner In Depth*, Steven Ricks, TR7 Productions

11. *Don't Knock Yourself Out,* Network 2007

12. *The Prisoner In Depth*, Steven Ricks, TR7 Productions

13. As above.

14. As above.

15. *Six into One, The Prisoner File*, Channel 4 1984

16. As above.

17. *Photoplay*, September 1968

18. As above.

19. http://twitchfilm.com/interviews/2009/01/tcm-private-screeningsinterview-with-ernest-borgnine.php

20. *Photoplay*, September 1969

21. As above.

22. *The Prisoner In Depth*, Steven Ricks, TR7 Productions

23. As above.

24. *Inside the Prisoner*, Ian Rakoff, Batsford Books, 1998

25. As above.

26. http://www.theunmutual.co.uk/interviewskanner.htm

27. http://confluencefilmblog.blogspot.com/2009/11/appear-disappear-reappear-interview.html

28. *Six Into One, The Prisoner File*, Channel 4, 1984

29. *Don't Knock Yourself Out*, Network 2007

30. *Six Into One, The Prisoner File*, Channel 4, 1984

31. As above.

32. As above.

33. http://www.theunmutual.co.uk/interviewsmaher.htm

34. *The Prisoner In Depth*, Steven Ricks, TR7 Productions

35. As above.

36. *Six Into One, The Prisoner File*, Channel 4, 1984

37. *The Prisoner In Depth*, Steven Ricks, TR7 Productions

38 As above.

39. http://www.theunmutual.co.uk/interviewskanner.htm

40. *Six Into One, The Prisoner File*, Channel 4, 1984

41. *The Box*, issue 1, January 1991

42. *Daily Sketch*, February 1968

CHAPTER 7
Fall-Out: The USA

1. *Six Into One, The Prisoner File*, Channel 4, 1984

2. Source unknown.

3. *Six Into One, The Prisoner File*, Channel 4, 1984

4. *TV Times*, February 1968
5. *Cosmopolitan*, December 1969
6. *Six Into One, The Prisoner File*, Channel 4, 1984
7. *Inside the Prisoner*, Ian Rakoff, Batsford Books, 1998
8. As above.
9. *Cosmopolitan*, December 1969
10. *TV Guide*, May 1968
11. *The Prisoner In Depth*, Steven Ricks, TR7 Productions
12. *Cosmopolitan*, December 1969
13. *Don't Knock Yourself Out*, Network 2007
14. As above.
15. *Inside the Prisoner*, Ian Rakoff, Batsford Books 1998
16. *The Prisoner In Depth*, Steven Ricks, TR7 Productions
17. As above.
18. *Sunday Telegraph* magazine, August 1984
19. *TV Guide*, May 1968
20. As above.
21. *Premiere* magazine 1995, Lagardère Digital France

CHAPTER 8
Kings and Desperate Men

1. Arnold Hano interview in *TV Guide*, September 1977
2. *The Box*, issue 1, January 1991
3. *Premiere* magazine 1995, Lagardère Digital France
4. *TV Times*, February 1968
5. *Daily News*, July 1977
6. Arnold Hano interview in *TV Guide*, September 197
7. As above.
8. As above.
9. As above.
10. As above.
11. As above.
12. http://confluencefilmblog.blogspot.com/2009/11/appear-disappear-reappear-interview.html
13. *Premiere* magazine 1995, Lagardère Digital France
14. Arnold Hano interview in *TV Guide*, September 1977
15. As above.
16. *The Village*, issue 4
17. *TV Times*, March 1977
18. Private email communication with the author.
19. *Titbits*, March 1980
20. As above.
21. *Premiere* magazine 1995, Lagardère Digital France
22. *Cronenberg on Cronenberg*, David Cronenberg, 1996
23. http://somecamerunning.typepad.com/some_came_running/2009/01/patrick-mcgoohan-19282009.html
24. *The Mail On Sunday* magazine, April 1984

25. As above.
26. *Sequence* magazine, published in New Zealand since the 1940s
27. http://www.illuminationsmedia.co.uk/blog/index.cfm?start=1&news_id=201
28. As above.
29. 'The LA Tape', Patrick McGoohan 1984
30. 'The LA Tape', Patrick McGoohan 1984
31. *Premiere* magazine 1995, Lagardère Digital France
32. Time magazine, February 1985, William A Henry III
33. Source unknown.
34. *Philadelphia Enquirer*, February 1985
35. *South Florida Sunday*, February 1985
36. *Philadelphia Enquirer*, February 1985
37. Google News
38. From a variety of internet sites on Patrick McGoohan – source unknown.

CHAPTER 9
An Enigmatic Legacy

1. *Number Six*, issue 31 1991
2. *The Box*, issue 1, January 1991
3. As above.
4. As above.
5. As above.
6. *The Box*, issue 1, January 1991
7. Private communication with the author.
8. *In The Village*, issue 1, Winter 1994
9. *New York Times*, September 1992
10. *The Observer*, December 1991
11. *National Enquirer*, February 1992
12. http://catholicism.org/more-on-patrick-mcgoohan.html
13. Original source unknown (this appears on various internet sites)
14. *Premiere* magazine 1995, Lagardère Digital France
15. *The Box*, issue 1, January 1991
16. http://www.wired.com/underwire/2009/07/qa-can-jim-caviezel-fill-patrick-mcgoohans-prisoner-shoes/
17. http://www.independent.co.uk/news/people/news/death-of-star-who-will-forever-be-more-than-number-six-1366704.html